6

HEROES, ANTIHEROES AND THE HOLOCAUST

American Jewry and Historical Choice

David Morrison

MILAH PRESS

Jerusalem   New London

First Published in 1995

Library of Congress Catalog Card Number 95-76846
Heroes, Antiheroes and the Holocaust: American Jewry and Historical Choice
 by David Morrison
With Bibliograhy and Index

1. Holocaust, Jewish (1933-1945). 2. World War, 1939-1945-Jews-Rescue.

ISBN   0-9646886-0-3

MILAH Press   Machon Yerushalayim L'Haskalah- MILAH
POB 267   6 King George Street
New London, NH 03257   Jerusalem, Israel

Painting on cover by Schwebel

Printed in Israel

10 9 8 7 6 5 4 3 2 1

ACKNOWLEDGEMENTS

Jews are a people with a memory. Contemporary Jews "know" there was a Holocaust. We cannot "understand" or relate to the horror that engulfed the Jews of Europe. The best one can do is "immerse" oneself in the phenomenon of the Holocaust; the death of six million Jews calls for some personal level of "response." These sentences are a poor paraphrase of the guidance and inspiration I have drawn over many years from Rabbi Irving Greenberg in my own coming to terms with the Holocaust. For that inspiration and for his reading this manuscipt and offering me help and encouragement I am immensely grateful.

Many years ago Richard Friedman introduced me to some of the out of print, difficult to find material that first awakened me to the contradictions and missing links in contemporary Jewish history. We have discussed together and struggled with these issues for two decades, and he was there to review this manuscript and make many helpful suggestions.

I heard Professor David Wyman speak more than ten years ago. His *The Abandonment of the Jews* was for me a monument to scholarly research and a model for the dedication to the pursuit of truth. Many years later I wanted to seek his consultation and guidance when I began the actual writing of this manuscript. But who was I to approach him and intrude on his time? With great trepidation I picked up the telephone. He welcomed me with a wonderful openness of spirit. We met later in New England, and he offered me much help and encouragement. When it was time to ask for suggestions on the raw manuscript, he combed it in detail and made extensive suggestions for strengthening the content, presentation and form.

My first free associations to this material, long before it began to take form on paper, were verbalized between gasps for air as I jogged through the hills of Jerusalem with my dear friend, Rabbi Shaul Feinberg. From that formative phase through the drafts on paper, he generously offered his encouragement and suggestions which were very gratefully received.

Fred Worms, my good friend and tennis partner, offered much help and guidance in the preparation of this book. His practiced eye caught many "typos" that even a professional editor missed. Those that remain are my responsibility only.

Professor Martin Gilbert and Professor Marc Saperstein provided important help and encouragement in this project.

Family support is essential in a project like this. My parents, Zelda and Max Morrison raised me with a love and respect for yiddishkeit and learning. There are no words to express my gratitude for all they have given me. My children, Marc and Valerie, encouraged me all along the path and, in many ways that only they could do, helped "raise" me. Wonderful support and encouragement were abundant from Jimmie and Emil Hess. And the daughter they raised? What would I do without you, Jo? That is a quesion I don't even want to try to answer.

To Jo,
who shares the dream.

CONTENTS

Abbreviations for Notes

AJC - American Jewish Committee (Archives in New York)
contains Proskauer, Waldman, Wertheim,
and Adler papers, as well as oral histories.

CZA - Central Zionist Archives (Jerusalem)
contains Wise, Mack, de Haas, Brandeis, and
Lichtheim papers, as well as papers of the
American Jewish Congress and various Zionist
umbrella groups.

JLC - Jewish Labor Committee (Archives in New York)
Contains Pat, Held papers.

PPF - Pro-Palestine Federation (papers at CZA)

PSCP - Palestinian Statehood Committee Papers (papers of
Bergson group are at Yale University, New
Haven). Oral interviews with Bergson are at
the Hebrew University Institute of
Contemporary Jewry, Division of Oral
Documents.

OTHER ARCHIVES

Hirschmann Papers - Diaries are at the Roosevelt Library in
Hyde Park; papers relating to music interests
are at the Music Section of the New York Public
Library.

Morgenthau Diaries - at the Roosevelt Library in Hyde Park

Silver Papers - Papers of Abba Hillel Silver are at The Temple
in Cleveland.

INTRODUCTION

The enormity of the Holocaust as a historical event makes great demands on historians. To identify and report everything that happened is a task of immense proportions. Interpreting these events, imputing cause and effect and coming to historical judgments compound the task.

The assessment of German actions and responsibility presents one level of difficulty. For an American Jewish historian to address the role of the Roosevelt administration and the Allies is an issue closer to "home," and greatly taxes the ability of the historian to chronicle and interpret events objectively.

Researching and writing the history of the American Jewish response to the Holocaust, especially for the Jewish historian, reaches the level of pain, and it is not surprising that controversy exists. There are those historians who charge that American Jews were indifferent and failed in their responsibility to their fellow Jews. They label as "apologists" their colleagues who assert that given the climate of the era in question, with the disunity and relative powerlessness of the Jewish community, there was little Jewish leaders could do. The latter group of historians tends to accuse the first group of moralizing; any indictment of American Jews is inappropriate.

My reading of the history of the American Jewish response to the Holocaust leaves me with a sense of incompleteness. The 20th historian Frederick Teggert wrote:

Actual inquiry begins when an individual encounters some specific difficulty in experience, as when he finds that the accepted account of some phenomenon is at variance with the facts. Every advance in knowledge, from the time of Thales or of Copernicus, has been made by someone who has resolutely faced a difficulty in thought...every difficulty in thought which is neglected or slurred over is a failure of duty in scholarship and constitutes a serious obstacle to the advancement of knowledge.[1]

Thus this current study. The archival data available to the researcher are immense. Many documents are included in this book that have never before been published. Excluded here is enough material to fill several volumes. The historian must decide what to use and what to leave out.

The focus in this book is on the choices available to Jews during the 1930s and 1940s. I am at one with the historian, Peter Gay, when he says: "...a historical event is always the product of numerous causes, immediate and remote, public and private, patent and concealed. The inquirer's impulse to fasten on a single cause appears to be practically irresistible: fame, it seems, awaits the historian who can find one cause where there had been two causes before...."[2]

While Gay is a psychoanalyst as well as a historian, he rejects as do I the methodology of putting the historical figure "on the couch" and trying to carry out a one-sided analysis.

Historians differ widely in their theories about the importance of the individual in history. Many draw on Hegel, Spencer and Marx in stressing the inevitability of the historical process. Man has choices, but they are choices strictly limited by the social, economic and political forces which move history forward.

Other historians ascribe great importance to the role of the individual in history. The noted Jewish historian, Lucy Dawidowicz, cautions:

By attributing historical responsibility to the medieval mind, the Renaissance spirit, the Industrial Revolution, mass culture, secularism, or inevitability, some historians have managed to evade the attribution of human responsibility for the occurrence

---

[1]Teggart, Frederick, "Causation in Historical Events," Journal of the History of Ideas, Jan, 1942, pp. 3-29.

[2]Gay, Peter, *Art and Act: On Causes in History - Manet, Gropius, Mondrian* (New York: Harper and Row, 1976), p. 7

of historical events....History is at bottom an account of what men did and achieved, and the historian's task is to untangle that meshwork of human character, behavior, and motive whose intertwining creates the very material of history.[1]

What is most lacking in the documented history of the American Jewish response to the Holocaust is an understanding of the Jewish leadership as people. Without an insight into these leaders as flesh and blood people, one learns little of the forces that motivated their actions. Stephen Wise is depicted appropriately as a preeminent Jewish leader, but he emerges from what has been written as little more than a symbol. We learn nothing of the passions that drove him, and he was a very passionate man. In addition, much of what we read about him points out one of the potential traps of historical writing - the propensity to propagate myth.

Note the following references to Wise's relationship with Roosevelt. They come both from historians identified with the group that believes American Jewish leadership fell short and from the group that the "accusers" label as "apologists":

His well-publicized friendship with FDR...The doors of the White House were always open to Wise....[2]

Dr. Stephen Wise...confidant of President Franklin Delano Roosevelt...; To Wise...the election of Franklin Roosevelt seemed like the coming of the Messiah....[3]

---

[1] Dawidowicz, Lucy, *The Holocaust and the Historians* (Cambridge: Harvard U. Press, 1981), p. 146.

[2] Friedman, Saul S., *No Haven For the Oppressed* (Detroit: Wayne State U. Press, 1973), p. 129.

[3] Kranzler, David H., *Thy Brother's Blood: The Orthodox Jewish Response to the Holocaust* (New York: Mesorah Press, 1964), p. 3 ("confidant") and p. 66 ("coming of the Messiah").

Wise was an influential figure in American domestic politics; he had been on close terms with President Wilson and was the one Jewish leader who could reach Roosevelt.[1]

These depictions are wide of the mark. Delving into the more than one hundred reels of microfilm that hold his papers, one comes to understand much about Stephen Wise. Critical to this analysis is an examination of his relationships with Louis Brandeis, Julian Mack, Felix Frankfurter, Jacob de Haas, and others. To date, a clear presentation of these relationships is missing from recorded history..

In addition to the leaders just mentioned, one must come to know Ira Hirschmann, Louis I. Newman, William Ziff, Ben Hecht, Irving Bunim, Eliezer Silver and many more of the "cast of characters" that appeared on this stage of history. Only then does the range of human choices come into focus.

Most of the studies available begin their narrative late in the 1930s and give scant attention to the earlier decades of the 20th century. Yet Wise, Brandeis, Frankfurter and de Haas were all active in American Jewish life before World War I. Inevitably, these earlier experiences helped shape their responses to the Nazi threat.

Thus Part I of this book includes history from the earliest days of the 20th century and ends on the eve of World War II. Part II chronicles the war years. Who was Peter Bergson? More importantly, what did he do, and how much support did he receive from American Jewry?

While the primary focus is on American Jewry, there was much communication between American Jews and Jews abroad, and these contacts are an important part of the history.

Part III examines the writing of this history. There is a fascinating parallel between the tension among the Jewish leaders who lived the historical events and the historians who have written about them.

A section of Part III is devoted to the questions of when information about the Holocaust was available - when the world "knew." Many have addressed this question, but the answers have more often been obfuscating than elucidating, perhaps because the question is inexact and incomplete. When did we know *what*? And when crucial information became available, did *knowing* significantly change anyone's behavior?

---

[1]Lacquer, Walter, *The Terrible Secret* (Boston: Little, Brown, and Co., 1980), p. 10.

If it did not, then why have historians been so preoccupied with these questions? To what extent is what the reader of history "knows" dependent on what material the historian makes available?

Those scholars who ponder the complexities of historiography consistently address the limitations that each generation of historians bring to their research. *The* definitive history can never be written. More than fifteen years ago, a group of historians of the Holocaust came together to compare notes. Nathan Rotenstreich, who coedited the book that resulted from the conference wrote:

Our attempt to interpret the Holocaust "a generation after" is probably an inadequate attempt, one that will be reconstituted in the generation to follow; but it is still necessary, because sheer silence toward the phenomenon is also not adequate. Reflection is closer to memory than silence. Mere silence can easily be taken as the first attempt at suppression, and such an attempt can easily be taken as readiness to forget.[1]

Much has already been written about the American Jewish response to the Holocaust, and much needs to follow. It is my hope that this book helps further our understanding of a difficult and painful period.

---

[1] Bauer, Yehuda, & Nathan Rotenstreich, editors, *The Holocaust as Historical Experience* (New York: Holmes & Meier, 1981), p. 273.

PART I

AMERICAN JEWRY ORGANIZES

Prologue

We are having terrible days and nights. In the morning the bad news starts and during the night we cannot sleep expecting the worst. The papers only publish what the government permits. I cannot imagine that people abroad know how much the poor Jews have to suffer here. I cannot describe to you how desparate [sic] our situation is. If the foreign countries do not help us soon, we are lost....How many poor Jews have already been tortured to death. They even cut "Jakenkreuze" [Swastikas] into their flesh. These are real middle ages. Many Jews are in prison and it is doubtful if they ever leave it alive....[1]

I am an attorney from Berlin....It is impossible for me to put into a few words everything that I have seen and heard and lived through in the last few weeks in Germany....Daily there were attacks upon people of my acquaintance who were known to have Democratic or Socialistic views, or simply because they were Jews....You will probably have heard by this time of the pogrom in Koenigsberg of which the most important Jews of the community were victims. Here in Zurich I received from an absolutely reliable source the confirmation of the terrible reports from Koenigsberg. The relatives of the Jews who had been attacked and wounded did not dare even to bring the poor

---

[1]Letter dated 3/22/33, CZA, Wise papers, Reel 82.

victims to the hospital in Koenigsberg....It was only foreign protests, especially that of America which prevented even worse happenings....[1]

The reports piled up on the desk of Rabbi Stephen S. Wise, prompting him to write to his friend and mentor, Judge Julian Mack:

I am going through days and nights of hell, for I am mindful of our awful responsibility. But if you had seen the documents that we have seen you would know that...silence is acquiescence.[2]

A few days later, he continued pouring out his heart to Mack:

I wonder whether many Jews realize that we are facing today... a Jewish upheaval which parallels, if it does not surpass in significance, the upheaval of 1881....the trouble, Mack, is that none of us is quite alive to the fact that this may be the beginning of a world-wide movement against us, a world-wide conflagration, a world-wide undertaking against the Jews.[3]

Writing to Judge Mack's daughter, Ruth Mack Brunswick, Wise reiterated his concern: "The situation, as far as Jews in Germany is concerned, is as grievous as it can be...the Germans are saying that we are spreading atrocity tales. That is not true...."[4]

Further reports poured out of Europe:

Being arrested in Berlin on the pretext that I am spying for Jews, so I want the world to know the atrocities that I saw

---

[1] Letter dated 3/29/33, ibid.

[2] Letter dated 3/29/33, ibid., Reel 115.

[3] Letter dated 4/1/33, Voss, Carl Herman, editor, *Servant of the People: Selected Letters* (Philadephia: Jewish Publication Society of America, 1969), p. 177.

[4] Letter dated 4/6/33, ibid., p. 183.

there in person. Seventy people in one cellar without any air only the light of one electric small bulb - without pillows or a bed or a chair to sit on, only the stone floor with a lavatory in the same room. There are people with broken arms, with broken heads - blood running over all their faces without any medical care fed only with a piece of hard bread and black coffee. I met there people that fourteen days already had the same food....I spoke to a young boy who told me that the Nazis came into his home and wanted him to beat his father up. He refused to do so and they gave him a terrific beating and as the blood gushed from his nose and mouth on to the table they made his mother and sister lick it up....[1]

Frustrated by the lack of a response from President Franklin Roosevelt, Wise wrote in one of his frequent letters to Mack:

The [American Jewish] Congress will have to do the very, very lamentable thing of crying out against the President who has not by a single word or act intimated the faintest interest in what is going on....Roosevelt ought to know the story. Of course, F.F. [Felix Frankfurter] must have told Roosevelt much, but there is still much to be told....[2]

Wise decided to write directly to Frankfurter, the Harvard Law professor who had personal access to Roosevelt:

I have been waiting, I confess, day after day in the hope that you might send some further information about your talk with Headquarters. I did not want to ask your sympathy but I do want you to know that I am having an awfully hard time of it with the Jewish masses who cannot be expected to understand why no word has come from the administration in all these weeks.

Sharpening his protest, Wise continued:

---

[1] Statement by Morris S. Sonders, dated 4/13/33, CZA, Wise papers, Reel 82.

[2] Letter dated 4/15/33, ibid., Reel 115.

Frankly, if I were the head of the American Jewish Congress, as I am merely the honorary head, I would resign tomorrow. I would make public announcement that I resigned in order to permit someone else to serve as president who might have such access to the President of the United States as is denied to me.[1]

Attempts by Frankfurter and Supreme Court Justice Louis Brandeis to placate Wise in the absence of a statement from Roosevelt failed, and Wise again wrote to Frankfurter:

Last Sunday you telephoned me that you and LDB [Louis Dembitz Brandeis] were persuaded that the President was alert to the meaning of events in Germany, especially in relation to the peace of the world, and further, that in his own way, he would at the right moment give effective evidence of his concern over the occurrences in Germany which must have aroused his moral nature and have evoked his constructive statesmanship. However, the presence of wide popular demands for mass demonstrations, organized boycotts etc. is becoming increasingly heavy and all but impossible to resist....Prayerfully hope for some word by the President in whatever form he may choose to express his own deep feeling and that this word will be spoken at once.[2]

Writing to a friend, Wise a few days later depicted the pressure on him:

Yes, I am in the midst of a hideous job as far as the Jews of Germany are concerned....I have reason to know in many ways that what I succeeded in doing through the American Jewish Congress in channeling the protest of American Jewry and, above all, of non-Jewish America, did much to make life livable for the Jews of Germany. It is a war of extermination that Hitler is waging, and it is a deliberate thing planned since the

---

[1]Letter dated 4/15/33, ibid., Reel 109.

[2]Letter dated 4/16/33, ibid., Reel 82.

25th of February, 1920, when the Hitler program was first issued....[1]

The bad news was unrelenting as documented by this telegram:

BERLIN NOT AMERICA NOT EVEN COUNTRIES BORDERING GERMANY CAN HAVE FULL PICTURE INSULTS TORTURES HOPELESSNESS WHICH JEWS UNDERGOING GERMANY STOP....EVERYTHING THAT WAS TRUE FIRST DAYS HITLER REVOLUTION IS STILL TRUE NOW EVEN DRASTICER [sic] STOP JEWS STILL DISAPPEAR LATER FOUND IN MORGUES....SUICIDES AMONG JEWS ASSUMING UNIMAGINABLE PROPORTION STOP TRAGEDY GREATER BECAUSE EVEN GERMANS ALL CLASSES FORMERLY ENEMIES OF HITLERISM ARE GRADUALLY ACCEPTING IT PATRIOTICALLY THUS JEWS FIND THEIR FRIENDS OF LONG AGO CONVERTED ANTISEMITES ANXIOUS SEE JEWS OUTLAWED IN ORDER SHARE THEIR PROPERTIES BUSINESS JOBS.[2]

A despairing Rabbi Wise cried out in a letter to his good friend, Alexander Kohut:

I am looking into the depths of hell. Sometimes I feel as if I could hardly live through it and as if I hardly cared....I heard a man who had seen Hitler within nine days say...Hitler will not rest until he has destroyed the Jewish people. "His [Hitler's] word to me was, 'I will do the thing that the rest of the world would like to do. It doesn't know how to get rid of the Jews. I will show them!'"[3]

Wise was not the only Jewish leader alarmed by events. Dr. Cyrus Adler, the president of the American Jewish Committee, wrote to Secretary of State Cordell Hull:

---

[1]Letter dated 4/18/33, Voss, op. cit., p. 185.

[2]Telegram dated 4/22/33, CJA, Wise papers, Reel 82.

[3]Letter dated 4/26/33, Voss, op. cit., p. 87.

I have not tried in speech to be eloquent to you, dear Mr. Secretary, but I think you should realize that this is not and should not be treated as an internal German question. If Germany says in effect that the Jews are not fit to be members in good standing of a modern State, that is an attack upon every Jew throughout the world.[1]

A short time later, Wise asserted himself in his continuing effort to break through the silence of the Roosevelt administration. He wrote to Mack:

We have decided on two things. To bring all the pressure we can through letters and telegrams from all the Jews of this country to bear upon the President, the State Department and Congress demanding action. I think I have been a little guilty in restraining such action up to this time. I dare not do it any longer. I have no right....[2]

Writing to the famous scientist, Albert Einstein, Wise relayed the reports flowing into the United States:

We here in America get not only the most terrible letters from individuals, lawyers, doctors, judges, who have escaped from Germany into surrounding countries...but we have also heard from [James G.] McDonald, the secretary of the Foreign Policy Association, who declares that Hitler said to him, just three weeks ago: We will annihilate the Jews in every way. They do not belong to the White race and they will no longer be tolerated in Germany. We are going to destroy them and we are going to show the rest of the world how it can and should be done....[3]

The stream of protest letters from Wise to Frankfurter continued:

---

[1]Cited in Morse, Arthur, *While Six Million Died* (New York: Random House, 1968), p. 122.

[2]Letter dated 5/4/33, CZA, Wise papers, Reel 115.

[3]Letter dated 5/9/33, Voss, op. cit., pp. 187-188.

It may be of course that FDR has exacted some promise from the German government. One devoutly hopes so, for he was in a position to ask almost anything for securing Hitler immunity from French attack or invasion. He has saved Germany from France. He has saved the world from war. In heaven's name, why can't he be moved to save the Jews of Germany? Does he not know? Does he not care?[1]

A few days later, a fresh report from Europe reached the American Jewish Congress:

The present situation of the Jews of Germany is deplorable beyond any words of mine to describe....What you will decide to do is of course your own concern; all I can say, in conclusion, is that what you do should be done quickly. Either muffle your ears to the weeping and wailing of the children of Rachel, and harden your hearts to this cry of humanity itself and thus let the worst crime of our age proceed to its ordained end in the deliberate extinction of nearly a million men, women and children or else come quickly and strongly to the rescue....[2]

The following month, Wise wrote to Mack of pressure for silence coming from the White House in the person of Sam Rosenman, a Jewish Justice of the New York Supreme Court and a speechwriter for Roosevelt. Rosenman had written to a Jewish leader:

You should not ask the President to make a declaration or any public act. As for receiving a delegation or deputation, it is out now. If you are going ahead with your resolution, form and language should be submitted to the State Department.[3]

---

[1] Letter dated 5/17/33, CZA, Julian Mack papers, Reel 83a.

[2] Report dated 5/22/33, ibid., Reel 83.

[3] Letter dated 6/3/33, ibid., Reel 83a.

The question of whether public protest could harm German Jewry pressed on the minds of the Jewish leadership in the United States. Wise addressed this question when writing to Mack:

I had an illuminating conversation with some men yesterday - Dr. [Emanual] Libman, and Dr. [Leopold] Lichtwitz who, according to Libman is one of the greatest metabolism men in Europe, and Dr. [Benjamin A.] Bernstein, friend of [Albert] Einstein and Morris Cohen....I happened to say that we were nervous about doing a certain thing because of the possible hurt to German Jews. Both of them believe in this thesis and restated it again and again - "You cannot hurt the Jews of Germany. They are finished. You may help them. You cannot hurt them." I really felt, Mack, as though I had been struck a blow between the eyes to hear two distinguished German Jews, one of whom (Bernstein) is about as Jewish-looking as Hitler, speak in these terms....[1]

From Stuttgart came additional information:

...the homes of members of the Jewish Benevolent Association were searched and four hundred men, women and children ranging in age from twelve to eighty were rounded up. They were forced to lick the dirty pavement....When an old man defended himself...the crowd attacked and severely beat him. At the end of the day, sixty Jews were detained for further punishment.[2]

The same month, Wise gave an update to a friend:

Things get worse and worse in Germany. Today I had a report which it will become necessary for me to verify...that sixty-five Jews in Halle-on-the-Salle were taken to a local hospital and operations performed on them in order to sterilize them.

---

[1]Letted dated 6/7/33, Voss, op. cit., p. 190.

[2]Quoted in Morse, op. cit., p. 190.

Four of them died, eleven are crippled, and all the rest have been permanently and curelessly sterilized....[1]

An officer of the Joint Distribution Committte, Dr. Jonah B. Wise [no relation to Stephen Wise] added his concerns about the silence of the Roosevelt administration at a meeting in New York:

It is difficult for Americans - Jews and Gentiles alike - to understand the silence of President Roosevelt in the face of one of the great human disasters of our time. The tragic and needless sufferings of the Jews in Germany are such that it should have been impossible for the President of the United States not to have spoken a word of warning and condemnation to the German government. I am aware of the niceties of diplomatic procedure and the amenities of international life. But in a crisis such as exists in Germany today diplomatic discretion must yield to moral indignation.[2]

Back from a fact-finding trip to Europe, Stephen Wise reported to the American Jewish Congress, recounting life in German concentration camps: "The average life in a concentration camp is from three to six weeks, except for very young, tough people. That is the testimony I got from everybody...."[3]

In October of the same year, the *New York Times* carried a story of a former inmate at a concentration camp near Berlin. There were accounts of drunken guards severely beating inmates and the names of his fellow inmates who had committed suicide.[4]

Despite the continuing misery, the White House maintained silence and Wise's protests to Mack became increasingly bitter:

---

[1]Letter dated 6/21/33, Voss, op. cit., pp. 190-191.

[2]Quoted by Morse, op. cit., p. 121.

[3]Report dated 9/23/33, CZA, Wise papers, Reel 87.

[4]Morse, op. cit., pp. 157-159.

"We have had nothing but indifference and unconcern up to this time."[1]

The White House silence did not reflect a lack of direct documentation. The American Consul General in Germany dispatched to his superiors the story of a German Jew, a decorated veteran of World War I. The man had been released from a German concentration camp, and was then requested to report to the police. Receiving a call from the police telling her to come to the station for "good news about your husband," his wife hurried there only to be shown his dead body. The Consul General wrote: "There is an element of brutality and hardness in the German character which I have never before believed was there, but which we must recognize as existing."[2]

The disturbing reports cited above were all dated the same year.

The year was 1933.

---

[1] Letter dated 10/18/33, Voss, op. cit., p. 195.

[2] Morse, op. cit., pp. 155-156.

CHAPTER I

A Group of Powerful Men

Adolf Hitler came to power in 1933, only fourteen years after the end of "The Great War," World War I. The leadership of the American Jewish community which would largely determine the American Jewish response to this threat was mature, experienced. Many had been involved in leadership positions even before World War I, and their views were shaped and informed by the momentous events of those early years.

The often described division of the Jewish leadership into Zionists, non-Zionists and anti-Zionists has served to oversimplify the varied and complex factors that determined what a given leader did and did not do in the 1930s and 1940s. Differences over Zionism did exist, but must take their place alongside other significant factors such as money, power, ego, personal and family relationships, and religious identification.

To be sure, there were different perspectives on many issues. This begs several questions: (1) What were the points of disagreement? (2) Was there disagreement on all key issues or were there important areas of agreement? (3) In what way did the points of disagreement and the points of agreement affect the vigorousness of the response to the crisis of world Jewry?

The leaders of the American Jewish Committee, American Jewish Congress, Zionist Organization of America, and other Jewish organizations were individuals active in arenas other than these organizations. Many issues divided the leadership within each organization, and some important issues bound together the leadership across organizational lines. Other Jewish personalities completely outside the sphere of these organizations had a profound impact upon the response to Nazism.

In this chapter are described the beginnings of the official Jewish organizations. Also examined are the Armenian massacres during WWI, as there are parallels to the Holocaust which cannot be ignored. What did the world know of the Armenian genocide? When did the news get out? What was the role of the State Department and how did their response to the Armenian massacre presage the State Department response to the Nazi treatment of Jews a generation later?

The Kishinev pogroms and other anti-Jewish disturbances in Russia directly influenced the emergence of the American Jewish Committee and the American Zionist movement. Each new organization inevitably included among the criteria for its coming into existence the desire to be more "democratic" than the already established organizations.

In 1906, Dr. Cyrus Adler, in a letter to the *American Hebrew*, complained that current organizations were unrepresentative, and called for the establishment of an authoritative group comprised of delegates from all states. This was followed by a meeting in New York of a group of thirty-four people who "shared a common concern for the fate of world Jewry, a concern intensified by developments in czarist Russia."[1]

This was the backdrop to the first official meeting of the American Jewish Committee. The number of members was set at sixty, and the constitution provided for "five-year terms for members to be elected by district advisory councils, with one-fifth of the members to leave office each year." [2]

The leading figures were Judge Mayer Sulzberger, Louis Marshall, Cyrus Adler, and Jacob Schiff. Schiff was the towering figure of the group which to a large degree represented wealthy American Jews of German background. Sulzberger was president until his death in 1912. He was succeeded by Marshall who served until his death in 1929. Cyrus Adler then served until his death in 1940.

Many of these same leaders founded the Joint Distribution Committee - the JDC, in 1914. The JDC is an important philanthropic organization while the American Jewish Committee, the American Jewish Congress, and Anti-

[1]Cohen, Naomi, *Not Free to Desist: The American Jewish Committee, 1906-1966* (Philadephia: Jewish Publication Society of America, 1967), pp. 3ff.

[2]Ibid., p. 16

Defamation League of B'nai B'rith are often classified as "defense" organizations concerned with the rights of Jews.

Louis Marshall was named president of the JDC, and Schiff's son-in-law, Felix Warburg, the treasurer. Warburg soon became chairman and remained at the helm until 1932.

At the time Cyrus Adler published in the *American Hebrew* his call for what became the American Jewish Committee, there was a young journalist at the *American Hebrew* named Louis Lipsky. Lipsky became a leading figure in the American Zionist movement, and wrote from the inside some of the most insightful history of that period. In tracing American Zionist origins, he writes: "The Zionist movement can be considered to have made its appearance through the reaction of the American Jewish community to the Kishinev pogroms of 1903...."[1]

Like Lipsky, Jacob de Haas was a journalist. He attended his first Zionist Congress as a reporter. He became committed to Herzl's dream of a Zionist political movement that would enable large numbers of European Jews to escape endemic discrimination by settling in their ancient homeland. Eager to enlarge his field of activities, Herzl encouraged de Haas to go to America and gave him a letter of introduction. The first president of the American Zionist Federation, Richard Gottheil, sponsored de Haas' relocation. In 1902 De Haas received an encouraging letter from the secretary of the American organization telling him: "I believe there is a large field of activity for you in this country, and I further believe that it is to the very best interest of Zionism here that you should come at once."[2]

Jacob de Haas was born in London in 1872, the descendent of a Dutch Sephardic family. He came to America as secretary of the Federation of American Zionists, a nascent organization headed by Rabbi Judah Magnes. After a few years, de Haas, despairing of the direction of the American organization, returned to journalism. He moved to Boston and bought the *Jewish Advocate*, but soon retraced his steps to play a central role in American Zionism.

Louis Lipsky, who served as the New York correspondent of de Haas's *Jewish Advocate,* left us this insight into de Haas' dilemma: "He was a Herzlian Zionist in an environment which,

---

[1]Lipsky, Louis, *Memoirs in Profile: A Memoir of Early Days* (Philadelphia: Jewish Publication Society, 1975), p. 52.

[2]Letter dated 3/14/1902, CZA, de Haas papers, A404, folder 30.

in his view, was more cultural than political. He felt himself alone...he was at odds with the Federation until he met Mr. Brandeis and began conversations with him that led to his gradual conversion."[1]

Lipsky painted a colorful portrait of de Haas:

> He remained English in his manner and speech all his life; he never rid himself of the London fog in his throat....He was a rebel and took delight in attacking the conservative leaders of the Jewish community. He was contentious and loved to pick a quarrel....He carried himself with a Bohemian swagger, spoke of political affairs with mystic allusions to what he might reveal if he were free to speak, and had an endless fund of gossip about the leading figures in the Zionist Movement....he smoked a cigar with savage intensity, drank beer like a German and had a bizarre taste in matters of the theatre....[2]

Contentiousness was a trait de Haas had in common with Stephen Wise, and the relationship between the two men was never cordial.

In June, 1918, in Pittsburgh, the Federation of American Zionists became the Zionist Organization of America. The President was Judge Julian Mack, a partner in what came to be known as the "Brandeis-Mack Group." The friends and colleagues in journalism, Louis Lipsky and Jacob de Haas were named executive secretary and secretary, respectively.

Just as many of the founders of the American Jewish Committee and the JDC were the same men, so too did most of the same men establish both the ZOA and the American Jewish Congress. During World War I a Jewish Congress Committee was formed which involved members of the Federation of American Zionists and other groups with an interest in Jewish settlement in Palestine. Though the American Jewish Committee had come into existence to make Jewish life more representative, many people considered this very same group undemocratic and determined to create a congress which would organize along democratic lines.

---

[1] Lipsky, op. cit., pp. 216-224.

[2] Ibid.

On December 15, 1916, the American Jewish Congress convened its first meeting in Philadelphia and named Judge Julian Mack as presiding officer. The American Jewish Congress had delegates claiming to represent over 700,000 Jews. In general it can be said that they favored continued Jewish settlement in Palestine and were vocal in demanding equal rights for Jews in all the states of Europe.[1]

Judah Magnes, mentioned as an early leader of the Federation of American Zionists, was sought by many organizations as a leader. Magnes was married to the daughter of Louis Marshall and was a favorite of the leadership of the American Jewish Committee and Joint Distribution Committee. Lipsky writes of his first meeting with Magnes:

I met Judah Magnes when he returned from his studies in Germany, probably in 1903. I was advised by Mrs. Phillip Cowen, the wife of the publisher of the *American Hebrew*, to see an American young man who should interest me as a curious personality. I met Dr. Magnes the next day in a kosher restaurant on Canal Street. He insisted that it be kosher. He was a tall, spare, young man with a light beard, who smiled generously with an easy friendliness, and confessed without provocation that in Berlin he had been converted to orthodoxy, that he had attended a Zionist Congress and knew Theodor Herzl....

Lipsky's profile of Magnes captures the restlessness of this fascinating personality. "He was greatly excited by life. He liked to be free to change his music....To the surprise of all of his friends, he made his way to the pulpit of Temple Emanu-El, resigning that post shortly in a clash of opinion about liturgical practices...."[2]

Magnes "chose sides" with the American Jewish Committee in its burgeoning conflict with the American Jewish Congress. Like Cyrus Adler and Magnes' father-in-law, Louis Marshall, he was involved in the development of the Conservatives' Jewish Theological Seminary. He moved to Palestine in 1923

---

[1]See the detailed report by de Haas in: CZA, Wise papers, Reel 107.

[2]Lipsky, op. cit., pp. 224-231.

and was the first chancellor of Hebrew University, serving in that capacity from 1925-1933.

Magnes was a committed and principled pacifist. His championing of a binational state for Arabs and Jews in Palestine brought him into frequent conflict with Wise and other American Zionist leaders.

The power behind the group that made up the JDC and American Jewish Committe was Jacob Schiff. Schiff, while a man of short physical stature, was a giant in American finance until his death in 1920. From a wealthy banking family in Germany, he joined Kuhn Loeb in New York in 1873. His experience, intelligence and aggressive nature won him two major prizes in 1875 - the hand in marriage of the daughter of Solomon Loeb and full partnership in the firm. His specialty was railroad finance. Working with E.H. Harriman, he acquired the Union Pacific Railroad in 1897.

The term "assimilationist" is often misused in describing differing outlooks among American Jewry. While Schiff shared with other leaders of the American Jewish Committee the fear that political Zionism would undercut the efforts of American Jews to establish beyond doubt their "American-ness," he did not shrink from using his power overtly in the service of identifiably Jewish causes.[1]

Outraged by the pogroms against Jews in czarist Russia, he took pride in helping the Japanese finance the Russo-Japanese War. The Japanese and Russians had competing interests in Korea and Manchuria. Diplomatic efforts to mediate the dispute led to broken agreements, which, in turn, led to war. On February 8, 1904, Japan attacked Russian ships in Port Arthur, Manchuria.

When Japan sought major loans in London and New York, Schiff "shocked Japan's financial commissioner, Baron Korekiyo Takahaski, by volunteering to underwrite half the ten-million pound loan." The Japanese victory in the war stunned the Western world.[2]

Orthodox, Reform, and Conservative denominational lines were much more blurred in the first two decades of this century than is the case now. Judah Magnes was courted by all three groups. Schiff was a major supporter of the Reform

---

[1]Ibid.

[2]Chernow, Ron, *The Warburgs: The 20th - Century Odyssey of a Remarkable Jewish Family* (Random House: New York, 1993), pp. 110.

Temple Emanu-El in New York, but he and Felix Warburg also contributed generously to the Jewish Theological Seminary. While these men were not dedicated Zionists, Solomon Schechter, who came from England to the United States in 1902 to become president of the Seminary, lent his support and prestige to the Zionist cause.[1]

Cyrus Adler, one of the prime movers behind the formation of the American Jewish Committee, became president of the Jewish Theological Seminary in 1915 after Solomon Schechter died. A scholar by training, he had been a professor of Semitic languages at Johns Hopkins University.

Adler was vigorously opposed to the goals of Zionism, but Lipsky, while noting the incongruity, included Adler in his book of profiles of Zionist leaders, writing:

> He was a man of faith....He should have been a Zionist by reason of faith, for he was a Sephardi. There were many Sephardim in the American movement who affirmed Zionism....Cyrus Adler loved the formal, the ritual, the traditional; but emotion seldom shook him. Therefore he was a stranger to the birth of Zionism and alway resentful of its existence and its successes.[2]

Louis Dembitz Brandeis, an early Zionist leader, protested to the "non-Zionist" Schiff-Warburg group over the route that Joint Distribution Committee funds took from the United States to Polish Jewry. Millions of dollars were channeled through the Aid Society of German Jews which included Max Warburg. Brandeis protested to Felix Warburg that the German group supported the ban on immigration of Polish Jews into Germany.

Louis Lipsky, who was always allied with Chaim Weizmann and thus in the Zionist camp opposite to Brandeis, wrote of Brandeis:

> Louis D. Brandeis became a Zionist too late in life. His personality was matured and fixed, and his way of life was trained in habit....He looked American, he lived American...he

---

[1] See Bernard G. Richards' chapter in: Cohen, Israel, *The Zionist Movement* (New York: Marstin Press, 1946), Chapter 22.

[2] See Lipsky's profile of Adler in Lipsky, op. cit. pp. 268-272.

was already distinguished in that way of life as a fighting lawyer for public causes. In all of his past his Jewish heritage had played no real part except as auxiliary to his basic concepts. He had to be recalled to his memory of the Jewish past that lived in his subconscious self.[1]

Brandeis was born in Louisville, Kentucky in 1856, and thus was already 58 when Jacob de Haas lured him into the Zionist fold. Where de Haas was flamboyant, Brandeis was ascetic. De Haas was loquacious while Brandeis was brief in speech and in writing. The correspondence in Brandeis' collection of papers at the Central Zionist Archives in Jerusalem consists of succinct, hand-written notes, barely legible. For de Haas, Jewish politics and Jewish journalism were his life; Brandeis made his name as an outstanding attorney and jurist. Zionism was a time consuming activity for only a brief period of his life. Despite these differences, the bond between these two men was genuine and lasting. In 1922, six years after he had ascended to the Supreme Court, Brandeis called de Haas his "teacher and companion."[2]

President Wilson named Brandeis to the Supreme Court in 1916. The two years previous to this were Brandeis' busiest years of activity at the head of American Zionism. Thereafter he presided from behind the scenes, the undisputed leader of the "Brandeis-Mack" group, sometimes referred to as the "Brandeis-Mack-de Haas" group.

It was Judge Julian Mack who was the first president of the Zionist Organization of America and of the American Jewish Congress. Mack was born in San Francisco in 1866. His family was part of the Reform movement in San Francisco. While unflinchingly identifying with Jewish organizations, he considered himself non-religious. His family moved to Cincinnati during his school years. It was there that he finished high school, and from high school he went straight to Harvard Law School. Mack distinguished himself at Harvard as one of the organizers of the renowned *Harvard Law Review* which first appeared in 1887, the same year he graduated *cum laude*.[3]

---

[1] For Lipsky's excellent profile of Brandeis, see Lipsky, op. cit., pp. 201-211.

[2] Ibid.

[3] See the forward by Horace Kallen in: Barnard, Harry, *The Forging of an American Jew: The Life and Times of Judge Julian W. Mack* (New York: Herzl Press, 1974).

Mack, like Brandeis, had no aspirations to high office in Jewish organizations. Leadership roles came to Mack by virtue of his stature and Brandeis' unwillingness to hold formal office. He admired Louis Marshall, and was involved in the top leadership of the American Jewish Committee for the first decade of its existence. However, with the growing polarization between the Committee and the Zionist movement, Mack resigned from the American Jewish Committee.

In Chicago, Mack was a noted law professor at Northwestern University, and, in 1903, he was encouraged to run for the Circuit Court. He was successful and served as either a state or Federal Judge for thirty-eight years.

While active in the formative years of the American Jewish Committee, American Jewish Congress and the ZOA, by 1923, when he was 57 years old, Mack wrote to Wise in response to Wise's desire to push for a World Jewish Congress: "The more I think about it, the more I feel we must go on in our way, that the real leadership of the WZO requires younger men than either [Brandeis] or myself....But I cannot get up any enthusiasm for a World Jewish Congress on Palestine, unless we are assured of the cooperation of practically all elements, and I haven't the faintest hope that this will come about in the next few years."[1]

Wise blamed de Haas for being over-protective of Brandeis' time and had only an occasional, formal correspondence with Brandeis. Mack, however, recognized Wise's talents and served as a mentor to him for many years.

An early insight into Wise's temperament is gleaned from a letter written during his tenure as head of a Reform congregation in Portland, Oregon. The exact date is unclear, but the year was most likely 1906. Wise wrote to Lipsky about the omission of some of Wise's notes in a document printed in the *Maccabean*, a monthly published by the Federation of American Zionists. The nature of the document is not spelled out, but Lipsky's response is pertinent:

You doubtless appreciate the fact that I am not the editor-in-chief of the *Maccabean*, and that any censure you may administer to me is unjust unless you make it general enough to include the entire Editorial Board....The omission was due to no

---

[1]Letter dated 3/20/23, CZA, Wise papers, Reel 114.

slight opinion of your style of writing, but rather to the aggressive, or I may say, the pugnacious tone of the notes.[1]

When Wise returned to New York from Portland, he was interviewed for the prestigious pulpit at Temple Emanu-El, America's largest Reform congregation, then guided by the dominating personality of Louis Marshall. Wise demanded the freedom to speak his mind, but Marshall asserted the right of the Board of Trustees to be the final authority on any matters pertaining to the Temple, including what was said from the pulpit.

Many years later, Wise's daughter, Justine Wise Polier, recalled the clash: "...Father wrote an open letter to Marshall on freedom of ministry, and a great battle ensued, in which Marshall said Father had never been offered the pulpit...."[2] Wise set up his own Free Synagogue which served as one of his stages of operation for years to come.

In 1919, Marshall was honored at a dinner. Mack, a friend of Marshall and a member of the organizing committee for the event, received this letter from Wise who protested his exclusion from the dais:

I have your letter of July 21 in which you give me further information concerning the Marshall dinner and reception....From your letter and the daily press I gather that virtually every member of the delegation is to speak at the dinner excepting myself....I wish to tell you that I consider it an entirely unfriendly, not to say, viewing our relations, disloyal thing in you to be ready to speak at the dinner and the meeting from which I, your associate in the Congress and as vice-president of the ZOA have been shut out....That you should assent to so viciously insulting an attitude...is somewhat but not wholly surprising.[3]

---

[1]Letter dated 12/16/05, Wise papers, Reel 113.

[2]Oral History Library, American Jewish Committee. Interviews of Justine Wise Polier were held in 1980.

[3]Letter dated 7/23/19, CZA, Wise papers, Reel 114.

Wise was a man of enormous energy and ambition, acknowledged as one of the leading orators of an era which honored great oratory. He held many leadership positions throughout the first four decades of the 20th century, yet he was always alive to perceived slights, and he thrived on conflict.

In addition to Brandeis and Mack, two other distinguished attorneys and jurists-to-be were involved in these beginning years of the major Jewish organizations. Felix Frankfurter, through his mentor, Brandeis, came to be involved in Zionist work, and Samuel Rosenman was an early member of the American Jewish Committee. However, both of these men left active Jewish organizational work behind early in their careers. They will appear with Henry Morgenthau, Jr. as central figures in Part II of this work; all three men had close access to President Franklin Roosevelt.

When Wise established a branch of his Free Synagogue on the Lower East Side, he attracted the attention of Orthodox Jewry. American Orthodoxy adhered to traditional observance, but was alert to the fact that the open forums and other educational opportunities which Wise's Free Synagogue offered in the English language filled a need.

Concerned about keeping younger people involved in Orthodoxy, three members of the Orthodox community approached Judah Magnes. Magnes often participated in *minyans* in an Orthodox *shtibel*. He willingly joined in the planning stages of a new Orthodox organization that was to take the name "Young Israel." In the early years there was considerable tension between a Conservative-leaning group within the new movement and a group that, while accepting the need for programming in English, was concerned that pure Torah principles would be diluted.

Enter Irving Bunim. Bunim was born in Volozhin, Lithuania, a city known as a major center of Torah study. Before his father brought him to America when he was nine years old, young Bunim was exposed to the horrors of pogroms and the constant fear of death. In America, Bunim's strong social conscience led him at age sixteen to the Socialist party, but the anti-religious bias of the Jewish Bundists quickly disillusioned him.

Bunim joined the Young Israel group and became the most vocal advocate of adherence to Orthodox principles. He was married in 1927 and joined his brother-in-law in a fabric business. When his brother-in-law moved to Palestine in

1932, Bunim bought the business, named it Eden Textiles and turned the family business into a highly successful enterprise which made him a wealthy man. Irving Bunim became synonymous with Orthodox causes and brought his own approach to the Nazi threat in the 1930s and 1940s. His work with Young Israel received a high compliment from Rabbi Joseph B. Soloveitchik, who said: "Young Israel, led by Bunim, did no less than save a whole generation of Jewish youth."[1]

Bunim and all Jewish leaders of the time were influenced by the First World War. Like all global conflicts, WWI made and broke many careers. The Jewish leadership was active on many fronts - working toward the Balfour declaration and minority rights for Jews in Europe, defining terms for the peace treaty that would formally end the war, and negotiating financial and political conditions that would shape the post-war era.

At the outset of the war, when American military involvement seemed far away, Jacob Schiff felt the tug of his German roots. He aided Germany financially and told a friend: "My sympathies are naturally altogether with Germany, as I would think as little to side against my own country as I would against my own parents."[2] But the sinking of the Lusitania in 1915 jolted his confidence in his fatherland, and by 1918 he was calling for a total allied victory to "utterly and permanently do away with Germany's military establishment."[3]

However, Schiff's enmity toward czarist Russia deriving from the relentless persecution of Jews never faltered. In 1915, President Woodrow Wilson lifted the ban on loans to the warring nations, and leaders of American financial markets received a delegation of British and French officials seeking loans. J.P. Morgan and Company came through with a $500 million dollar loan, but Schiff demanded British and French assent to exclude their Russian allies from any arrangement with Kuhn Loeb. Such terms were unacceptable to the Allies.

When his partners met to consider a loan agreement, Schiff said: "I realize fully what is at stake for the firm of Kuhn, Loeb & Company...but come what may...I cannot stultify myself by

---

[1]Bunim, Amos, *A Fire in His Soul* (Jerusalem: Feldheim Pub., 1989), pp. 9ff.

[2]Chernow, op. cit., p. 166.

[3]Ibid., p. 181.

aiding those who, in bitter enmity, have tortured my people and will continue to do so."[1] There was no loan from Kuhn Loeb.

Schiff's brother-in-law, Max Warburg, was a German delegate to the economic talks at Versailles when World War I ended. He had discussions with John Foster Dulles who would more than three decades later become Dwight Eisenhower's Secretary of State. Dulles and his brother Allen, a future CIA director, were two Americans whose international careers were launched during this critical period. The family tradition of high public service was well established; a grandfather and an uncle had already served their country as Secretaries of State.

The young Dulles brothers agreed that after the war the political and economic structures of Germany and her defeated allies should be kept intact for reasons of international commerce.

Allen Dulles served in Turkey as an assistant to the US High Commissioner Mark L. Bristol. He went from there to the New East Section of the State Department and from that post aided Bristol in an attempt to cover up the Turkish massacre of the Armenians during the war. In a chilling note, Bristol averred: "The Armenians are a race like the Jews - they have little or no national spirit and poor moral character."[2]

The Armenians, in the 400 years of Ottoman rule, were one of many tolerated minorities. They were Christians and, like the Jews in the Ottoman Empire, were accorded *dhimmi* status under Islamic law. They enjoyed a certain level of autonomy in religious practice and self-governance. The Armenians were concentrated in Anatolia, on the Russian border, and there were Armenians inside Russia. Russian Armenians were prominent on the Russian side of the Russian-Turkish War of 1877-78. As the Ottoman Empire began to crumble, the Armenians flourished, setting up their own school systems and cultural forms of expression.

The Young Turks who led the 1908 revolution were Turkish nationalists and established secular institutions, overthrowing the religious Moslem order. They viewed the Armenians as a direct threat to their revolutionary plans. The evidence is overwhelming that the massacre of the Armenians was a deliberate, planned genocide with all the requisite

---

[1] Ibid., pp. 166-169.

[2] Simpson, Christopher, *The Splendid Blond Beast* (New York: Grove Press, 1993), p. 31.

infrastructure necessary for the success of such an operation. The Young Turks allied themselves with Germany and used World War I as a cover for their slaughter of Armenians.

The killing began with Armenians in the armed services. With close cooperation between Talaat Pasha, the Turkish Minister of the Interior, and Enver Pasha, the Minister of War, Armenian labor battalions were disarmed in 1915 and systematically exterminated. The civilian Armenian population was next.

....the public crier went through the streets announcing that every male Armenian must present himself forthwith....When they arrived, they were thrown without explanation into prison, kept there a day or two, and then marched out of the town...they had not long to ponder over their plight, for they were halted and massacred at the first lonely place on the road.

As did the Nazis in World War II, the Turks used their intended victims as slave laborers.

Beginning in late 1914 and accelerating over the next three years, the Turkish government rounded up Armenian men for forced labor, worked many to death building a trans-Turkish railway for German business interests, then shot the survivors....when the camps became full, the Turks expelled the people into the deserts of what is today Syria and Iraq.[1]

Did the world "know?" The American ambassador to Turkey was Henry Morgenthau, Sr. He kept in close touch with the State Department on the unfolding massacres. In 1915, Tallat Pasha told Morgenthau: "We have got to finish with them....No Armenian can be our friend after what we have done to them."[2]

Morgenthau cabled specific suggestions for intervention to the State Department. Two months passed without a response while Secretary of State Robert Lansing awaited guidance from

---

[1]Ibid.

[2]Morgenthau, Henry, III, *Mostly Morgenthaus: A Family History* (New York: Ticknor and Fields, 1991), p. 169.

his Near Eastern desk. The advice presaged the State Department response to Jewish massacres years later: "However much we may deplore the suffering of the Armenians we cannot take any active steps to come to their assistance at the present time."[1]

In 1915, the Allies, France, Britain and Russia, accused the Turks of "crimes against humanity and civilization," leading the perpetrators to offer a secret deal to stop the massacres in exchange for control over Palestine and what is today Syria. The Allies, already in conflict over which of them would control these areas after the war, apparently never seriously considered the offer.[2]

High Commissioner Bristol toiled to keep the press from areas where the Armenians were being massacred, and Allen Dulles supported him in the State Department. He wrote Bristol of the considerations the Secretary of State faced, telling him that Lansing "wants to avoid giving the impression that while the United States is willing to intervene actively to protect its commercial interests, it is not willing to move on behalf of the Christian minorities." Dulles grumbled about support for Greeks and Jews as well: "I've been kept busy trying to ward off congressional resolutions of sympathy for these groups."[3]

How much of what the State Department knew did the American public know? In 1915, the first year of the genocide, over one hundred articles appeared in the *New York Times,* and there was extensive coverage by many other widely read publications.

But in 1921, the world was tired of war, and commercial and political interests asserted themselves. The Armenians were forgotten.

There were, of course, other political factors that proved disastrous for the Armenians...but the systematic effort (chiefly by the Harding administration) to turn US public opinion towards Turkey was purely and simply motivated by the desire to beat the Powers [Britain, France and Russia] to what were

---

[1] Quoted by Morgenthou, ibid., p. 170

[2] Simpson, op. cit., pp. 30-31.

[3] Ibid., p. 34.

thought of as the vast, untapped resources of that country...it was not possible to bring about the desired change in public opinion without denigrating what the Armenians had suffered.[1]

And the perpetrators? Most of the leaders fled to the asylum extended to them in Germany. Despite the fact that the international commission dealing with war crimes at the post-war Paris Peace Conference confirmed and denounced the Armenian genocide, little was done.

Article 230 of the Treaty of Sevres of 1920 did not specify a forum in which the perpetrators would be tried, shifting to the Allies the "right to designate the tribunal which shall try the persons so accused."[2]

On Malta the British government held many Turks accused of war crimes but could not decide on a course of action. The confusion was reflected in the condition of imprisonment. The prisoners lived in apartments and were loosely supervised. Two high Turkish officials implicated in the Armenian massacres were able to escape. The British replaced the Treaty of Sevres with the Treaty of Lausanne which conspicuously omitted all reference to war crimes.[3]

Lord Curzon later reflected on the inaction: "I think we made a great mistake in ever letting these people out. I had to yield at the time to a pressure which I always felt to be mistaken."[4]

---

[1]Study done by Marjorie Dobkin, cited by Simpson, pp. 34-35.

[2]Willis, James F., *Prologue to Nuremberg: The Politics and Diplomacy of Punishing War Criminals of the First World War* (Westport: Greenwood Press, 1982), p. 157.

[3]Ibid., pp. 160-161.

[4]Ibid., p. 163.

CHAPTER II

Zionist Politics

Secretary of State Lansing was no more favorably disposed toward Zionism than toward the Armenian fate, putting forth the argument: "Many Christian sects and individuals would undoubtedly resent turning the Holy Land over to the absolute control of the race credited with the death of Christ."[1]

Lansing's Ambassador in Turkey was also opposed to Zionism. Morgenthau, a member of Stephen Wise's Free Synagogue, wrote Wise of his conversation with the Turkish Foreign Minister, Halil Bey, who had told him: "Just see how the Armenians are treated for their nationalistic tendencies!"[2]

Morgenthau went on to warn Wise of Zionist activities:

I beg of you for the sake of all the Jews that are living here, that you try to exert your influence to have no bomb thrown from America. It is utterly impossible to convince the Turkish authorities that Zionism is anything but a political move to create a Jewish state on Turkish territory.[3]

Morgenthau's views put him on a collision course with his rabbi. The clash came in 1922 when Wise, in an address on Zionism, strongly criticized Morgenthau's position. Morgenthau requested a copy of the address and, when it was

---

[1]Quoted in: Cohen, Naomi, *The Year After the Riots* (Wayne State U. Press, 1988), p. 19.

[2]Morgenthau, pp. 163-164.

[3]Ibid.

not forthcoming, resigned from the Free Synagogue. In a letter
to Wise he explained:

> I was reliably informed by someone who heard your
> address...that it contained a strong personal attack on me....I
> hoped, that upon my receiving the sermon, it might prove that
> your attack was not as abusive as I had been led to believe, but,
> if your attack was personal against me...I would be totally
> devoid of all self-respect, if I remained a member of the Free
> Synagogue.[1]

Wise and other American leaders were feverishly involved in
Zionist politics in the years between the end of World War I
and Hitler's rise to Germany's Chancellorship in 1933. A
knowledge of this activity is important to an understanding of
the status of American Jewish leadership as it faced the
beginning of this tragic era.

This chapter begins with negotiations over the British
Mandate for Palestine, describes the defeat of the Brandeis-
Mack group in 1922 in American Zionist politics, and the
"rematch" in 1930. The chapter ends in 1932 on the eve of the
Nazi era in Germany and a new era in the United States. Stephen
Wise is embroiled in open conflict with second-term New York
governor and presidential candidate Franklin Delano Roosevelt.

During the war, in 1917, the Balfour Declaration had
become a reality. While Chaim Weizmann in London was the
leader in most regular contact with the British, every aspect of
every draft of the proclamation was reviewed, refined and
subsequently approved by Brandeis in Washington. This was
followed by extensive negotiations concerning incorporation of
the Balfour Declaration into the wording of the British Mandate
over Palestine.

The Hashemite leader, Emir Feisal, signed an agreement with
Weizmann in January, 1919, in which Feisal seemed to
support Zionist aims. When shortly thereafter he inveighed
against a Jewish commonwealth in an interview with the
French publication *Le Matin*, Weizmann sought clarification.
There followed the often quoted letter from Feisal to Felix
Frankfurter expressing sympathy with the Zionist movement

---

[1]Letter dated 1/14/22, CZA, Wise papers, Reel 117.

and grandly stating: "We will wish the Jews a hearty welcome home...."[1]

Feisal was much too far out in front of his constituency. In Damascus, in July, 1919, the First Syrian Congress rejected all Jewish claims to Palestine. Many Zionists viewed Weizmann's contacts with Feisal as naive, and a British intelligence officer reported to Lord Curzon: "Dr. Weizmann's agreement with Emir Feisal is not worth the paper it is written on or the energy wasted in the conversation to make it."[2]

Weizmann was also having his problems with American Zionists. Wise and de Haas sparred over Wise's enmity toward Weizmann. Wise protested when de Haas reported to Brandeis and Mack that Wise was estranged from Weizmann.[3] However, less than six days later, Wise wrote to a friend that Weizmann was "a dangerous factor in the movement; and hard and regrettable as it may be, it will be necessary to curtail his power almost to the point of elimination."[4]

Frankfurter, writing to Brandeis from London, also sent negative comments about Wise's clash with Weizmann over wording of the British Mandate: "I am sorry to say that Wise seems to have lost sight of the object for which he was sent, namely to devote himself to Zionist matters....The result was that he was not taken seriously by Weizmann."[5]

Frankfurter also was critical of de Haas' attitude toward Weizmann: "He treats Weizmann as the bright young Zionist whom he knew, or knew of, some 20 or 25 years ago. It is essential not only now, but for the future for de Haas to understand that whether he likes it or not, Weizmann is the commanding figure in Zionism on this side of the water."[6]

Frankfurter's trip to Europe included a fact-finding mission to Poland to look into extensive reports of Jewish repression. Some months earlier, he had jousted with Colonel Edward

---

[1]Quoted in: Reinharz, Jehuda, *Chaim Weizmann: The Making of a Statesman* (New York: Oxford University Press, 1993), p. 274.

[2]Ibid.

[3]Letter dated 2/11/19, CZA, Wise papers, Reel 107.

[4]Reinharz, op. cit., p. 303.

[5]Ibid.

[6]Ibid., pp. 303-304.

House, President Wilson's top aide, telling him that American Jews might very well oppose the confirmation of Hugh Gibson as Minister to Poland because he was not perceived as sympathetic to Jewish concerns. This demonstrates that, in 1919, there was an awareness of American Jewish political muscle and the willingness to use it.

Once confirmed and on duty in Poland, Gibson complained of being overwhelmed by complaints of Jewish leaders and recommended that "Zionists and other trouble-makers" not be allowed into Poland.[1] Nonetheless Frankfurter got his visa.

The British claim to Palestine had to vie with French goals in the Middle East. The French laid claim to the northern Galilee which included several Jewish settlements. General Edmund Allenby, while believing that security concerns dictated British control of this area, gave in to the French in September 1919, and pledged to withdraw British forces from the northern Galilee. A line was drawn which brought Jewish settlements within the British area of influence but left to Syria, under the French Mandate, key water resources on which Jewish economic development depended.[2]

British officials had been privy to an American report summarizing the findings of a fact finding commission sent to the Middle East by the State Department in the summer of 1919 to study conditions there. The commission reported that Feisal was "a great lover of Christians" and commented on high hopes for Christian missions. They warned, however, that Jewish settlements could not be protected and advised strict limitations on Jewish immigration.[3]

One of the victims of the dispute over the border between the French and British Mandates was Joseph Trumpeldor. Trumpeldor had lost an arm while serving the Russian Army during the Russo-Japanese War of 1905. He later formed the Zion Mule Corps and, with Vladimir Jabotinsky, the Jewish Legion.

Tel Chai was at the far reaches of the Galilee and local Bedouins insisted on their right to be armed and keep the hated French officials out of the area. It was to a great extent for this purpose that they patrolled the area of Tel Chai. Conflict and

---

[1]Walworth, Arthur, *Wilson and His Peacemakers* (New York: W.W. Norton & Co., 1986), p. 473.

[2]Ibid., pp. 303-304.

[3]Walworth, Arthur, op. cit, p. 503.

misunderstanding developed with the outnumbered Jews in the area. Trumpeldor and six of his colleagues were killed in February, 1920.[1]

Weizmann's protest over British capitulation in the Galilee was to no avail. He also suffered a temporary defeat at the hands of Brandeis in meetings in Europe over Zionist organization. While both acknowledged the need to seek support for Palestine from Jews who were not enthusiastic Zionists, Brandeis rejected Weizmann's desire to include non-Zionist organizations on the proposed Provisional Council. Brandeis presided at the crucial meeting and forced through his formula. Stung by the defeat, Weizmann told Brandeis:

You have built a Monroe Doctrine around American Zionism. I consider it my duty to break through this Monroe Doctrine with full force. If the creation of a general Jewish organization causes you discomfort, you will have to face the choice of remaining Americans or joining the general Jewish organization....[2]

This set the stage for Weizmann's alliance with Lipsky and other American Zionists who would triumph over the Brandeis-Mack group a short time later.

Weizmann was not the only one upset about Zionist affairs. In 1920, a central General Actions Committee of World Zionism was chosen, and it included several Americans. Not included was Stephen Wise who resigned as Vice-President of the ZOA and poured out his resentment in a letter to Mack:

I had assumed that the service, political and propagandist, which it was my privilege to render to the movement especially during the last six years was not so much to be placed by the side of [others]...as by the side of that of Justice Brandeis and yourself....Do you know of any man who has been more loyal to Justice Brandeis than I have been....the fact is that Justice Brandeis presided at the evening sessions at which the elections

---

[1]See Katz's account of the Tel Hai incident in : Katz, Shmuel, "*Jabo* [Hebrew], Vol. I (Tel Aviv: Dvir Publishing House, 1993), pp. 301-306.

[2]Reinharz, op. cit., pp. 308-309.

were held. He should have noted the omission of my name, assuming as I do that the loyalties of friendship are not always to remain unreciprocated....[1]

Mack responded to his friend with some irritation: "...I have urged in vain that you should discuss the matter with LDB [Brandeis] and de Haas before taking this step. You leave me no alternative, however, but to present your resignation, and, of course, I shall have to do so."[2]

Another 1920 event of importance in the history of American Jewish leadership was the death of Jacob Schiff. This powerful figure, often associated with the "assimilationists" among American Jews, stipulated that his grandchildren were to forfeit the generous trusts he set up for them if they married non-Jews. Testifying to his skill and power was his estate of $35 million, an enormous sum in 1920.[3]

Louis Brandeis was now on the Supreme Court and the unquestioned leader of American Zionists. His view of Zionism brought him into open conflict with Chaim Weizmann. While Lipsky from his partisan stance beside Weizmann and de Haas in his championing of Brandeis left us somewhat partisan views on the history of the rift between the powerful Justice of the American Supreme Court and the confidant of high British officials, there is agreement on the essence of the dispute.

De Haas describes Weizmann's ties to Achad Ha'am, who had a vision of Palestine as a cultural and spiritual center of Judaism. World War I drove Achad Ha'am and his group to England where they saw the possibility of realizing Herzl's dream of a "charter for Palestine." De Haas wrote that Weizmann was drawn to a more political view of Zionism because "Jewish patriotism forced them to undertake the leadership of a movement which had...outgrown their own convictions."[4]

In Brandeis, de Haas saw a proponent of Herzl's diplomatic and economic approach to Zionism. Brandeis looked to building

---

[1]Letter dated 8/24/20, CZA, Wise papers, Reel 114.

[2]Letter dated 8/27/20, ibid.

[3]Chernow, op. cit., pp. 237-238.

[4]De Haas' views were detailed in an article, "Thirty Years After Herzl," which was published in the *Menorah Journal,* June, 1927 and can be found in: CZA, de Haas papers, 28.790.

an infrastructure based on solid economic principles that could accommodate 50,000 new immigrants a year, while Weizmann saw a more selective, gradual *aliyah.*

Weizmann championed the Keren Hayesod which de Haas viewed suspiciously as a means of bureaucratic control. "For the doctrinaires this plan had great advantages. It shelved acute consideration of practical questions...it demanded no reform in policy; it gave free play to all the factions in the movement."[1] By contrast, de Haas detailed Brandeis' plans:

The Brandeis formula had been in the winter of 1920-21 worked out into a practical program. It proposed, in the first place, the capitalization of a large land purchase - the triangle of the Negeb - the area of southern Palestine from Jappa to Rafa which Dr. Weizmann had undertaken to obtain the previous summer.[2]

De Haas mentions some of the consultants involved in the American's plan and their vision for southern Palestine.

...this area J.H. Cory, the California expert, Sir William Willcock, the well-known irrigation engineer, and Dr. R.H. Forbes, Director of the Arizona Agricultural Experimental Station, regard as superior to California for citrus development. In the second place, it proposed the capitalization of what were known as the "key industries" in Palestine. For the land purchase project a comprehensive campaign was outlined....the campaign slogan was intended to convey the idea that each share of stock [that investors bought] would equal in value one dunam.[3]

When Weizmann came to the United States in 1921, de Haas believed it was for "...the avowed purpose of consolidating his position as leader, which in his own view required the ousting

---

[1]Ibid.

[2]Ibid.

[3]Ibid.

of Brandeis and his principal advisors. Glittering generalities were more persuasive than cold technical considerations...."[1]

Lipsky, the American Zionist leader most closely allied with Weizmann, saw Weizmann as "the guide and protector," of the Zionist dream, and was critical of Brandeis' lack of emphasis on the need to develop the Jews in Palestine into a strong political entity. "Mr. Brandeis...seemed to have in mind a planned economy for a people not yet organized."[2]

Jehuda Reinharz also stresses the Brandeisian emphasis on infrastructure versus Weizmann's advocacy of cultural renaissance. Philosophical and organizational differences were important, but Reinharz puts his finger on perhaps the most crucial difference:

> While Weizmann and other European Zionists did not hesitate to sacrifice much of their time, and in some cases jeopardize their careers, Brandeis and his top American advisors were unwilling to do the same; their personal advancement in the world outside the Zionist orbit took first priority....[3]

The battle was joined, and though he stayed behind the scenes, Brandeis' memos to his colleagues leave no doubt that he was the commander.

> ...the objection to a personal fight with W. [Weizmann] is...not unwillingness to engage in personal polemics - (although they are usually inadvisable) - but that W's position with the British is such that we cannot pull him down publicly without topping over or seriously impairing our structure....We must figure with that fact just as we must figure with the fact that he is entirely untrustworthy....[4]

---

[1]Ibid.

[2]See Lipsky's discussion of Weizmann and this period in his *Memoirs in Profile*, op. cit., pp. 101-114.

[3]Reinharz, op. cit., p. 331.

[4]Letter dated 3/19/21, CZA, Wise papers, Reel 107.

As Weizmann's American colleagues steeled themselves for a fight, the question of a coalition was considered by Brandeis and his followers. One position paper by the opposition evoked this scholarly Brandeis lesson to his group:

The statement makes obvious the irreconcilable conflict....A coalition government is justifiable where in a great emergency party differences are sunk and their purposes postponed in the common devotion to a paramount purpose....But our differences are not as to means but as to ends. And the opposition differs from us in means - mainly if not wholly because they differ as to ends.

Changing tone, Brandeis ended this note in a combative manner:

Such opponents have no proper place in the Executive. Those of them allowed to survive...remain as before an obstacle and a danger. The proper place for such opposition is among the oats.[1]

A few days later, the ascetic Supreme Court justice issued another directive:

We must be aggressive against our foreign foes - and fight-fight-fight being careful always not to openly attack Weizmann personally. But we must with absolute frankness attack the policies which he espouses....[2]

As the pivotal convention approached, there was a brief, cool meeting between Brandeis and Weizmann, and a lengthy confrontation between Weizmann sitting opposite Julian Mack and Felix Frankfurter. Reconciliation being impossible, Weizmann told Frankfurter: "Your Zionism is not my Zionism.

---

[1]Ibid.

[2]Letter dated 3/22/22, ibid.

Your Jewishness is not my Jewishness. Your education is not my education. Your point of view is not my point of view...."[1]

At the ZOA convention in Cleveland, Mack, the on-scene leader of the Brandeis-Mack group, was soundly defeated. Mack and the entire group resigned from their positions in the American and World Zionist organizations.[2]

Stephen Wise's dilemma was acute. Brandeis and Mack had high judicial positions to command their full attention, but Wise was one American leader who *was* willing to give Zionism his full attention. Jewish politics was his life.

At first Wise allied firmly with the defeated group, writing to a relative:

Frankly I was disturbed for a little time when your letter came with its surprising note of confidence in, or rather hopefulness, over Weizmann....But you understand and clearly see that he is a man undeserving of confidence...we are to have nothing to do with the Organization....[3]

However, Wise was clearly uncomfortable outside the orbit of leadership. In June of 1922 he wrote to Mack:

...W. [Weizmann] is unchanged, purporting all the time to be frankness itself and yet if anything less frank than he was a year ago....The only thing I see anew is that he is not a man with whom one can work...it is unutterably sad that he alone should be at the helm, and Brandeis and you and Felix F. and the rest of us outside the range of service.[4]

The American Jewish Congress became Wise's personal fiefdom, but he was always seeking new and more visible forums. In a letter to Brandeis in 1923, he pushed the idea of a World Jewish Congress. There is no record of a response from

---

[1]Reinharz, op. cit., pp. 346ff.

[2]Lipsky, *Memoirs in Profile,* op. cit., pp. 216-224.

[3]Letter dated 6/14/21, Voss, op. cit., p. 112.

[4]Letter dated 6/26/22, CZA, Wise papers, Reel 114.

Brandeis, but Mack wrote to Wise and threw cold water on the idea.[1] It would be another decade before Wise realized his dream of a World Jewish Congress.

In 1925, Wise was busy organizing a conference to deal with Jewish relief in Eastern Europe. One recipient of an invitation was the same Louis Marshall with whom Wise had crossed swords over the Temple Emanu-El pulpit. Marshall believed Wise's efforts to be an unnecessary duplication of Joint Distribution Committee relief activity and enlisted the aid of his friend, Mack, to bring pressure on Wise.

Mack replied to Marshall: "I feel sure that Dr. Wise, to whom I am sending a copy of this, will agree with you that, in the light of the action of the JDC, the essential thing which the meeting next Sunday had been called to further has been accomplished and that there is no occasion for a new organization or a duplication of effort."[2] Wise called off the meeting.

Thus, in 1924, at the age of 50, Stephen Wise was still insecure among the leadership of American Jewry, but not without admirers. In a tribute to his service, noted Jewish writer and journalist Johan Smertenko, toasted Wise: "He formulated the battle-cry of the American Jewish Congress [and] uttered the words that changed the voice of Israel from the cry of a mob to the demand of a dignified people."[3] This praise in 1924 is significant, because twenty years later, in the midst of efforts to prod the Roosevelt administration to help the Jews of Europe, Smertenko became active in a group bitterly opposed by Wise.

Meanwhile, Weizmann continued his efforts to involve "non-Zionists" in the effort to develop Palestine. When traveling to the United States, he and his wife, Vera, enjoyed the company of Felix Warburg and his wife, Frieda, of whom Vera later wrote: "My husband liked beautiful women, but they had to have brains as well, which she had in abundance."[4]

Frieda Warburg testified to Weizmann's spell over her. Referring to their first social engagement at her home, she

---

[1] Letter dated 3/20/23, ibid.

[2] Letter dated 5/19/25, CZA, Mack papers, A405, 73.

[3] Document dated 3/17/24, CZA, Wise papers, Reel 1.

[4] Chernow, op. cit., p. 250.

said: "I had not felt warmly toward Dr. Weizmann up to that time, but he came and, like Caesar, he conquered me at once."[1]

The Warburgs journeyed to Palestine with Weizmann and had a joyous reunion with Judah Magnes, a long-time friend. Felix and Frieda retained their opposition to a Jewish political entity, but willingly supported Magnes' vision of Palestine as a cultural center. They gave Magnes $500,000 for an Institute of Jewish Studies at Hebrew University.[2]

In the period leading up to the 1930 "rematch" between the Lipsky-Weizmann camp and the Brandies-Mack group, another Reform Rabbi, Louis I. Newman, figures prominently. Newman was a friend and frequent correspondent of Stephen Wise. Both were dedicated Zionists, but they were to take sharply different positions in the face of the Nazi threat in the 1930s.

Newman, in 1926, set forth for Reform Jews a strong case for Zionism. After reviewing the early history of the movement when its founder, Isaac M. Wise (no relation to Stephen Wise) led Reform Jews in passing resolutions opposed to Zionism, he pointed out that politics existed also in the Reform camp:

Newman stressed that anti-Semitic agitation in the United States was aimed not at Zionists but at assimilated Jews.

> The fear of the Reformers that the establishment of a Jewish homeland in Palestine would give impetus to expulsion-propaganda is without foundation. Torquemada, Ferdinand and Isabella exiled the Spanish Jews though Israel had no center in Zion...the adversaries of Zionism, whether they be Reformers, Conservatives or Orthodox assimilationists, should rid themselves of the apprehension that their economic and political opportunities will be curtailed by the progress of Zionism.

Newman went on to give a ringing endorsement to Jewish nationalism:

> Reform Jews must emancipate themselves from their obsession against nationalism. They must free themselves from their morbid fears....A courageous self-analysis of its own policies

---

[1] Ibid.

[2] Ibid., p. 251.

will reveal the same tendencies which motivate the Zionist movement, namely a recognition that nationalism is the very keystone in the arch of Jewish life....[1]

Newman's friend, Wise, had made his peace with Lipsky's leadership of American Zionism, but the relationship was stormy. They went together to the Basle Congress in 1927, Lipsky as president and Wise as head of the Political Committee. But Wise again clashed with Weizmann and left the Congress in protest before its close.

In 1928, Wise declined to accompany Lipsky to a meeting concerning a loan from the United Nations. "After reading Dr. Weizmann's letter to you...I have reached the conclusion that I cannot join you in negotiations with respect to a project which is a confession of the bankruptcy of the Zionist movement...."[2]

As many American Zionists began to call for a return of Brandeis' leadership, Wise found himself in the middle. He was agitated by Brandeis' unwillingness to be an active leader, and asserted to his daughter that "we should have built up a leader, whether Mack...or myself or anybody, but not forever depend upon an impossible leadership which can never come to pass....If he [Brandeis] left the bench now, he could save the movement from Weizmannism and Lipskyism...."[3]

A big sticking point for Wise was de Haas' role. In a letter in April, 1928, he wrote to a colleague:

The so-called Brandeis-Mack group...may take the leadership in its hands. I shall probably cooperate with it, but I am not a part of the group. I may say to you in confidence, that my reason for it lies chiefly in the circumstance that...Justice Brandeis' nominal leadership means the actual leadership of Mr. de Haas.[4]

---

[1]Newman, Louis I., *Biting on Granite* (New York: Bloch Publishing Company, 1946), pp. 34-45. This book is a compilation of Newman's writings which includes the 1926 Zionist appeal.

[2]Letter dated 1/1/38, CZA, Wise papers, Reel 113.

[3]Letter dated 3/28/28, ibid., Reel 4.

[4]Letter dated 4/3/28, ibid., Reel 107.

De Haas, for his part, had no use for Wise. At the 1928 American Zionist Convention, there was an unsuccessful thrust at Lipsky's leadership by those favoring a return of the Brandeis-Mack group. In reporting to Brandeis about Wise's role in the convention, he wrote:

> Wise behaved according to his own vacillating character. If my judgement is worth anything he has lost certainly the respect of the [Lipsky] administration; clearly that of the majority of us. By reason of his vocal ability he will be courted again and again for that purpose and for no other.[1]

Wise reported his perceptions of the convention to Louis Newman:

> The victory for Lipsky...seems overwhelming, but as you will see it is Pyrrhic in character....The opposition over-reached itself. Had it cried out solely against incompetence, a lowering of morale, etc., and made a place for Lipsky in other than administrative work, a far better showing could have been made....[2]

In a more personal note to his son he railed against de Haas' and Brandeis' "fatuous bitterness" toward Lipsky.[3]

Wise's anger boiled over in 1929 when Weizmann, after many years of trying, was able to establish an expanded Jewish Agency. He had found a firm ally in Wise's old nemesis, Louis Marshall. The leader of the "non-Zionist" group, Marshall was the architecht of Weizmann's dream, drafting the documents which brought the expanded Jewish Agency into existence. The delegates gathered in Zurich, and once again Wise was on the outside looking in.

In words, pungent even by Wise's standards, he attacked the compact between Marshall and Weizmann.

---

[1]Letter dated 7/6/28, ibid., CZA, de Haas papers, A404.

[2]Letter dated 7/12/28, ibid., CZA, Wise papers, Reel 117.

[3]Letter dated 10/10/28, ibid., Reel 122.

The bitter address prompted a lengthy front page article in the popular Jewish publication, *The Forward.* The article is worth examining in some detail as it is a trenchant, insightful analysis of Stephen Wise.

What is the key to the enigmatic character of the Pastor of the Free Synagogue? How explain his capriciousness and petulance, his inconsistency and inchoateness, his flights of rhetoric and tilting at windmills, his flamboyancy and loquacity? How reconcile his many notable achievements for American and for world Jewry with his indubitable vanity and egotism? How account for his acerbity, his querulousness, his cantankerousness, his virulence? And how, in brief, account for that speech of last Sunday morning....

The article carrying the byline of Nathaniel Zalowitz went on to offer some answers to the questions raised:

Rabbi Stephen S. Wise lives his life in the key of passion. It is largely in this way that we can comprehend his baffling nature....The moment you begin to regard Dr. Wise as a thinker or a leader you are lost in the maze of his contradictions. As long as you bear in mind that clear thinking and consistent action are alien to his nature you will readily forgive him his faults and be grateful for his extraordinary gifts.[1]

Wise's battle with Marshall and Weizmann was cut short by Marshall's death later in 1929. Felix Warburg inherited the mantle of the American Jewish Committee, JDC, "non-Zionist" leadership but did not have the forceful leadership qualities of his predecessor. The extended Jewish Agency never became a meaningful reality.

Louis Newman, a supporter of Brandeis, tried to convince his friend, Stephen Wise, to make a commitment to their camp. Wise responded by writing to Mack suggesting himself as a mediator between the two groups: "I might, of course, address a formal communication to you and to Lipsky, urging that there be a meeting on neutral ground - say, my study - but I do not

---

[1] Document dated 1/13/29, CZA, Mack papers, A405, 7b.

wish to do this nor could I do it unless I knew in advance that you and your associates were hospitable to the proposal."[1]

Mack responded pointedly: "I am perfectly willing of course to discuss anything and everything with you at any and all times. I care for no conference of any kind or at any time with Lipsky.[2]

As the pivotal Zionist Convention in the summer of 1930 drew near, Newman called on Wise not to let his feelings toward de Haas interfere with the goal of the return of the Brandeis-Mack group to leadership. Wise responded testily saying he would not even attend the convention and would "probably though not certainly refuse to serve as an officer of the ZOA even under the Brandeis-Mack leadership."[3]

At the Cleveland convention, a political compromise was fashioned. Lipsky agreed to step aside in favor of an eighteen man executive which later chose Robert Szold as their chairman. De Haas essentially barred Wise from holding an office, stating categorically to Mack: "I will not be a party to SSW holding any office at this time....none of us can afford the risk of perpetual irresponsibility of the SSW type."[4]

Wise was appointed to a committee chairmanship. Irrepressible as ever, he soon had the new leadership meeting on his turf. In one of his frequent reports to Mack, he exulted: "We had a good meeting of the 'Gang' at my home on Saturday morning." The Gang included de Haas.[5]

Wise and de Haas found common ground on British policy in Palestine during this time period. The Arab riots which rocked Palestine in 1929, wiping out the Jewish community in Hebron, shocked the Jewish world. The British sent two commissions to study conditions in Palestine and rewarded Arab aggression with the Passfield White Paper. This document set strict limits on Jewish land purchases and immigration.

Wise set out to author a book on the subject and, in part because of illness, called on de Haas to do the actual writing. The two rivals were co-authors of *The Great Betrayal*,

---

[1]Letter dated 2/20/30, CZA, Wise papers., Reel 114.

[2]Letter dated 2/22/30, ibid.

[3]Letters dated 5/13/30 and 5/17/30, ibid., Reel 117.

[4]Letter dated 7/4/30, CZA, Mack papers, A405, 98a.

[5]Letter dated 12/29/30, CZA, Wise papers, Reel 114.

published in 1931. In the Forward, Wise set forth the purpose he and de Haas shared in the writing of the book:

Upon the issuance of the Passfield White Paper...it seemed that after the tumult of protest should die, it would be needful to set forth the facts lest men forget....It is a serious, in truth, a grave task to which we set ourselves, the graver because of a life-long reverence and affection for all that is English. We do not indict a people. We do indict a government, which rendered a terrible disservice to its people by bringing their honor into question....

Heaping praise on his co-author, Wise charged that the recent British action represented a pattern, not a single incident:

Mr. de Haas' almost unique command of the vast documentary material has made it possible for us to trace, step by step, the march from the high promise of November 2, 1917, to the base breach of October 20, 1930 - the descent from Balfour to Passfield. It would be unfair not to state with unmistakable clearness that the Passfield White Paper was not a bolt from the blue. It was the culmination of a sinister policy rather than its commencement....[1]

Weizmann's response to the White Paper was typical - he protested strongly in private letters to British officials, but when he was stonewalled, backed off from confrontation. In trying to assure the British that the Jews had no intention of displacing the Arabs, he went so far as denying that he saw the importance of a Jewish majority in Palestine, saying that a majority was not a guarantor of security nor necessary for development of Jewish civilization and culture in Palestine.[2]

At the 17th Zionist Congress, de Haas and Wise, along with a newly formed "Group B" of American Zionists (as opposed to

---

[1]Wise, Stephen S. and Jacob de Haas, *The Great Betrayal* (New York: Brentano's, 1930). On microfilm at NY public library.

[2]Katz, op. cit., Volume II, p. 811.

"Group A" headed by Lipsky and faithful to Weizmann), joined in voting censure of Weizmann. Wise had compassion for his fallen opponent who was not returned to the World Zionist presidency. Wise wrote to his children:

> ...So much has happened and yet so little may be told excepting that last night (Sunday), the whole thing came to a climax. I could have wept for Weizmann, because after all, fifteen years of work, good, bad, and indifferent, was ended by a vote of censure. He deserved it and I voted for it. At the same time it was a sad spectacle....It was a terrible parliamentary struggle in which Motzkin and the Presidium helped us to get the vote on censure first, but we got it and it went through by about 125 to 110. Weizmann has already told friends that if we Americans had not come over in the spirit of the vendetta to punish him for 1921, the vote of censure would never have been passed.[1]

At this point in his career, Wise came into conflict with Franklin Roosevelt. Roosevelt was elected governor of New York in 1928 and re-elected in 1930. As the governor of the most populous state in the country, his name figured early in the speculation for the presidential elections of 1932. Facing persistent calls for action against Tammany Hall corruption in New York City, he equivocated. That his handling of the issue was weak and vacillating is agreed upon by two of Roosevelt's major biographers.[2]

Tammany Hall was an ingrained part of New York politics. Roosevelt calculated that while wounded by revelations of corruption, the powerful political machine would in 1932, as in previous national elections, have a major influence.

The most damaging revelations of abuse by the Tammany bosses came when the US attorney, Charles Tuttle, uncovered strong evidence that the wife of an appointed city magistrate had delivered $10,000 in cash to a Tammany leader. The money was purportedly part of a stock sale which was revealed

[1]Letter dated 7/14/22, CZA, Wise papers, Reel 122.

[2]The account which follows is based on: Schlesinger, A., *The Crisis of the Old Order : 1919-1933* (Boston: Houghton, Mifflin Co., 1956), pp. 394-395 and Davis, Kenneth S., *FDR, The New York Years, 1928-1933* (New York: Random House, 1979), pp. 166-172.

to be fictitious. The evidence was referred to Thomas Crain, the Manhattan district attorney.

When Crain, himself a Tammany faithful, dismissed the scandal by announcing that he was not able to get indictments from a grand jury, he received an open letter from a member of the City Affairs Committee accusing him of corruption and calling for intervention from the State level. The City Affairs Committee member who penned the letter was Rabbi Stephen S. Wise.

Roosevelt blunted criticism temporarily by appointing a commission of inquiry headed by Judge Samuel Seabury. Seabury was not a newcomer to the public eye. He had been the New York State Democratic gubernatorial candidate in 1916, and his name figured in the speculation for the upcoming presidential sweepstakes in 1932.

The confrontation sharpened when the Seabury Commission report in late 1930 detailed accounts of corruption in the Walker administration. Roosevelt rode the political fence and temporized.

When he publicly criticized the City Affairs Committee in 1932, the New York Governor drew a stinging reply from Wise and Holmes, a colleague on the committee:

If we have seemed to bombard you, it must be because any activity in the public interest appears like a bombardment to an official sunk in a stupor of indifference or lost in the absorption of political planning and plotting for his own political advantage.[1]

Wise added insult to injury a few months later in his privately published newsletter, *Opinion.* Wise held Roosevelt responsible for his own bad press and added: "It remains to be seen whether he wills to extricate himself honorably from a dilemma which has arisen because of a lack on his part of basic courage and the absence of capacity for true and fearless judgement."[2]

Wise continued to pound the Walker administration and included among his targets the Jewish *Morning Journal*, a

---

[1] Letter dated 4/1/32, CZA, Wise papers, Reel 68.

[2] Letter dated 8/8/32, ibid., Reel 9.

popular publication of the Orthodox Jews of eastern-European extraction. The leaders of the paper, Wise accused, had "peculiarly subterranean and nauseous relations to City Hall." He labelled his co-religionists as a "wretched crew of traitors to everything decent, civic and Jewish alike, who must never again be suffered to speak or to act in the name of the Jewish people."[1]

Louis Newman had by this time come to the New York pulpit of Rodeph Shalom, the congregation that Wise's father had served. Wise was instrumental in helping Newman secure the position. When Newman tried to modify the rhetoric of his old friend towards Roosevelt, Wise sharply rebuked him:

> I must say to you frankly that I am not interested in the least about what you write concerning Governor Roosevelt....I could not with self-respect vote for a person of his quality as a candidate for the presidency. I have not reached a decision whether I shall take an active part in the campaign. I may conceive it to be my duty to do so. I may even go through the country...in order that people who believe in him and trust him may know...that he is a man of no moral courage whatsoever and of no political integrity.[2]

In 1933, Roosevelt was in the White House and Hitler was Chancellor of Germany. Wise had to channel his appeals on behalf of German Jewry through Mack and Frankfurter. That Wise's attacks on Roosevelt were not forgotten is testified to by a letter of May, 1933, from Mack to Frankfurter: "You doubtless saw the miserable editorial...urging that he [Wise] be kept out of all touch with the powers that be in Washington, because he knew, as everyone knows, how FDR felt about him."[3]

---

[1] Letter dated 10/12/32, ibid.

[2] Letter dated 7/19/33 ibid., Reel 117.

[3] Letter dated 5/22/33, ibid., Reel 115.

CHAPTER III

Revisionist vs. Socialist Zionists

After the return of the Brandeis-Mack Group at the Cleveland convention in 1930, Stephen Wise wrote to Jabotinsky: "The main thing is that we shall now have a militant organization prepared to stand against the American non-Zionists.... "[1]

Wise combined in one dynamic, restless personality the drive for daring, activism, and fierce independence, on the one hand, and the insecure need for approval and reassurance from authority figures on the other hand.

Fifteen years after Wise's death, his friend, Horace Kallen, a philosopher and educator, captured this side of Wise in an oral history:

Stephen became what you might call...a spirit of free, positive Jewishness, a spokesman for it, and he showed a capacity for deference to leadership, to authority, Brandeis' authority, Brandeis' leadership, taking orders and carrying them out, even ruthlessly, that one wouldn't suspect in a person so spectacular and egocentric.[2]

It was natural that Wise would be drawn to Jabotinsky. Brandeis had consistently disappointed him by refusing to take active leadership in American and World Zionism. In 1933,

---

[1]Letter dated 7/2/30, CZA, Wise papers, Reel 102.

[2]American Jewish Committee, Oral History Library, Horace Kallen interview, Aug-Sept, 1964.

Brandeis was 77 years old and had been on the highest court of the land for 17 years. Felix Frankfurter had also left behind his brief flurry of Zionist activity and was well established as a brilliant Harvard professor of law.

Weizmann was the acknowledged international Zionist leader, but Wise had long despaired of Weizmann's conciliatory brand of leadership. Jabotinsky, by contrast, was a dynamic, forceful Zionist leader with an international reputation as an orator that exceeded that of Wise himself.

Vladimir Ze'ev Jabotinksy was a classical Zionist in the mold of Theodor Herzl. Herzl along with Max Nordau and Joseph Trumpeldor were his models for what Jewish leadership should be. Born in the enlightened city of Odessa, Jabotinsky was not a traditional Jew of the *shtetl*. A true Renaissance Man, he was imbued with democracy and classical 19th century liberalism. He wrote and lectured in several languages, writing original articles, books, and poetry as well as translating Edgar Allen Poe into Russian and Chaim Nahman Bialik from Russian into Hebrew.

Jabotinsky saw in Herzl, Nordau and Trumpeldor men of clear vision and resolute action. The signs of danger to the Jewish people were everywhere, and rising tides of nationalism throughout Europe meant that only with a nation of their own could the Jewish people be physically safe and spiritually free to propagate their rich heritage in the modern era. He decried the *galut* mentality of the Jewish people and believed that self-defense was necessary not only for physical survival but for the spiritual liberation from a subservient posture.

Jabotinsky was the personification of a leader *among* men as opposed to a leader *of* men. Small in stature and peering out from behind thick glasses, he was the image of an intellectual, but he would not limit himself to the passive exposition of theories. In the formation of the Jewish Legion he worked arduously along with Trumpeldor, a military man by training. At the outset when the British offered only a mule corps, Jabotinsky was disappointed and distanced himself from Trumpeldor, but later admitted that Trumpeldor was right in taking what was offered and joined with him.

An early ally in Jabotinsky's efforts to attain British approval for a Jewish Legion was Chaim Weizmann. Despite markedly different temperaments and leadership styles, the two natives of Russia were friends, and Jabotinsky lived with

Weizmann and his wife for several months in London. Weizmann told Jabotinsky:

> I cannot work like you, in an atmosphere where everybody is angry with me and can hardly stand me. This everyday friction would poison my life and kill in me all desire to work. Better let me act in my own way; a time will come when I shall find a means to help you as best I can.[1]

Weizmann did in fact labor behind the scenes to facilitate British approval of the Jewish Legion, and many years later he wrote about Jabotinsky's efforts to form the Jewish Legion:

> It is impossible to describe the difficulties and disappointment which Jabotinsky had to face. I know of few people who could have stood up to them, but his pertinacity, which flowed from his devotion, was simply fabulous. He was discouraged and derided at every turn.[2]

Colonel John Henry Patterson, the British military leader who commanded the Jewish Legion, also testified to the opposition Jabotinsky faced: "Had it not been for the incredible stupidity of the Old Men of Zion who strenuously opposed Jabotinsky's endeavors, I am certain that a Jewish Army of at least one hundred thousand men would have been formed."[3]

Jabotinsky chose to be an active role model for the new recruits under Patterson's command and saw combat with the Legion. Patterson wrote of Jabotinsky's instincts under fire: "Never shall I forget the keenness with which he led the machine gun section when we made our attack on the Umm Es Shert ford over the Jordan. He was the first man to reach the

---

[1]Schechtmann, Yosef, *Jabotinsky, a Biography* , Vol I (Silver Springs: Eschel Books, 1986), p. 224. Published originally in 1956 as *The Vladimir Jabotinsky Story.*

[2]Weizmann, Chaim, *Trial and Error* , op. cit., p. 167.

[3]Jabotinsky, Vladimir, *The Story of the Jewish Legion,* forward by Col. Patterson (New York: Bernard Ackerman, Inc., 1946).

historic river and thereupon immediately placed his guns in a strong position to resist any counter-attack by the Turks."[1]

Among the recruits in the Legion were two young Socialist Zionists who played a crucial role in the politics of the Labor Zionist Movement, Berl Katznelson and David Ben-Gurion. Katznelson, the beloved conscience of the labor movement, led a minor rebellion among the Jewish legionnaires. He objected to the floggings which were administered for disciplinary reasons and demanded that military orders be given in Hebrew to stress the Jewish consciousness of the group. This did not set well with the British military command, and Katznelson had to back down.[2]

At war's end, the British disbanded the Jewish Legion and rejected the request for an armed Jewish defense organization. From Jerusalem Jabotinsky prodded Weizmann to be realistic about the anti-Jewish bias of British officials in Palestine and the danger of their consistent undermining of the Balfour Declaration: "My dear friend, it will grieve you, but I must say that the whole official attitude here is one of apologizing to Arabs for Mr. Balfour's *lapsus linguae*."[3]

Jabotinsky's reading of the situation is reinforced by a memo written at the time by a British politician who by name accused two British officials of anti-Semitism. In addition, Colonel Richard Meinertzhagen, a British official in Palestine, wrote in his dairy in 1919: "We should inform the Palestine administration in no uncertain voice that anti-Jew sentiments must not be tolerated in official circles in Palestine."[4] Jabotinsky's worst fears were realized when in April of 1920, Arab mobs shouting "*El Dowleh ma'anah*" - the government is with us - attacked Jews in Jerusalem, killing five and wounding over two hundred. Jabotinsky, who headed the defense of Jerusalem, was arrested by the British with several of his men. In a perverted demonstration of "even-handedness," the British court sentenced two Arabs who were convicted of raping Jewish women to 15 years in prison, and handed out the same sentence to Jabotinsky and his men for their defense of

---

[1]Cited by Schechtman, op, cit. Vol I, p. 270.

[2]Shapira, Anita, *Berl: the Biography of a Socialist Zionist* (Cambridge: Cambridge U. Press, 1984), p. 81.

[3]Reinharz, op. cit., p. 278.

[4]Ibid., p. 279.

the Jewish population. The news of Jabotinsky's arrest spread on a Saturday, and Rabbi Yitshaq HaCohen Kook, the chief Rabbi of the *yishuv,* authorized the *Shabbat* signing of petitions protesting British injustice.[1]

Shabbat was followed by a general strike in Jerusalem with all shops, schools and official Jewish institutions closed. *Kuntress,* the newspaper of Ahdut HaAvodah which was an amalgamation of two labor factions united by Katznelson and Ben-Gurion, hastened to defend Jabotinsky and to

> confess the crime committed by Palestine Jewry who for two years treated this question [of defense] with 'so what,' hoped for miracles and did not plan concrete actions...they called the man who forecast what was to be expected an imposter.[2]

Support for Jabotinsky was world-wide. The *London Times* characterized the sentencing of Jabotinsky and his men as "apparently vindictive punishment. Lt. Jabotinsky is well and honorably known in this country." *The Manchester Guardian* wrote:

> If Mr. Jabotinsky was in possession of firearms, if he organized a Defense Corps and even used it...there is prima facie evidence that he may have been perfectly justified, owing to the failure of the military authorities to discharge their proper duties.[3]

The official paper of the Zionist Organization of America, *The New Palestine,* joined in praise of Jabotinsky: "London newspapers are calling Vladimir Jabotinsky "The Jewish Garibaldi. He deserves this distinction and will wear it nobly."[4] The reference was to the popular 19th century Italian hero who liberated and united Italy.

---

[1]Schechtman, op. cit., Vol I, p. 343.

[2]Ibid., p. 356.

[3]Ibid., pp. 350-351.

[4]Ibid., p. 357.

Jabotinsky, like Weizmann, retained his belief that a Jewish state would arise with the cooperation of the British. The unmistakable difference between them was that Jabotinsky insisted on open confrontation of overt anti-Jewish policies of British officials in Palestine in order to mobilize British opinion behind the Jewish position. Weizmann preferred to protest in private and, when his protests did not succeed, to consider them temporary setbacks that would only be worsened by continuing to press British officials.

As for his attitude toward the Arabs, Jabotinsky set forth his basic principles in an article called "On the Iron Wall." This article, written in 1923, was prophetic and forms the basis of the Israeli approach to the Arabs of the Middle East in the present day. Jabotinsky made clear his attitude of respect for the Arabs and their claims of sovereignty, and in distinct terms rejected any idea of turning the Arabs out of the land of Israel. The key was not the Jewish attitude toward the Arabs, Jabotinsky claimed, but the Arab attitude toward Zionism.

And what was the Arab attitude toward Zionism? Jabotinsky wrote that the Arabs understood well Zionist aims, and that Zionists should not treat the Arabs as fools who could be deceived. It was natural for them to oppose the idea of a Jewish majority in Palestine. "On an agreement of wills between us and the Arabs of the land of Israel it is impossible to dream. Not now and not in the future which appears on the horizon."[1]

Did that mean that there was no hope of peaceful coexistence with the Arabs? Jabotinsky rejected this idea. The only way to accommodation with the Arabs was to become strong enough to convince them that the Jews were in Palestine to stay, to erect an "Iron Wall" that the Arabs knew they could not break down.

The Jews had to be strong in self-defense and strong in negotiations. Jabotinsky was at his logical best in a follow-up article on his "Iron Wall" thesis. He presented the Talmudic case of two men who claimed the same *tallit* (prayer shawl). One says he found the *tallit*, and the other makes the same claim. The judge decides they should halve it. Jabotinsky continues:

...only one of the disputants was obdurate, and the second, the opposite, decides to surprise the world with his "gentlemanliness." He says: We found the *tallit* together, I claim

---

[1] Cited by Katz, op. cit., Vol II., p. 611 .

only half, and the other half belongs to my opponent. As opposed to this attitude, the second man stood with full force on his opinion: I found it, all of it is mine.

The judge is faced with a new situation. Jabotinsky continues:

The judge says: on the one half [of the prayer shawl] there is no dispute. The first disputant himself admits that it belongs to both of them. The dispute therefore is only on the second half. Therefore, we will divide it in two. And in sum the stubborn man received three-fourths and the "gentleman" only one-fourth. And rightfully so. It is good to be a gentleman, but it is not necessary to be a fool.[1]

In May, 1925, Jabotinsky and his colleagues decided to form a separate movement within the World Zionist Organization. At a coffee house in Paris, they considered names such as "Democratic" and "Activist" but decided on "Revisionist" because Weizmann's leadership had taken Zionism far from Herzl's Zionism.[2] There was immediate support in Palestine for the new movement. The Jewish newspaper *Ha'aretz* wrote:

The activism of Jabotinsky and his movement are a natural reaction against the passive stand and the "realism" that spread through the Zionist ranks in recent years....If the Revisionist Movement will put an end to this passive stance, will awaken national political thought and renew political action of the Zionist Organization, it will surely fulfill its task.[3]

While Jabotinsky distanced himself from Weizmann over political issues, the Labor Movement did so over economic issues, resisting any non-Socialist leadership. Katznelson and Ben-Gurion united most of the labor movement, but HaPoel

---

[1] Ibid., pp. 612-613.

[2] Ibid., p. 619.

[3] Ibid., p. 621.

HaTzair, the Young Workers, maintained their inependence. When they set up the first moshav, an act seen by Ben-Gurion as a dangerous deviation, Ben-Gurion warned the members of the moshav that they were "sitting on the border. Beyond you lies capitalism."[1]

The Fourth Aliyah in the mid-1920s was less socialist in its orientation. Fewer and fewer settlements were established and more workers became wage earners in small enterprises. Ben-Gurion and Katznelson had to make peace with the new developments. At the end of the decade there was an economic crisis and key Labor institutions like the newspaper *Davar*, and the building contracting company Solel Boneh were on the verge of bankruptcy. The executive of the World Zionist Organization had agreed to help pay the debts, but due to budgetary problems of their own, had to withdraw the offer.

Katznelson, though generally more conciliatory than Ben-Gurion, warned against conceding leadership of world Zionism to non-Labor elements. In 1927, he proclaimed: "There is no future for Zionism unless it is conquered by the Labor movement, and no other way for the worker: Labor must take over the Zionist movement completely so that our spirit prevails in the economy and in cultural affairs."[2]

Thus was launched negotiations to unite Ahdut HaAvoda with HaKibbutz HaMeuchad. In May, 1929, the two came together to form Mapai. Remaining independent was the far left-wing faction, HaShomer HaTzair, which refused to compromise their strictly Marxist principles.[3]

Stephen Wise was much more naturally drawn to the liberal, democratic principles of Jabotinsky than to the Socialism of the Labor Zionists. In 1931 when Wise and de Haas published their condemnation of the British government over the Passfield White Paper, Jabotinsky, despite having been imprisoned by the British ten years earlier, wrote to Wise indicating his belief that they [the Zionists] had only themselves to blame:

---

[1] Shapira, op. cit., p. 155.

[2] Ibid., p. 159.

[3] Ibid., p. 162.

Personally I don't feel as yet prepared to say that England has failed. As a lawyer I think that, taking British public opinion as a sort of Court of Appeal, you sometimes lose a good suit not because the Court is rotten, but because your advocates are rotten....[1]

When Wise was invited to a meeting of the Central Committee of Zionist Revisionists of America in 1930, he was not able to attend, but sent a note: "With most cordial greetings, and recognizing the truth that the time has come for a very significant revision of many things in the Zionist movement, beginning with much of our so-called leadership."[2]

In 1934, Wise received a letter from a Robert L. Baker, of *Current History* Magazine, asking for a clarification of Jabotinsky's philosophy. Wise responded:

I hasten to answer your inquiry of January 18th. It is not easy in a sentence or even in a paragraph to tell you just what the Revisionist Wing of the Zionists wish to revise...what they really desire is the enforcement of the Balfour Declaration....There is nothing revolutionary or incendiary about the Revisionist movement. It does nothing more than demand the fulfillment of the English Government's pledges and obligations which have not been honorably fulfilled up to this time.[3]

The clash between Labor Zionists and Revisionist Zionists heated up. Jabotinsky, working from Europe after 1929 because after a trip abroad the British barred him from reentering Palestine, condemned the growing Socialist domination of the *yishuv*. Ben-Gurion "declared war" on the Revisionists, and authorized the use of force, saying it was necessary "to create the proper atmosphere and fight the war

---

[1]Letter dated 7/2/30 , CZA, Wise papers, Reel 102.

[2]Letter dated 12/16/30, ibid.

[3]Letter dated 1/17/34, ibid.

using any and all means, even harassment of those who defy organized labor."[1]

At Kfar Saba, in 1930, farmers had hired some new immigrants who were members of Betar, the Revisionist youth movement. The Betar members refused to be registered as Histadrut workers and the farmers backed them up. Ben-Gurion came to Kfar Saba and failed to persuade the young people to comply. As a consequence, the Histadrut workers removed them by force.[2]

Ben-Gurion's efforts to control all employment suffered defeat at a small biscuit factory in Jerusalem. The owner, Yaacov Froumine, hired a woman who was not a member of the Histadrut. The Jerusalem Labor Council demanded that she be dismissed, but Froumine refused and requested arbitration. This was ignored by the Histadrut and the Histadrut workers at Froumine walked out. Froumine hired Betar workers to replace the strikers and again asked for arbitration. Ultimately the Histadrut was forced to back down. The Histadrut members returned and worked alongside the young Betar workers.

The use of force and insistence on trying to deny jobs to Betar members caused a rift between Ben-Gurion, Mapai's labor organizer, and Berl Katznelson, Mapai's intellectual and spiritual leader. Katznelson's biographer writes that "Ben-Gurion wanted to blackball Betar workers all over the country and throw the weight of the Histadrut into the 'decisive battle' against them....Berl disagreed."[3]

After Histadrut partisans attacked a Betar group in April, 1933, injuring several, Katznelson resigned from the Central Committee of Mapai in protest:

> I have been deprived of the emotional capacity to regard myself as a representative of our movement....What others regard as an expression of mass sentiment, closing ranks against the enemy, and strengthening class unity, I see as a delusion,

---

[1]Teveth, Shabtai, Ben-Gurion: *The Burning Ground, 1886-1948* (Boston: Houghton Mifflin Co., 1987), p. 376.

[2]For accounts of this violent period of labor unrest see, Teveth, pp. 367-378, Shapira, pp. 83-192, and Katz, Vol II, pp. 827-836. Teveth and Katz's biographies are strong in support of their subjects' points of view, while Shapira's account provides some balance between the two.

[3]Shapira, op. cit., p. 190.

destroying the inner force of the working class, handing it over to the forces of chaos and darkness among the workers, and destroying the social fabric....[1]

Katznelson was prevailed upon to withdraw his resignation, but soon the Socialists and the Revisionists were embroiled in another confrontation when Chaim Arlosoroff, the head of the political department of the Jewish Agency, was murdered on a Tel Aviv beach. Avraham Stavsky and Zvi Rosenblatt, Betar members, were arrested along with Abba Achimeir, another opponent of the Socialists. Arlosoroff's widow identified Stavsky as the trigger man and the Labor Zionists rushed to judgement.

The fact that all three men were ultimately cleared of the charges (Stavsky was convicted in the first trial and subsequently cleared) is almost beside the point. The Socialists were only too glad to seize upon the arrests to vilify the Revisionists. The murder occurred on the eve of the 18th Zionist Congress in Prague, and Ben-Gurion cynically accused Jabotinsky of creating the atmosphere that led to the murder. The Revisionists fired back with charges of a blood libel.

The invective was intense and the Revisionists were the losers. The Labor Zionists tightened their hold on the infrastructure of the *yishuv*, and Jabotinsky and his movement lost ground at the Zionist Congress.[2]

In the summer of 1934, when Stavsky was cleared of the charge that he murdered Arlossorov, he was called to the Torah in a Tel Aviv Synagogue. This infuriated the Laborites and intensified the bitterness between the two groups. Wise, arriving in London for a meeting, was asked about the situation:

Crossing the ocean I learnt to my unutterable joy that Stavsky had been discharged or acquitted....Whether or not Stavsky should have been honoured with an Aliyah in the Tel Aviv Synagogue, it is not for me to say, but that his ascent to the Torah should have been made an occasion for protests by the Party which does not ordinarily show very much concern for

---

[1]Ibid., p. 192.

[2]The Arlosoroff murder is covered in Shapira, pp. 194-200, Katz, pp. 879-894, and Teveth, pp. 422-428.

the Synagogue...and for violent action, passes my simple understanding.

Wise went on to give his view of the power of the Histadrut in Palestine:

Because the Histadrut has power, because the Histadrut is virtually the Jewish Government of Palestine and because the non-Histadrut members of the Jewish Government are more fanatically anti-Revisionist even than the Histadrut itself, we have the right to ask that it in turn demand of its followers moderation and a spirit of conciliation.[1]

While Wise and the American Jewish leadership followed these events in Palestine closely and differed as to their support for Jabotinsky or for the Socialists, Ira Hirschmann was an American Jew who was not a member of any Jewish organization and most likely knew nothing about the debate raging between the Socialists and the Revisionists. He was innocent of any ideological bent. His response to Hitler's rise to power was dictated from within, and his story contributes much to the study of individual choice in history.

Hirschmann was an accomplished pianist and travelled to Germany in August, 1932, to attend master classes given by Arthur Schnabel, one of the leading concert pianists of the time. Hirschmann tells of his chance encounter with Adolf Hitler:

Walking through the streets of Weimar, the city of Franz Liszt and Goethe, I saw a crowd outside a meeting hall. I learned that a political meeting was getting under way inside. As I pushed my way through the crowd to the rear of the hall...my attention was immediately riveted to the speaker on the platform, a wild-eyed mustached man with an inappropriate resemblance to Charlie Chaplin.

---

[1]Letter dated 7/29/34, CZA, Wise papers, Reel 82.

Hirschmann was taken aback by the raucous response of the people around him, and wrote of the deep and lasting impact the phenomenon had upon him:

> The Sieg Heils would forever echo in my ears and the frenzy of these Bavarian burghers, awakened by the rasping oratory of this Austrian madman, would never quit my consciousness....Until this day in Weimar, I had had confused, certainly unresolved feelings about my Jewish heritage. Having come from a home where the traditional holiday rituals were the total of our observance, only the ceremonials, the songs and the tragic history of Jews held any appeal for me...the dream of a Jewish state was not in me....I had no desire to escape my background: I merely sat on the sidelines - a spectator.[1]

Hirschmann was raised in Baltimore, the sixth of seven children. He began studying piano at age nine, and music became a guiding passion in his life. Another early influence was his exposure to politics. His father who had immigrated from Riga to the United States at age seventeen, took him to a session of the 1912 Democratic Convention in Baltimore.

> I had my first look at history as it was being made....A dark horse, the Governor of New Jersey and former President of Princeton, Woodrow Wilson, won the nomination...my bloodstream was invaded for the first time by the political bug, a virus that was to lead me in and out of countless scrapes and high adventures in the years to follow.[2]

Hirschmann studied briefly at Johns Hopkins University then went to work as a copywriter for an advertising firm. His drive and management skills soon propelled him to the position of advertising manager for Lord & Taylor, a major department store in New York.

His attention focused on Hitler by his visit to Germany, Hirschmann took notice of the effort in 1934 to organize a

---

[1] Hirschmann, Ira, *Caution to the Winds* (New York: David McKay Co., 1962), pp. 41-43.

[2] Ibid., p. 6.

boycott of German goods. He spoke out, saying New York's department stores should join the boycott and was promptly invited into the office of Joseph Pridday, the president of Lord & Taylor, to explain why he was agitating to involve the prestigious store in a political issue. The ownership and top management of Lord and Taylor was not Jewish, but Hirschmann was successful in convincing them to join the boycott.

Hirschmann's activity brought him an invitation to meet Justice Brandeis. Hirschmann penned a colorful description of the meeting:

> I was immediately struck by the unadorned, almost ascetic atmosphere in Brandeis' home. Books ,ined the walls from floor to ceiling in several rooms....He bore a strong resemblance to Abraham Lincoln with his protruding lower lip and aristocratic, aquiline nose which arched into his soft brooding eyes beneath a massive forehead. Impassive, almost masklike, his face would come alive and his thoughtful eyes would light up when he was making a point. Brandeis told me how he, the product of a department store family in Louisville, Kentucky, like Theodor Herzl had become a Zionist rather late in life....[1]

The meeting with Brandeis impressed him, but Hirschmann did not become involved in Jewish organizational life. He was, however, drawn close to New York politics through his friendship with Fiorello La Guardia. Hirschmann was a friend and tennis companion of Ernest Gruening, at that time the editor of *The Nation*, and later a Senator from Alaska. Gruening introduced him to La Guardia and Hirschmann worked in his New York mayoral campaign.

When La Guardia triumphed at the polls he offered Hirschmann a city commisionership. "It was a great temptation, but after much soul-searching I decided that the warm friendship which had sprung up between us might not endure....For the time being I stayed at Lord & Taylor."[2]

A year later, La Guardia called on Hirschmann to manage the campaign of his hand-picked candidate for City Comptroller.

---

[1] Ibid., p. 46ff.

[2] Ibid., p. 63ff.

Hirschmann reluctantly agreed to consider the position only to pick up the paper the next day and read that he had been appointed to run the campaign. Hirschmann's candidate was badly beaten and he discovered through the experience that he was "not cut out for the unavoidably dirty and tough game of politics."[1]

In addition to the boycott issue, two other incidents illustrate Hirschmann's independent character and personal courage. The first was when he found himself at odds with La Guardia. Hirschmann accepted an appointment from his friend to the Board of Higher Education since it was a non-paying job, comforting himself that this was a non-political appointment. He soon discovered how wrong he was.

Bertrand Russell was appointed as a visiting lecturer at Hunter College. His reputation as a radical pacifist aroused a storm of protest, and the Board of Higher Education met to decide whether or not to approve the appointment. As Hirschmann prepared to leave home for the meeting, La Guardia telephoned and said he did not want Russell appointed. At the meeting Hirschmann listened to the debate and, persuaded that academic freedom was the overriding issue, he cast the deciding vote in support of Russell's appointment.

An irate La Guardia ordered Hirschmann to come to City Hall and sign a letter of resignation. Hirschmann refused and soon received a summons to appear before a Commissioner of Investigation to be questioned about his "political background and alleged affiliations with left-wing organizations." Hirschmann consulted his attorney who referred him to Charles Burlingham.

Burlingham, along with Judge Samuel Seabury, who had headed the investigation of corruption by former Mayor Jimmy Walker, were major influences in New York politics and had chosen La Guardia to head their Fusion ticket for Mayor. "It was often said that La Guardia listened only to God and Burlingham and there was some question about the former," Hirschmann recounts. The "inquisition" was called off and after a year's hiatus, Hirschmann and La Guardia resumed their friendship.[2]

The second incident indicative of Hirschmann's willingness to take risks for what he believed in involved his love of music. While studying piano with Arthur Schnabel, he had met Otto

---

[1]Ibid.

[2]Ibid., pp. 119-126.

Klemperer and Arturo Toscanini and maintained an active correspondence with them.[1]

Toscanini left Italy in protest over Mussolini's Fascism and led a group of eleven well known artists in resigning from the Wagner Festival in Germany. He came to New York as Music Director of the New York Philharmonic Orchestra. When he resigned, apparently over a dispute with management, Wilhelm Furtwangler was hired to replace him.

Furtwangler, as the "First State Conductor" of the Berlin State Opera, had raised no protest when Jewish musicians were dismissed from his orchestra and had been rewarded with various Nazi honors. Hirschmann bombarded Philharmonic Board members with telegrams of protest. His career was once more on the line when two of the Board members who were also on the Board of Gimbals department store, controlled by Saks Fifth Avenue, tried to silence him.

Hirschmann continued his fight and gained backing from an unexpected source. Felix Warburg invited him to his Fifth Avenue home (now the Jewish Museum) and congratulated him on his effort. Ultimately Furtwangler withdrew his name.[2]

Hirschmann's activism also led him to involvement with the New York School for Social Research. The school developed a plan to set up a University-in-Exile and offer positions to distinguished scholars from all fields whose freedom was threatened by the development of Fascism and Nazism in Europe. Hirschmann rose to become chairman of the Board and was at the center of efforts which successfully brought many leading intellectuals out of Europe. The most famous figure who came to the University in Exile was Albert Einstein, and Hirschmann was at the head table at the dinner honoring his arrival. The master of ceremonies at the dinner was Felix Frankfurter.[3]

The boycott of German goods that occupied Hirschmann was one that Stephen Wise initially opposed. However, once it gathered steam, he reversed himself to claim credit for the boycott on behalf of his American Jewish Congress. The Vice-President of the Congress, Samuel Margoshes, was also the Editor of the Yiddish newspaper *Der Tag* (*The Day*). Margoshes

---

[1]This correspondence is among the Ira Hirschmann papers, New York Public Library, Music Division, Box 1.

[2]Hirschman, *Caution to the Winds*, op. cit., pp. 94-100.

[3]Ibid.

had proposed the boycott resolution in the American Jewish Congress. At the end of 1934 Margoshes journeyed to Germany and reported on his findings at a mass meeting.

Margoshes reported that the Jews of Germany saw no other choice except emigration and requested that the American Jewish Congress petition Roosevelt to permit more refugees into the United States. He told the gathering that 65,000 Jews had already left Germany and that "before the year 1934 is over, they expect no fewer than 200,000 Jews, out of the 600,000 now in Germany, to have left the country."[1]

The American Jewish Congress was the only organizational platform Wise had in 1934. He appeared far from the coveted ZOA presidency as attested to by a letter he wrote complaining:

There is no Zionism in America, because there is no Zionist leadership in America....Rothenberg [ZOA President] had the insolence to say, "Is the house burning?" What can be said of a man or men who ask...whether the house is burning - as we read from hour to hour that Austrian Jewry is in greater peril even than German Jewry, and tomorrow may see Hitlerism triumphant over Austria![2]

The ZOA newspaper, *The New Palestine*, was equally critical of Wise and his organization. In an article in the December 21, 1934, issue it stated:

The American Jewish Congress is now engaged in repairing its broken fences. That it has suffered reverses must be admitted even by its best friends. Appalling weakness have been revealed on two fronts. It overextended its lines when it commits itself to the convocation of a World Jewish Congress in advance of adequate preparation.

The other area that the ZOA publication attacked was the very claim to existence of the American Jewish Congress - its democratic nature:

---

[1]Report dated 11/29/34, CZA, Wise papers, Reel 88.

[2]Letter dated 2/9/34, Voss, op. cit., p. 198.

The leaders of the American Jewish Congress have engaged in discussions about democracy with such assurance and confidence that it seems almost unbelievable that they could have gone ahead for so long a time without making a reasonable effort to realize their democratic ideals in a supporting constituency. The present leaders of the American Jewish Congress have been uttering wrathful denunciations of anti-democratic forces in Jewish life at a time when its own democratic constituency has become reduced to a fraction of what it was in the heyday of its existence.[1]

Thus, at the end of 1934, Wise was a vocal critic of Weizmann and of Franklin Delano Roosevelt, fulsome in his praise of Jabotinsky, and involved in a bitter exchange of words with the Zionist Organization of America. Within two years, he had completely reversed himself on all four issues. What prompted these changes? In what way were these monumental reversals connected to the plight of European Jewry?

---

[1] *New Palestine*, 12/21/24. Copy found in YIVO, American Jewish Comittee, Box 1, #48.

CHAPTER IV

The New Stephen Wise

As the atmosphere enveloping European Jewry grew darker and darker in 1935 and 1936, there was a flurry of activity among the Jewish leadership. Could world Jewry meet what was universally agreed to be the biggest threat in Jewish history? Would they? In this chapter we focus on these dramatic years and their portent for the years to come.

In December of 1934, Stephen Wise wrote to a non-Jewish friend that Hitler and Germany "have taken much of the joy out of life, and I confess I have terrible fears for the future."[1]

Wise's concerns were shared by Jonah Wise who after a trip to Europe reported to the executive secretary of the American Jewish Committee, Morris Waldman:

The situation of the Jews in Germany has reached the lowest ebb. The utter hopelessness of the position of every man, woman and child of Jewish blood within the Reich became so apparent to me that it blotted out all the details, and makes it impossible to draw a picture other than one of the blackest despair.

His assessment of the state of mind of the Nazi leaders was no less chilling:

I was surprised to learn that for a fortnight prior to my arrival, a radical change had taken place in the attitude of

---

[1]Letter dated 12/12/34, CZA, Wise papers, Reel 5.

Germany toward the Jews. The "Party" is convinced that the rest of the world does not and will not concern itself about the Jewish question, and that it and its leaders have a free hand....[1]

The American Jewish Congress and the Jewish Labor Committee, which came into being in 1933 as a response to the Nazi threat to their fellow workers in Germany, jointly held a Halt the Hitler Menace, in New York in 1935.

Jacob Fishman, editor of the *Jewish Morning Journal,* outlined the danger and excoriated the Roosevelt administration for its silence:

This policy of extermination was foreshadowed last Spring, when...one of Hitler's trusted lieutenants, speaking in Hitler's name, disclosed that the German Jews would be "liquidated" within the next five years....And what about our government in Washington? Neither the White House nor the State Department has as yet uttered a word of displeasure at the renewed Nazi outrages....One has a right to ask: What has become of the noble tradition of this free Republic to raise its voice on behalf of oppressed and maltreated minorities?[2]

Samuel Untermeyer, president of the non-sectarian anti-Nazi League, also called on Roosevelt to act:

The various forms of savage cruelty inflicted upon the German Jews and the still further brutalities that are avowedly in store for them, to which the German people have been educated, are beyond human endurance and have aroused the enmity, amazement and contempt of the world. The failure of our government during these (almost) three years of constantly increasing cruelties inflicted upon those helpless people to protest against this reversion to the Dark Ages has surprised and excited the indignation of the non-Jews as well as the Jews of the world. There was ample precedent for such official

---

[1] Letter dated 4/8/35, YIVO, AJC, Box 14, file 267.

[2] Document dated 5/22/35, Taminent Institute, Robert F. Wagner Labor Archives, JLC, Reel MN.

protests, and on far less provocation. It is late in the day, but not too late, for our Government to act....[1]

Samuel Margoshes, editor of *The Day* and an activist within the American Jewish Congress, called for pressure on the White House:

...With regard to the American government and its silence on the anti-Jewish atrocities in Germany: When the 242 members of the House of Representatives descended the other day on the White House to ask President Roosevelt to raise his voice against the persecution of Catholics in Mexico, President Roosevelt did not try to hide under a wall of silence....Is it because the Catholics in the United States can bring greater pressure to bear than we can....If the doors of the White House will yield not to logic, but only to pressure, by all means, let's apply that pressure and plenty of it.[2]

Margoshes pressed his appeal for political pressure in a meeting of the Joint Consultative Council which included members of the American Jewish Committee, American Jewish Congress, B'nai B'rith and Jewish Labor Council. A decision was made to concentrate activity on pressuring the President. The minutes reflect:

...Dr. Margoshes proposed the setting up of a delegation of one thousand to be comprised of outstanding representatives of Jews and non-Jews from the forty-eight states of the Union for the purpose of bringing pressure to bear on the Governors of their States, their representatives in Congress, with a view to enlisting their support in soliciting action by the President of the United States....Dr. Margoshes' plan was approved in

---

[1]Ibid.

[2]Ibid.

principle and a subcommittee was appointed to draft a plan in writing.[1]

Meanwhile the Nazi heel ground deeper. Not long after the protest conference in New York, the National Socialist Party of Germany met in Nuremberg and passed the Nuremberg Laws of September 15, 1935. Whether one was an observant Jew or a convert to Christianity, the Nazis defined as a Jew anyone having one Jewish grandparent. Germans were warned that any marriage or extramarital relations between Germans and Jews was punishable by imprisonment.

Although the American Jewish Committee did not participate in the protest meeting in New York, they issued a statement upon the enactment of the Nuremberg Laws:

> The Jewish situation in Germany today is controlled by the Nuremberg laws of September 15, 1935....Compared with preceding legislation, the Nuremberg laws are perfidious and undoubtedly lend themselves much more readily to bring about...the complete destruction of the Jews of Germany....

And how did the American Jewish Committee assess the state of mind of Jews in Germany?

> ...it may be said that all the Jews regard the present situation as hopeless. Until the Nuremberg laws were promulgated, the Jews still clung to hope in various possibilities, such as that the force of public opinion of the outside world might bring about an alleviation of their situation....The Jews now see that all these grounds for hope are...illusory. Therefore, a new wave of emigration may be looked for. Until now, many Jews had postponed their departure from Germany in the hope of being able to save their property or to realize on their assets, but if the conditions of the past three months continue, many Jews

---

[1]Minutes dated 8/1/35, CZA, Wise papers, Reel 88.

will be satisfied to escape from Germany merely with their lives....[1]

A non-Jewish group monitoring the ominous signs from Europe was the Pro-Palestine Federation, the PPF. The head of the PPF was Charles Edward Russell who was in frequent correspondence with Wise. His executive director was Ben Elias, a Jew.

In 1933 a proposed merger of the PPF and the ZOA was turned down by ZOA's Morris Rothenberg. The PPF had little more success in trying to work with the American Jewish Congress. The general disarray of that organization was attested to by Russell's letter to Elias in July, 1933, turning down the idea of any further work with the Congress because of "bitter experience" and "unpaid bills....if the Congress is to defeat every effort I make...I should be foolish to expose myself again."[2]

By the end of Hitler's first year in power, Russell had come to the same conclusion as Jewish leaders. Writing to Elias, he said: "It is useless to hope for any amelioration of the status quo in Germany....We should therefore give to the movement to assist the exodus of the German Jews our most earnest support."[3]

The PPF found support for their efforts from the familiar figure of Jacob de Haas. In December, 1933, de Haas agreed to be the chairman for a luncheon honoring the leadership of the PPF. Elias wrote to Russell about the response to de Haas' endorsement: "Only a few days after invitations went out in the name of Mr. de Haas, acceptances poured in from all those who were hitherto standing aloof from our work....Men like Wise, Szold, Rothenberg, etc., who have maintained a passive attitude in the past...."[4]

Wise wrote a supportive letter to Elias in February, 1935, praising Russell's "soul-stirring address,"[5] whereas a year

---

[1] Memo dated 10/22/35, YIVO, AJC, Box 14, file 267.

[2] Letter dated 7/31/33, CZA, PPF papers, F42, #32.

[3] Letter dated 11/23/33, ibid., #33.

[4] Letter dated 12/21/33, ibid.

[5] Letter dated 2/8/35, ibid., #30.

earlier he had responded curtly to Elias' complaints of lack of cooperation from the ZOA. Wise told him "I am not one of the leaders of the Zionist movement in this country or anywhere else. I have no place of leadership: I hold no office in the Zionist organization."[1]

Wise, however, had no intention of remaining bereft of a ZOA leadership position. He began laying the groundwork for a challenge to Rothenberg's leadership of the ZOA while pushing his long latent, but not forgotten idea of a World Jewish Congress. Though Mack had discouraged him in 1923, Wise now pushed forward. First he had some political fences to mend.

Wise watched with some discomfort the steady rise of influence of the Socialists in Palestine. By the end of 1934, Ben-Gurion and Berl Katznelson were well on their way to their goal of Socialist control of the World Zionist movement. Ben-Gurion had orchestrated an attack on Jabotinsky and the Revisionist Zionist Movement, using the Arlosoroff murder to arouse anti-Revisionist passions.

However, when in October, 1934 Ben-Gurion and Jabotinsky chanced to meet in Europe, the Socialist leader and the champion of liberal democracy were taken with one another. In a series of meetings they negotiated an agreement that would recognize Revisionist workers' rights in Palestine but not jeopardize Labor control of governing institutions.

In the United States, the *Boston Jewish Advocate* heralded the pact: "A new era opened in Zionist history when Vladimir Jabotinsky...and David Ben-Gurion signed an agreement which ends the bitter internecine struggle which has rocked the Zionist movement...."[2]

Ben-Gurion found out just how fragile was his hold on the Socialist coalition he headed when the agreements he signed with Jabotinsky were rejected by the Histadrut. Jabotinsky and Ben-Gurion exchanged warm personal letters, but Ben-Gurion had been chastened and turned his attention toward building his bridges with Chaim Weizmann.

The Revisionists responded by pulling out of the World Zionist Organization and forming their own New Zionist Organization.

The majority of American Zionist leaders were oriented toward Weizmann and Ben-Gurion, and after the agreement

---

[1]Letter dated 5/17/34, ibid.

[2]*Boston Jewish Advocate*, 10/10/34.

between Jabotinsky and Ben-Gurion fell through, there was renewed polarization between Weizmann supporters and Weizmann detractors led by Louis Newman, de Haas, and Wise.

How then explain Wise's speech just days after the Histadrut voted down the rapprochement with Jabotinsky? Wise took to the podium of the Free Synagogue to denounce Jabotinsky's movement using all of the most polemical code words like "fascist" and "militarist" with which Jabotinsky's detractors demonized him.

Perhaps it is no coincidence that within a week of the address Wise received this letter from the honorary president of the New England Zionist Region:

> This is to supplement my telegram of yesterday, by stating that I am happy to be able to be in complete agreement with you with reference to your views as expressed...relative to Revisionism. The Zionist Region of New England rejoices in being able to identify itself with your views and policies in Zionism....I sincerely hope that you will take your proper place in the active leadership of the Zionist Organization.[1]

A day later, another official of the New England Zionist Region wired his congratulations, and from that day on the New England region was solidly in the Wise camp in his bid for the ZOA presidency. The same week, the *New Palestine*, the official organ of the ZOA which had attacked Wise and his Congress movement just a few months earlier, splashed the news of Wise's speech across its front page, hailing it as "one of the most brilliant addresses of his career."[2]

Wise heard promptly from de Haas about his attack on Jabotinsky and Revisionism.

> Your Free Synagogue address on Jabotinsky is I fear me neither clear nor convincing in its distribution of praise and blame of him and others, nor as to your own position. Jabotinsky is not a fascist and you know it. You recently discussed with him his political outlooks, and he made it plain, as indeed every word he

---

[1]Letter dated 3/14/35, ibid.

[2]*New Palestine*, 3/15/35.

has written clearly corroborates, that he is an old-fashioned Liberal who believes the less government the better. He made the point that no self-respecting author or orator can live either under a fascist or a communist regime.

Lest Wise forget about his own past objections to Socialist excesses, de Haas listed them:

The Histadrut did raise the "Arlosoroff martyr" issue to carry the 1933 Congress. It did, as you admit, attempt to force the Revisionists out of the organization. It did carry on a bloody riot in Haifa. It has attempted here by coercion, pressure, boycott, etc. to prevent Jabotinsky's getting a hearing. Some of its leaders have preached class war. Its policies in Palestine have aroused the indignation of men like Dizengoff. It did attack Rabbi Kook and exhibited marked discourtesy to him. It has underbid the opposing union in Palestine in order to oust those who do not accept its rule. It does use the immigration certificates to consolidate its power both in Palestine and the Galuth.

The majority "Group A" (as opposed to "Group B" which supported Jabotinsky's New Zionist Organization) of the American Zionists were supporting the Histadrut-Weizmann coalition and de Haas pointedly told Wise (wrongly, it turned out): "As you will not stomach this program, you will...vote the other way [at the upcoming World Zionist Congress]." Reminding him that Jabotinsky was attempting to "revise" Zionism back toward the Zionism of Herzl, de Haas continued:

You slam Jabotinsky because he said, "A generation must devote itself single mindedly to the upbuilding of the Jewish State." Well, that is the essence of the teaching of Herzl, of whom you avow yourself a follower. That was the creed of Nordau. Both of these men were prepared to lead an exodus beyond anything that Jabotinsky has proclaimed.

Returning to Histadrut discriminatory practices, de Haas wrote:

The ugly part of the business is that the investigation of the views of immigrants is applied to the have-nothings...."Social justice" does whip the poor into line as socialists. I am not so purblind that I cannot see the charm of this system. I speak by the book. This discrimination is practiced in New York as well as in Poland. I believe the Chasid and the Misnagid, the Orthodox, Conservative and the Reform Jew, the follower of the Chofetz Chaim, have at least the same rights as the avowed atheistic follower of Karl Marx and Lenin. I look at facts and judge by results. Totalitarianism is totalitarianism whether it masks as communism, fascism, Histadruth or Toaism....[1]

Family considerations also figured into Wise's denunciation of Jabotinsky. The ideological clash between communism and fascism was an international issue, and Wise's son, James, who edited his father's newsletter *Opinion*, was an admirer of communism who vigorously attacked those who did not agree with him. When the heads of the American Jewish Committee, Jewish Labor Council, and B'nai B'rith issued a joint statement repudiating the Hitler declaration that Jews were Communists, James Wise characterized the joint statement as "concocted out of fear for themselves, libels against Soviet Russia and lies about the Jewish people." [2]

The younger Wise's flirtation with communism translated into support for the Jewish Socialists in Palestine. In *Opinion*, James began writing articles condemning Jabotinsky and Revisionism. When Jabotinsky wrote to the senior Wise about these attacks, Wise reassured Jabotinsky of his own support for him while asserting his son's editorial independence. The tension between father and son over this issue was ended when the elder Wise joined the attack on Jabotinsky. When, in 1936, the convention of Reform rabbis denounced both fascism and communism, Stephen Wise would not sign the resolution on communism.

In the debate over communism and fascism, the Catholic Church made a clear choice, a choice that was noted by Jewish groups. The American Jewish Committee considered a resolution condemning communism, but rejected the idea on the grounds that they did not make any statements about political

---

[1]Letter dated 3/13/35, CZA, Wise papers, Reel 107.

[2]*Boston Jewish Advocate*, 10/29/35.

movements. The executive secretary, Morris Waldman, in an analysis sent to Cyrus Adler, defended this cautious approach. He noted that the role of the Catholic Church was a factor that must be considered. His analysis is important, because it shows that the Church was not at all averse to bringing political pressures to bear in its own interests, and it demonstrates the role of anti-communism in determining the Church's attitude toward the Nazis:

Apparently the Catholic Church regards communism as its chief enemy, and is willing to come to terms with, if not actually to encourage, fascist governments. The Vatican has come to terms with Italy and Germany; it has encouraged the establishment of a fascist corporative state in Austria; it is undoubtedly helping the fascist rebels in Spain. The recent offer of the German Catholics to help the Nazis in their fight against communism cannot be blinked as an outright offer of alliance provided concessions of unique concern to the Catholics are made.

Waldman then turned to this phenomenon as it impacted politics in the United States:

In this country too, the Catholics have in their zealous campaign against communism ignored or soft-pedaled the totalitarianism of the fascist states. I have a number of clippings of speeches of Catholic dignitaries who cry out against communism but make no mention of Nazism; and who attack Russia and Mexico without mentioning Germany. Even Al Smith has done that recently. It is only natural when the enormous power of the Catholic Church is girded for battle against communism that Jews should become concerned about the effect of their abstinence from this campaign....At the same time, we cannot afford to act hastily and injudiciously under this Catholic pressure. We must give full consideration to the question whether in joining such a movement we will not be committed to policies and methods that will be repugnant to us and even dangerous for the Jews, particularly since such a movement will no doubt be carried on under Catholic direction and control....[1]

Stephen Wise skirted this ideological debate, trying instead to unite Zionists behind his push for a World Jewish Congress. He defined the fight as one between Zionists and non-Zionists, the latter term being synonymous in his mind with the American Jewish Committee which he also labeled "assimilationist."

It may be that Harold Laski, head of the British Jewish Board of Deputies, and Cyrus Adler, president of the American Jewish Committee, were two of the "assimilationists" that Wise had in mind. In November, 1934, Laski wrote to Adler that his Board had turned down a proposal for a World Jewish Congress. Laski had asked Wise for a statement "...of his work for the Congress, but still, I am not in possession of that precious document....I think it was born of the exhibitionist tendencies of Dr. Stephen Wise."[2]

Wise was certainly correct that the American Jewish Committee opposed his World Congress. Judge Joseph Proskauer, a leader of that organization, said unequivocally:

We are already regarded in many quarters as a sort of international people. If we let the notion back of the World Congress idea go without protest, we will be giving our enemies the best alibi for anti-Semitism they have ever had. We must fight. We cannot afford to let it pass by in silence. Our objective should be so to undermine the movement and, if possible, to smash it entirely.[3]

Wise thundered back at Proskauer and the American Jewish Committee:

---

[1] Waldman to Adler, 10/20/36, YIVO, AJC, Adler papers, Box 1, file 4.

[2] Letter dated 11/18/34, YIVO, AJC, Adler correspondence, Box 1.

[3] Cited by Medoff, pp. 34-35.

The World Jewish Congress is needed today to deal with the fundamental aspects of Jewish life and to forever banish from Jewish life the notion that relief and philanthropy can become the cure-all of Jewish wrongs and Jewish misery....the World Jewish Congress must once and for all proclaim that Jews are brothers. No brother ever saved another through the medium of relief....Out of the accursed notion that charity, relief and philanthropy will solve all Jewish problems come something more grave and more tragic. That is the control of Jewish life by the philanthropists....

Wise was scornful of the notion that a World Jewish Congress would induce anti-Semitism:

What an illustration we Jews could give, if only we had the courage to do so, of real Jewish solidarity! I have no patience to discuss the question whether Jews should meet together to discuss their common problems in an open and public way. The reasons for doing this are so obvious that to dwell upon them would be insulting to the intelligence of the Jewish people. The best proof of the unutterable status of the Jews is revealed by the fact that there are Jews of seeming significance who are fearful of meeting with Jews from other lands lest such meeting involve an impugnment of their national loyalties. That dread in itself calls for a Congress to deal with it. The psychoses which constitute that dread should be allayed and banished from Jewish life.[1]

Not all of the opposition to a World Congress came from the American Jewish Committee. Jacob de Haas disapproved of the idea no less than Wise's new view of Jabotinsky. In an open letter to Wise published in Jewish newspapers in Boston and Chicago, he went on the attack with an open letter to Wise:

Nearly three years have elapsed since you and your associates set out to fight Hitler....All your comings and going to Washington, like the journeys of the American Jewish

---

[1]This letter was published in Boston's *Jewish Advocate*, 4/7/36, and in the *Chicago Jewish Chronicle*, 4/17/36.

Committee, and the delegations of other organizations, produced zero. Hitler has won....This chapter of German Jewish existence is closing. The futility of American Jewish leadership of every stripe has pranced the world stage for three years. In the early dawn - I know you are an early riser - has the futility and impotence never struck you?[1]

Wise sailed for Europe for the World Zionist Congress at the time the international gathering prepared to welcome back to leadership the man who had been ousted four years before, the man Wise had castigated for many years - Chaim Weizmann. Wise joined the celebration, announced his contrition, and supported Weizmann fully.

Wise's embrace of Weizmann was too much for Rabbi Louis I. Newman, Wise's good friend for many years. In an article for the *Jewish Advocate*, Newman wrote: "Apparently a desire to see the World Jewish Congress come into being has led Doctor Wise into channels otherwise repugnant to him. It is not a pleasant story and should be passed over with a minimum of comment." Newman recalled the "old" Stephen Wise and lamented his loss:

Our memory goes back to the days when Rabbi Wise was warning...of the results which inevitably follow and did follow, the infirmity of Weizmann's negotiations with Great Britain....He is not acting in character, in fact he has placed restraints upon himself which a few years would not have been deemed possible....Doctor Wise has too many commitments and responsibilities to act in the role of the Great Adversary.[2]

Wise protested the article, but Newman held his ground. Defining in clear terms the minority view within Zionism, he wrote in the Chicago *Jewish Chronicle:*

The rapid development of Palestine...has brought about unusual conditions in the field of Zionist organization. Just as the

---

[1] *Chicago Jewish Chronicle*, 1/36; copy can be found in Wise papers, CZA, Reel 117.

[2] *Boston Jewish Advocate*, 9/24/35.

situation is unsettled in Palestine itself, so in the Jewish world the forms of political effort are still fluid and uncrystallized. Because the Laborites and their sympathizers at present [dominate]...does not signify that this circumstance is either healthy or will continue to exist when Zionist affairs become more stable. Hence the acclaim with which many persons greet the numerical preponderance of the Social-Laborites in Zionist life is not an index that Utopia has arrived. It merely indicates that a few enthusiasts have mistaken the semblance for the reality.

Newman then spoke to the need for a healthy opposition.

Every political-economic movement needs an opposition in order to fulfill the duty of vigilance by which those in power may be held to the essential purposes they are expected to preserve. The Revisionists under Vladimir Jabotinsky are the only group in contemporary Zionism who serve as an effective opposition party.

Newman outlined the reasons for which he, as well as Wise, and the entire Brandeis-Mack group, had opposed Weizmann:

Once more it is necessary for Zionists to be on guard against attrition within the movement. From 1919 to 1930 there was a steady regress in Zionism. Warning voices were raised against the procedures by which Weizmann fell into the indifference of the hostile mood of the Mandatory officials, and these prophecies of disaster came to their tragic fulfillment in the Arab outbursts of 1929 and the Passfield White Paper of 1930. Weizmann was forced from the Presidency because American Zionists possessed a party of critics, determined that a new order should prevail in the leadership of the movement.

In concluding, Newman sounded a call for support for Jabotinsky's New Zionist Organization:

Jacob de Haas, once a key figure in the Brandeis-Mack party, has kept himself independent and untrammeled, thinking of the needs of Zionism rather than the integrity of any party or the prestige of any would-be leader. Last year it became necessary to form "Group B" in the United States in order to counteract the aggressive Labor propaganda both within and outside the circles of official Zionism...."Group B" must inevitably incline towards the New Zionist Organization....it is the duty of the New Zionist Organization to act, then, as a rallying center for the Opposition, and to offer a shelter for its representatives when they are hounded and harassed by the party in control.

Another source of opposition to the World Jewish Congress idea from within the ZOA came from Abba Hillel Silver who was rapidly emerging as a rival to Wise. He wrote to Wise in May, 1936, to say: "I wish I could see eye to eye with you on the subject of the World Jewish Congress...I regard the project as unwise and doomed to futility."[1] The strengths of the two men, as well as their weaknesses, were similar. As early as 1930, Silver showed his antipathy to Wise. Newman, at that time still in San Francisco, had written an article about the oratorical prowess of two rabbis at the Zurich Congress, and somewhat disparaged the role of one versus the other. The article was based on information given him by Wise's son. Silver wrote to Newman that while he was not named in the article, he knew he was being referenced:

In as much as Wise and Silver were the only two American Rabbis at Zurich, the allusions are not too subtle. Jimmie [Wise's son] might have told you that the "customarily striking effort" of his father at the Congress was so poor and flat that he went around, apologetically, among the delegates saying, "wasn't that a rotten speech my father made?" And everyone agreed with him....I know how unhappy you were over my visit to San Francisco last February....I promise you dear Newman boy, that if you don't behave yourself, I shall come to San

---

[1]Silver papers, Series 1, Folder 56.

Francisco again soon, and give you another taste of the man who is "well-known as an orator."[1]

Newman returned fire, telling Silver that Wise was a man "whose shoelatches neither you, Silver, nor I are worthy to loose."[2]

After the Lucerne conference in 1935, when Wise embraced Weizmann, Wise wrote to a friend about Silver's role at the convention, saying that Silver was "ruthless at Lucerne to everybody. He [sic] interests lie not in the Congress, but in his being Chairman of something or in making a speech at the right moment. He was a horror to the delegation."[3]

In 1936, Silver backed Rothenberg's reelection as ZOA president. Wise recounted to his son, Jim, that Silver had told him: "If you become president of the Zionist Organization of America you will draw upon its head all the bitterness which is felt at present against the World Jewish Congress."[4]

A few days later Wise wrote to Lipsky that Silver "opposes with equal vigor and warmth my acceptance of the Presidency of the ZOA and of the entire Jewish World Congress program."[5]

Yet Wise was confident of victory and even contemplated leaving the Rabbinate. In a letter to one Harold Jacobi in June, 1936, he wrote:

An attempt will be made by a group of my friends, including George Medalie, Maurice Levin, Abraham I. Spiro, Max Osenfield, Louis Sturtz, to secure a fund which will be used for two purposes:

1) To push the circulation of *Opinion* in the hope that it may be brought to 40,000 or 50,000 and thus bring about a much wider circulation the things I am writing for *Opinion.*

---

[1]Letter dated 1/12/30, Wise papers, 117.

[2]Letter dated 1/18/30, ibid.

[3]Letter dated 11/7/35, ibid, Reel 5.

[4]Letter dated 6/30/36, ibid, Reel 122.

[5]Letter dated 7/1/36, ibid, Reel 113.

2) It is hoped to provide a fairly modest income, at most $100 to $150 per week, which is to take the place of the equally modest income I receive from the Synagogue when, in the near future I find it necessary, in the interest of *Opinion* and my work for Palestine and The American Jewish Congress to lay down the duties of my office as Rabbi.[1]

The 39th annual ZOA convention met in 1936 against the backdrop of renewed Arab violence in Palestine. Just as the disturbances of 1929 and the inadequate Zionist response to them had been used as a campaign theme to oust Weizmann from world Zionist leadership at that time, so too did Wise and his followers, who were on the outside looking in, use the disturbances in 1936 to point to the need for new leadership for American Zionists. To avoid a divisive convention, a compromise between the Wise and Rothenberg camps was reached which allowed Wise to become president in exchange for an amendment to the bylaws which barred any president of ZOA from being reelected to a second term.

After his election Wise solicited the approval of Brandeis, writing him: "I hope I have your congratulations upon being unanimously chosen as the President of the ZOA. For me it means that my fellow-Zionists want an uncompromisingly vigorous Zionist...leadership. And they shall have it."[2]

Brandeis responded, but not exactly as Wise wished. Brandeis urged Wise to solicit help from de Haas. When Wise said he could not do so, the Supreme Court Justice persisted, stating that "de Haas erred grievously in seceding from the WZO, but he is a Zionist and by long years of activity has shown his devotion to the cause; he has served it well, in many ways...your administration needs the aid he can give."[3]

That Brandeis, who disagreed with Jabotinsky's tactics of aggressive political pressure, shared Jabotinsky's views on one crucial issue is illustrated by a letter Wise wrote to Frankfurter the same month: "LDB [Brandeis] feels strongly

---

[1]Letter date 6/12/36, CZA, Wise Papers, Reel 9.

[2]Voss, op. cit., p. 211.

[3]Letted dated 9/23/37, CZA, Wise Papers, Reel 107.

that...we should insist that Transjordan must again be brought within the limits of the Jewish National Home."[1]

With the ZOA presidency in hand, Wise sailed in August for Europe for the World Jewish Congress. His mentor, Julian Mack, was elected honorary president and Wise was elected chairman of the Executive.

As he successfully orchestrated these triumphs, Wise had one more fence to mend. It is not clear how it was arranged, but Wise was able to see Roosevelt in January, 1936. Roosevelt, it seems likely, was shoring up support for his reelection campaign. Wise wrote to Albert Einstein at the same time announcing his "coup" and displacing blame for Roosevelt's silence on Nazi atrocities from the President to one of Wise's favorite targets - the Warburgs.

> I may say to you in strictest confidence that I saw the President yesterday for the first time in a long while (because of a serious difference which arose between us years ago). Unfortunately, and I tell it to you with sorrow...his first word was "Max Warburg wrote to me lately that things were so bad in Germany...there was nothing that could be done." You see how this bears out our theory that Max Warburg and his kind do not really desire to help. The President threw up his hands as if to say, "Well, if Max thinks nothing can be done, then nothing can be done."[2]

Wise's attacks on Roosevelt were over. In March, 1936, he couched his appeal for a United States denunciation of Hitler in terms of fear that failure on Roosevelt's part to respond to Hitler might help Republicans. That Wise's one meeting with Roosevelt did not signal ongoing access to the President is obvious from the fact that this appeal was directed to Frankfurter:

> I am terribly afraid that the Republicans are going to make capital of what they, without knowing, will hold to have been F.D.R.'s inaction re Nazism. I believe that it would be a mistake

---

[1]Letted dated 10/10/36, Wise papers, Reel 109.

[2]Letted dated 1/13/36, Voss., op. cit. p. 208.

to wait until it be too late....I am not for a moment thinking of any benefit to the Jewish cause. I am thinking chiefly if not solely of making F.D.R. absolutely invulnerable in this matter....If I felt I had the right to do so, I would write directly to the President....But I think the thing ought to be done verbally. I know how the President values your counsel, how distinterested he knows you to be and how completely devoted to him personally and to his Administration.[1]

That there was a *quid pro quo* for getting out of the Roosevelt dog house was demonstrated in May, 1936, when Frankfurter, wrote to Mack: "Tell Wise we think there should be no holler against Royal Commissions. He should lie low."[2]

The reference is to the British Commission "studying" the Arab violence in Palestine and the expectation that the British would side with the Arabs just as after the Arab violence of 1929 they had issued the Passfield White Paper restricting Jewish immigration and land purchase rights.

In contrast to his sharp criticism of the 1929 White Paper, Wise was not only silent on the Royal Commission, but pressured the Pro-Palestine Federation to postpone a program protesting British policy in Palestine. "I have received Dr. Wise's letter but find nothing in it to alter my conviction....The Royal Commission will recommend nothing that it knows is contrary to American public opinion." And a day later, he followed with another letter saying he had written "to Rabbi Wise declining to consent to a postponement of the meeting...."[3]

Despite the fact that Roosevelt remained silent about the Jewish misery in Europe, Wise wrote to his son in June, 1936: "I wonder whether you feel as I do that Roosevelt made a glorious speech on Sunday night. I know you doubt his sincerity, but he does seem to me to be on the way and I grow less and less fearful that he will capitulate."[4] And to another family member the same week: "Are you preparing to vote for

---

[1] Letter dated 3/2/36, CZA, Wise papers, Reel 109.

[2] Letter dated 5/20/36, ibid.

[3] Russell to Elias, Letters dated 10/9/36 and 10/10/36, CZA, PPF papers, F42, 35.

[4] Letter dated 6/29/36, CZA, Wise papers, Reel 115.

Roosevelt? I had a most charming note from him today and we will have to vote for him."[1]

When Roosevelt was reelected for his second term, Wise wrote to a friend in Israel:

> Firstly, I must tell you we are very, very happy over Roosevelt's reelection....We have in him a warm and understanding friend. He and I have made up, and I spent October practically going throughout the country in his behalf.[2]

As Roosevelt's second inauguration drew near, Samuel Margoshes tried to direct Wise's attention to the plight of Polish Jewry, complaining of the inaction of the American Jewish Congress:

> I hope you will not deem me unduly critical when I say to you that I was terribly disheartened by last night's meeting of the Governing Council. I had hoped that of all the committees of the Congress the Governing Council would best understand the crying need for immediate action on the Polish Jewish situation, and that it would rush to support any suggestion calculated to bring about such action. Instead I found divided counsels plus indifference. Not only was last week's decision to call a conference on Poland forgotten, but various attempts were made to stall and delay any kind of action....I am quite on the verge of losing my patience.[3]

Thus, as 1936 drew to a close, Margoshes, Newman, de Haas and others drawn to aggressive action in dealing with the tragedy of European Jewry were more and more estranged from the man who had been one of them. But Stephen Wise had learned his lesson. For many years, he was *against* Chaim Weizmann, *against* Franklin Roosevelt, *against* the Zionist Organization of America, and an admirer of Jabotinsky. What

---

[1] Letter dated 6 6/30/36, Wise papers, Reel 4.

[2] Wise to Irma Lindheim, 11/18/36, Voss, op. cit., p. 217.

[3] Letted dated 11/19/36, Wise papers, Reel 87.

had these positions netted him? He held no office in the Zionist Organization of America, no office in the World Zionist Organization, and was denied contact with a popular new American administration.

Now he was *for* Chaim Weizmann, *for* Franklin Roosevelt, and a renouncer of Jabotinsky. Where was he? He was president of the Zionist Organization of America, chairman of the Executive of the World Jewish Congress, and telling the world famous scientist, Albert Einstein, in "strictest confidence," that he had met with the President of the United States.

CHAPTER V

Years of Warning, 1937-1938

In 1937 and 1938 the violence against Jews continued unabated and climaxed in the horror of *Kristallnacht.* There was a clear division among those leaders who both recognized the nature of the threat and translated that recognition into plans for rescue and those leaders whose perceptions and actions *could* suggest they did not "know" how severe was the threat.

In March 1936, Abba Hillel Silver argued in public that German Jews should stay in Germany. He was countered by Jacob de Haas who asserted that Jews were suffering the "gravest crisis in Jewish history since the days of Bar Kochba," and that "whether we will it or not the liquidation of the German Jews is in progress."[1]

The same dichotomy was playing itself out in the fate of Polish Jewry. Jabotinsky, who warned against the worsening condition of European Jewry, was negotiating with Polish leaders for the emigration of large numbers of Jews from that country. Stephen Wise, in the meantime, circulated in January, 1937, an internal memorandum to the Governing Councils of the new World Jewish Congress making it clear "in the most emphatic terms that it cannot be a party to any scheme of the Polish government which looks to a place for Polish-Jewish emigrants...."[2]

And what in fact was going on in Poland as it was reported in the Jewish press in the United States? The *Chicago Jewish*

---

[1] *Boston Jewish Advocate,* 3/10/36.

[2] Memorandum dated 1/19/37, CZA, Wise papers, Reel 87.

Chronicle in January reported "renewed anti-Jewish rioting" at Warsaw University and the assessment of the Jewish Telegraphic Agency that "In these circumstances it is no wonder that thousands of Polish Jews are anxious to emigrate."[1]

In February the same newspaper headlined on the front page: "5 Dead in new Polish anti-Semitic Wave." The article told of a Jew who was the victim of an axe attack whose skull was fractured and whose nose was cut off.[2]

The same month Jabotinsky testified before a British Royal Commission that Jewish immigration needs amounted to 1,500,000 over the next ten years, and demanded that the doors of Palestine be opened to them.

Stephen Wise heard directly from Jewish representatives in Poland. In two memos sent to him in March 1937 he was warned:

I want you to know, dear Dr. Wise, that this prognosis of the political developments which we are facing in Poland is not the result of my own observations alone....I assure you that these are the well-considered conclusions of those Polish Jews who know the situation thoroughly, who bear the brunt of Polish-Jewish troubles....

And what was this assessment?

It must be added that in the last stage - if that stage is reached - we will face physical annihilation of Jews. What is happening now will be mere child's play in comparison with what must happen if anti-Semitic youth becomes an important factor....It must be clear that even the more decent people in the Government Camp will not worry too much if they have to attain their aims by a flow of Jewish blood. Here it will be done with more physical brutality than even in Germany.[3]

---

[1] *Chicago Jewish Chronicle*, 1/22/37.

[2] Ibid., 2/5/37.

[3] Letter dated 3/11/37, CZA, Mack papers, A405, 82.

Wise wrote to Julian Mack of the tepid response of Secretary of State Cordell Hull toward the Nazis: "He interprets Hitler's war upon civilization...as a 'row', and that is very sad." Making clear his own priorities, Wise added: "In the interest of Palestine, we are going to do what we can to let that pass from the scene. We cannot press the Hitler button and the British-and-Palestine button at one and the same time."[1]

The activist camp of American Jewish leaders suffered the loss of their most forceful voice in March 1937 when Jacob de Haas died. The *Chicago Jewish Chronicle* memorialized de Haas, calling him "a doer, not a talker, and as a result he was elbowed out of the way by the orators whose greatest triumph has been the decimation of the Zionist movement...."[2]

That Wise was not pushing the "Hitler button" is documented by a memorandum he circulated to several Jewish leaders including Mack, Brandeis and Silver. His memo, referring to himself throughout as "SSW," detailed his visit to the State Department. The fate of European Jewry was not mentioned.[3]

At the same time he circulated this memorandum, Wise wrote to a congressman from New York who intended to introduce legislation to ease the restrictions on emigration. Wise, who had throughout his battle for a World Jewish Congress castigated those who said it would only stir up anti-Semitism, wrote the congressman:

I wish I thought it were possible for this measure to be passed without repercussions upon the Jewish community in this country. I have every reason to believe, unfortunately, that any effort that is made at this time to waive the immigration laws will result in a serious accentuation of what we know to be a rising wave of anti-Semitic feeling in this country....[4]

The bad news from Poland continued with the March 5 report of the death of a five year old boy and continued push by Jews to

---

[1]Voss, op. cit., pp. 218-219.

[2]*Chicago Jewish Chronicle*, 3/26/37.

[3]Memo dated 4/5/37, CZA, Mack papers, A405, 24.

[4]Cited by Medoff, Rafael, *The Deafening Silence* (New York: Shapolsky Publishers, 1987), pp. 33-34.

emigrate, and a March 22 story which headlined: "50 Jews wounded in Polish riot; damages are put at $400,000."[1]

In May the *New York Times* carried the story of the Pro-Palestine Federation presenting a petition to the British Ambassador to the United States for Britain to open the gates of Palestine. "The petition, in expressing the opinion of enlightened Christian leadership...stressed the intolerable suffering of the millions of Jews in the European holocaust."[2]

Elias, executive director of the PPF, complained to his president, Russell, about the passivity of Wise:

> It appears the Zionists are being led by their leaders the wrong way. Dr. Wise seems to take the promises made by Roosevelt and Hull...while we know that these good fellows forgot their promises the minute they finished....Dr. Wise...advises the Pro-Palestine Federation not to undertake to do anything until he gives the word....[3]

When the British Peel commission recommended a partition of Palestine that would leave the Jews with a vulnerable strip of the historic area, Wise was opposed but allowed himself to be reassured by administration promises of opposition. The PPF executive, Elias, wrote directly to Wise to appeal for more assertive action:

> Now, dear Dr. Wise, it seems to me that all the promises made to you, to me, and to the Christian delegation by the White House and Secretary Hull have so far remained mere promises....The thing for us to do then is to increase, in turn, our own pressure upon Washington....I intend to immediately mobilize a powerful group of Congressmen and Senators...so as to compel action by the State Department.[4]

---

[1] *Chicago Jewish Chronicle*, 5/21/37.

[2] *New York Times*, 5/30/37; Article found in CZA, PPF papers, F42, 38.

[3] Letter dated 6/3/37, ibid., F42, 35.

[4] Letter dated 7/1/37, ibid., F42, 30.

PPF president Russell agreed with Elias' assessment:

I have had for some time a feeling that our friends of the ZOA were not in sympathy with us and did not share our views as to the necessity of swift and resolute action. I have written Wise two letters but had no answer....It is not exhilarating to learn that Dr. Wise puts faith in the administration to make a move toward salvation for Palestine.

Elias continued the frequent correspondence expressing his own despair:

...it seems to me that Dr. Wise was depending upon the interference of the United States government. That causes me the deepest distress. If the hope of the Jews is placed in official action by this government without any show of protest by the Jewish population and its sympathizers, the Jews are doomed to a terrible disappointment...it is the same old error that the Jews so often make. Appeal to the government, get some one in a position of authority to give the glad hand, let the President do it, get Mr. Hull's good word, but do nothing for and by themselves....

Elias' assessment of the situation was that the British were vulnerable to pressure from the United States:

Great Britain is now dependent upon the good will of the United States. The United States is in the last analysis ruled by public opinion. If Great Britain perceives here a manifestation of hostile public opinion it will take great heed to its steps in opposition to that opinion....[1]

At the 1937 World Zionist Congress, Weizmann supported the British Partition Plan, while Wise was back on the attack against the man he had embraced at the Congress two years before. The Jewish Telegraphic Agency reported that one

---

[1] Letters dated 7/17/37 and 7/22/37, ibid., F42, 36.

session of the Congress "began with a dramatic attempt by Dr. Stephen S. Wise, President of the ZOA, to [resist] the overwhelming partition forces by a slashing attack on the executive and Dr. Chaim Weizmann."[1]

Monitoring news of the Congress from the United States, Elias took heart and wrote to Russell:

> While Jewish leaders, groping in the dark, blundered and failed, your counsel inspired Dr. Wise to take a bold and courageous stand at the Zionist Congress. This resulted in a serious division among the delegates....Wise and his friends will soon be back here and together we shall launch one of the most formidable campaigns in the history of the Zionist movement.[2]

Two months after Elias' expressed optimism, he lamented Wise's limited action:

> Dr. Wise is president of the ZOA which is officially on record in favor of negotiating with Great Britain. Although, personally, Wise is against partition, he lacks the courage to resign his position in the ZOA. It is a tragedy....I have written to a dozen Zionist Districts, asking them if they would welcome an education anti-partition campaign and all answered in the affirmative.[3]

In October, 1937, Wise received a confidential report from the World Jewish Congress representative in Poland:

> We are facing an immediate upheaval. As long as an attempt can be made to write I am doing it. No one knows how long this possibility will exist....As far as Jews are concerned the program of Rydz-Smigly [Polish government ministers] is total annihilation of all possibilities for the Jews to remain in Poland.

---

[1]CZA, Wise papers, Reel 122.

[2]Letter dated 8/11/37, PPF papers, F42, 36.

[3]Letter dated 10/14/37, ibid.

They will not stop before anything. If it will be necessary they will use the youth for physical attacks on a scale unknown heretofore.[1]

In a now familiar pattern, Stephen Wise allowed his instincts toward firm action to be tempered by writing to those he knew would counsel caution. In a plaintive letter to Mack in which he reviews "the world Jewish situation," he asks for advice:

I know Felix [Frankfurter] feels that the "Skipper" [Roosevelt] ought to be spared. Have we the right to omit to do anything which holds out the faintest promise of relief for our people?....I lie awake at nights. I have ceased to be able to sleep. I cannot shake off the awful responsibility...Give me your judgement.[2]

We do not have a record of Mack's response, but Wise again busied himself with organizational affairs. On November 28, 1937, the American Jewish Congress decided to organize a nationwide plebiscite to form a "united democratic front against anti-Semitism." Four questions were framed to be answered by respondents, two dealing with reorganizing American Jewish communities on a democratic, representative principle, one asking if the respondent favored the establishment of a free Jewish State in Palestine, and a fourth asking whether there should be a continuation of the boycott against German goods.[3]

Many voices rose to expose the presumptiousness of this effort by the American Jewish Congress. Morris S. Lazaron, a member of the American Jewish Committee wrote of years of pledges by the American Jewish Congress for a democratically elected Jewish body, but concluded that "the Congress is still more or less a skeleton organization that serves as a sounding board for a few leaders."[4]

Elias wrote to Russell in agreement:

---

[1]Letter dated 10/31/37, ibid., Mack papers, A405, 82.

[2]Letter dated 12/20/37, Voss, op. cit., pp. 222-223.

[3]Medoff, op. cit., pp. 36ff.

[4]Document dated 12/5/37, CZA, Wise papers, Reel 113.

Chaos and confusion reign supreme in the minds of its leaders who seemingly have no policy whatsoever. They lack the courage of expressing their convictions, and in this respect, our mutual friend, Dr. Wise, is the worst offender.[1]

From within the American Jewish Congress, Wise received private counsel for more direct action. The editor of the Congress' publication *Opinion*, M. Boraisha, sent frequent memos to his boss. In December, 1937, he alerted Wise to criticism from the Yiddish newspaper *Der Tag* (*The Day*). The newspaper disparaged the idea of a plebiscite and asked why the American Jewish Congress evaded "its own positive program of internal activity."

Boraisha's memo included his own concern about his organization:

The trouble with this article is that we cannot tell Mr. Niger [the author of the article] how we are tied up in various ways with those whom we would have to fight openly if we really came out with a program of democratizing American Jewish life. Another trouble is Mr. Niger is among the most prominent of Yiddish publicists in this country and his word counts. In this case I really don't know where to find words to cover up the lack of a definite policy and program.

In the same memo, Boraisha pressed on Wise the plight of Rumanian Jewry and the need for forceful action:

The Roumanian catastrophe will not only destroy the million Roumanian Jews but will influence the fate of the Jews in other countries. It will strengthen the hands of the Fascist groups in Poland and weaken our position there. Today's Yiddish papers already report that Austria and Bulgaria have closed their borders from Roumania....It is an emergency great enough to

---

[1]Letter dated 12/5/37, CZA, PPF papers, F42, 36.

justify the immediate creation of the United Front Mr. Lipsky is speaking about. It is up to you to issue the call....[1]

A few days later, Boraisha sent Wise more bad news from the Yiddish press, this time from the pen of Jacob Fishman, Wise's colleague on the American Jewish Congress' Governing Council:

Jewish diplomacy has proven itself bankrupt in the most dangerous crisis in Jewish history, and it does not mean that only one tendency, that of the "sha-sha" Jews and shtadlonim is bankrupt, but even the so-called democratic tendency in Jewish diplomacy is just as helpless and powerless....

In a passage that could have been attributed to de Haas were he still alive, Fishman wrote:

What did the American Jewish Congress learn from its five years of unsuccessful struggle against Hitlerism and its struggles against Polish, Roumanian, Hungarian and other anti-Semites? What did the same Congress learn from its unsuccessful interventions with the New Deal Government which holds to its "splendid isolation" every time when there is need of a strong word against these anti-Semitic countries? It is easy to believe that Roumania would not at present act the way it has if President Roosevelt would not only console us with fine words of tolerance, but raise his voice the way Theodore Roosevelt did thirty years ago.

Fishman added his own opposition to the idea of a national plebiscite:

Does the American Jewish Congress study these questions? If one should judge by what we hear publicly about the Congress, one gets the impression that the main problem at present is democratic elections. At a bitter time like this the Congress is

---

[1]Memo dated 12/31/37, Wise papers, Reel 90.

involved in a "shibboleth" which is tied up with inner American problems and could not influence the situation at all.[1]

Fishman's attack on the policies of his own organization is important because it demonstrates that the choices that were available for responding to the Jewish misery in Europe were not just the choices of one organization versus another, but that within a given organization, there were clear and sharp differences.

On March 12, 1938, the Nazis marched into Austria, and Austria's 185,000 Jews were subjected to all the infamies visited on German Jews for five years. The *New York Times* of March 20 reported conditions in Austria:

> The death carts of the Anatomical Institution are busy daily collecting the bodies of those poisoned by their own hands or by those nearest and dearest to them. Death seems to them the kindest fate to those, well-favored or humble, for whom once smiling Austria has become a vast prison from which there is no outlet....Is this Vienna...with its truckloads of palefaced citizens being hurried through the streets to vanish through the great gates of the central prison - for many of them the first stage of the journey to the concentration camp?[2]

After Austria fell, Wise and other members of his group met with representatives of the American Jewish Committee and some non-Jewish groups in the wake of an attempt by Jewish congressman from New York, Samuel Dickstein, to introduce legislation that would allow unused refugee quotas to be allocated to those fleeing Hitler. Those gathered agreed unanimously:

> ...such of the organizations as have personal contact with Dickstein or Celler [Emanuel Celler, also of New York], should endeavor to persuade them against going ahead with the hearing...if the hearing is held, the organizations represented at

---

[1]Memo dated 1/3/38, ibid.

[2]Cited by Morse, op. cit., p. 200.

the conference, if they do appear [before the Congressional hearing], will take the position that the proposed legislation is inadvisable....[1]

Thus on the eve of the Evian Conference called to consider the world refugee crisis, Wise and his conferees raised the upcoming conference as a reason for discouraging Dickstein's initiative. The proposal for the conference had come from Assistant Secretary of State Sumner Welles. Welles had hit on the plan as a way to quiet clamor for increased United States help for the refugees.

Welles, a career State Department operative, had close personal access to Roosevelt. Kenneth Davis, Roosevelt biographer, paints this picture of Welles:

Welles was a son of privilege, the scion of a wealthy and historically distinguished family....Tall and handsome, as trim of figure as Roosevelt had been before the polio attack, he was intimidatingly aristocratic in manner, seemingly cold and aloof....His mother and Roosevelt had been the closest of friends. Aged twelve, he had been a page in service of the groom at the wedding of Franklin and Eleanor in 1905. He was, like Roosevelt, an alumnus of Groton and Harvard. His entrance into the Foreign Service in 1915 had been facilitated by Assistant Secretary of the Navy Roosevelt.[2]

The Evian conference was very well orchestrated. The French demanded that the British, French and US delegations meet in advance of the conference to coordinate their positions. Among the British positions was that the subject of Palestine must be left off the agenda. Despite this close coordination, Wise blamed the British for the inevitable lack of accomplishment at Evian, writing in his *Opinion*, of "American generosity and British caution" and of "the appalling disappointment of Evian."[3]

---

[1]Medoff, op. cit., p. 43.

[2]Davis, *Into the Storm*, op. cit., pp. 186-187.

[3]see Medoff, p. 45.

Present at Evian was Ira Hirschmann whose experience with the New York School of Social Research and its new University in Exile sensitized him to refugee issues. He approached Felix Frankfurter about becoming a delegate to the Evian conference. Hirshmann perceived that Frankfurter was doing him a favor (rather than protecting the administration's interests in strictly limiting Jewish input at Evian) by suggesting he go to the conference informally. "[Frankfurter] convinced me that my interests would be best served if I did not join the delegation."[1]

Within the Roosevelt administration, there were powerful voices more in tune to the suffering of the Jews. Harold Ickes, Secretary of the Interior, was asked to make a major address to Jewish groups after Nazi troops marched into Austria. He noted in his diary of March 30:

> The only reason I accepted this assignment was because I could get a national hookup which would give me an opportunity to say something to the country about recent developments of fascism, particularly with reference to the persecution of the Jews in fascist countries in Europe.

In his address he noted that "...in practically all of the nations in Europe that have gone fascist the Jews constitute the racial minority against which bitter hate is fanned into a searing flame."[2]

Meantime, Wise pushed his idea of a nationwide plebiscite with the same singlemindedness that drove him to establish the World Jewish Congress in the face of heavy opposition from Jewish critics. When a family member with whom he kept up a lively correspondence took note of the opposition to the plebiscite and urged Wise to "give in a little if you have to," Wise responded: "The fight is on. Win or lose, we shall go through with it."[3]

Appeals to keep the focus on the plight of European Jewry came from the Jewish community of Denver which sent

---

[1]Hirschmann, *Caution to the Winds*, op. cit., p. 101.

[2]Watkins, T.H., *Righteous Pilgrim: The Life and Times of Harold L. Ickes* (New York: Henry Holt and Company, 1990), pp. 664-665.

[3]Letters dated 5/26/38 and 5/28/38, CZA, Wise papers, Reel 4.

identical letters to the American Jewish Congress, American Jewish Committee, Jewish Labor Council and B'nai B'rith:

The tragic plight of millions of Jews throughout Europe - concentration camps, public degradations, mass disenfranchisements, confiscations, and ruthless expulsions of our people - the spectre of increasing race prejudice, intolerance and insecurity - these terrible forces of evil demand the most effective union possible of American Jewry at once.[1]

Only when Wise heard from the White House did he pause. In a June memo to two fellow leaders of the American Jewish Congress Wise wrote that FDR advisor Sam Rosenman told him that Roosevelt was displeased:

He [Rosenman] said the Chief used this term: "the whole thing is loaded with dynamite." First the four questions were read to him. He claimed that the Chief was filled with horror when he read the second question, which, I believe, although I am not sure [Wise was not correct], dealt with Palestine. He stated the Chief suddenly said to him: "Won't this enable Americans to say that the fellows who wrote the Protocols of the Elders of Zion had some justification?"

The Wise memo continued in a vein that indicates Wise was having second thoughts:

The Chief called SR's [Sam Rosenman's] attention to the fact that one of the days of the election is a Sunday, something which will give special offense to good Orthodox Christians... something which we will carefully have to consider. The important thing is that the Chief is terribly exercised. To use his phrase, which he used again and again, "this thing is loaded

---

[1]Letter dated 6/6/38, YIVO, AJC, Waldman papers, Box 2, file 34.

with dynamite: "And you know," the Chief said, "I am a friend of your people and I warn you against it."[1]

Wise did not question why Sunday, the Sabbath of "good Orthodox Christians" had anything to do with Jewish people voting on a plebiscite addressing Jewish community matters. Nor did he mention the suspicion that his sensitive antennae must have registered that Rosenman, a member of the American Jewish Committee which opposed the plebiscite, was protesting more on behalf of leaders of the Jewish organization than on behalf of Roosevelt. Whatever his suspicions, there was no plebiscite.

British policy in Palestine took on a new dimension in June of 1938 when Shlomo Ben Yosef was hung by the British. Ben Yosef had been guarding a settlement in the Negev and fired his gun at a suspicious car. No one was injured in the incident, but he was arrested, tried, convicted and hanged in less than three months. Ben Yosef, a member of Betar, cried out just before the trap door was opened: "*Yechi Jabotinsky. Lamut o' lichbosh et Hahar* - Long live Jabotinsky: To die or to conquer the mountain."[2]

Jabotinsky wrote to Ben Yosef's mother:

I do not deserve that such as your son should die with my name on their lips. But as long as fate shall permit me, his name shall live in my heart, and his pupils, more numerous than mine, will lead the way for a generation."[3]

The British were playing a high stakes game in Palestine. If Wise, who had coauthored *The Great Betrayal* in 1930, had lost his voice, William Ziff, a writer and a member of the Zionist Organization of America, had not.

Ziff published *The Rape of Palestine* in 1938, and it received wide circulation. The cover boasted: "Banned by the British. This book is forbidden in Palestine."

---

[1]Memo dated 6/7/38, CZA, Wise papers, Reel 108.

[2]Gurion, Yitshaq, *Heroes on the Gallows* (New York: Brit Trumpeldor, 1950), p. 42.

[3]Ben-Ami, Yitshaq, *Years of Wrath, Days of Glory: Memoirs From the Irgun* (New York: Robert Speller and Sons, 1982), p. 121.

On the first page of the book was a map of the area with these notations:

Anti-Zionist argument holds the Arabs to be a single people possessing a single patrimony. The nature of that inheritance hence is of direct interest. In Asia, the Arab countries with a population of 18,800,000 hold a territory as large as all of the United States east of Denver - some 1,300,000 square miles. If Egypt and North Africa also are to be considered an integral portion of this Arabic world, to these vast holdings must be added another 3,281,758 square miles; making a total land area half again larger than that of the continental United States.

On the apposing page was this quotation from Colonel Josiah C. Wedgewood, a member of the British House of Commons:

I hope the Hon. Members will believe me when I say that I am not pro-Jew; I am pro-English. I set a higher value on the reputation of England all over the world for justice than I do on anything else...but when I see this sort of thing going on, with the Government unable to put any argument on the other side, it makes me perhaps bitterer than even a Jew can be against the Government of Palestine today.[1]

Ziff did not know how accurately he was imagining a scenario that the Nazis would in time put into effect when he wrote:

Even if the Jews are to be murdered in a body, so as to do away with them and their problem together, it could only be done at the sacrifice of all existing liberty and culture. The eddies of such a monstrous proposition would not be lost until they had reduced Europe to a shambles. A population infected with such ideas is not likely to stop in its search for victims after the Jews have been butchered.

---

[1]Ziff, William B., *The Rape of Palestine* (New York: Argus Books, 1946). The 1946 edition is identical to the 1938 version except for a new Foreward and Epilogue.

The author asserted his belief in mankind and issued a poignant call to the Jewish people:

Despite the drab cruelty which obscures it today, it may be deemed certain that the world conscience still exists. If the Jews take the lead with stern unbending courage, yielding nothing that brave despair can hold, that conscience may be relied on to assert itself. They have at least no other choice, unless they are to go down in some general catastrophe which may well signal the end of civilized man on this planet. Meanwhile they can only fight on, sustained by that undimmed faith which valiant men have never questioned over the ages. It rings imperishably in the sad, beautiful words of Bialik:

Around the last dead slave,
      maybe tonight
The desert wind and desert
      beast shall fight...
Beyond the howling desert
      with its sand
There waits beneath the stars
      the Promised Land.[1]

Ziff's book caught the attention of the officials of the Pro-Palestine Federation. The new ZOA administration had written to Russell all but demanding that Elias be replaced as director of the PPF. Russell wrote Elias: "It is not possible for me to countenance the attack upon you after the unselfish, unremunerated and unremitting work you have done...." Elias responded that complaints about him by the ZOA "are not to be taken seriously....Moreover, we are not without Jewish friends. Mr. William B. Ziff has published his book, *The Rape of Palestine*, which I am mailing to you."[2]

In July, Wise ended his one term as ZOA president, reporting to his cousin about his rival within that organization, Abba Hillel Silver, that "Silver behaved very badly as he can always

---

[1]Ibid., pp. 191-193.

[2]Letters dated 10/17/38 and 10/30/38, CZA, PPF papers, F42, 36.

be depended upon doing...he is made up of eloquence and vindictiveness."[1]

Wise concentrated his organizational efforts on his American Jewish Congress. He planned a meeting in New York of representatives of 30 states and asked Roosevelt to send a message to the gathering. His loyalty to Roosevelt was rewarded by this reply:

> While I feel that a formal message at this time is not called for, I take occasion to reaffirm the sympathy which has always been felt in this country for those who have been oppressed in any part of the world on account of their beliefs.[2]

In the White House on November 8, 1938, Roosevelt sat anxiously listening to election returns. The news was mixed - Democrats would retain majorities in the Congress, but Republicans had cut into those margins with a gain of 81 seats in the House and 8 seats in the Senate. Probably unnoticed by Roosevelt was the story of a Jewish boy who had shot a German embassy official.

Hershel Grynspan was 17 years old when, on November 7, 1938, he walked into the German embassy in Paris and shot Ernst von Rath, the third secretary of the embassy. Grynspan was the son of Polish Jews who fled eastern Poland in 1911 for fear of the spread of pogroms against Jews in the Ukraine. At the time this area of Poland was controlled by Russia. His parents moved to Germany and there Grynspan was born.

As the Poles and Germans vied in their hatred of Jews, the Polish government, in March 1938, passed a law making it possible to revoke the citizenship of any Polish citizen who had been out of Poland more than five years. This was followed in October by a requirement that all Polish passports have a new stamp.

The Germans understood the intent of these moves and expelled 15,000 Poles living in Germany, among them Grynspan's parents.[3]

---

[1] Letter dated 7/6/38, CZA, Wise papers, Reel 4.

[2] Letter dated 10/29/38, ibid., Reel 108.

[3] See the account of Reed, Anthony and David Fisher, *Kristallnacht* (New York: Peter Bedrick Books, 1989), pp. 58-67.

Grynspan's parents were among those who were accepted by Polish authorities and made arrangements to live with family in Lodz. However, prior to leaving the border area they had sent to Hershel a postcard describing the desperate conditions there, leading to the shooting of von Rath.

When von Rath died on November 9, the Nazis whipped the German public into a frenzy of evil unprecedented in Germany in modern times. The *New York Times* correspondent on the spot filed the story:

Beginning systematically in the early morning hours in almost every town and city in the country, the wrecking, looting and burning continued all day. Huge but mostly silent crowds looked on and the police confined themselves to regulating traffic and making wholesale arrests of Jews "for their own protection."[1]

The *London Daily Telegraph* carried the story of its Berlin correspondent:

Mob law ruled in Berlin throughout the afternoon and evening and hordes of hooligans indulged in an orgy of destruction. I have seen several anti-Jewish outbreaks in Germany during the last five years, but never anything as nauseating as this. Racial hatred and hysteria seemed to have taken complete hold of otherwise decent people. I saw fashionably dressed women clapping their hands and screaming with glee, while respectable, middle-class mothers held up their babies to see the "fun."[2]

Over 7,000 Jewish stores and homes were destroyed, over 250 synagogues burned or otherwise demolished, and some 30,000 Jews were rounded up and taken to concentration camps. The death toll was over 200; the number of beaten and permanently injured is inestimable.

What was the reaction among the American public? We have this assessment from Kenneth Davis, Roosevelt biographer:

---

[1] Ibid.

[2] Ibid. p. 68.

It would be difficult to overestimate the height of the wave of revulsion against Nazi Germany that now swept over the American public. Father Charles E. Coughlin whose rabble-rousing activities had since 1936 become more and more violently anti-Semitic, condoned the Nazi violence as a necessary defense against "Jew-sponsored" communism, but his was almost the only influential American voice so raised publicly. Virtually every major US newspaper damned what the Berlin government had done....Within days, public meetings of religious and civic groups in nine of the largest American cities, including Father Coughlin's Detroit, adopted resolutions...calling for a strong US government response to the atrocities. So did dozens of similar meetings in smaller cities across the land.[1]

Among those horrified were a group of America's most influential literary figures including Eugene O'Neil, John Steinbeck, Edna Ferber and Thornton Wilder. Their message to Roosevelt was also printed in the *New York Times:*

We feel we no longer have any right to remain silent, we feel that the American people and the American government have no right to remain silent. Thirty-five years ago a horrified America rose to its feet to protest against the Kishinev pogroms in Tsarist Russia. God help us if we have grown so indifferent to human suffering that we cannot rise now in protest against pogroms in Nazi Germany. We feel that it is deeply immoral for the American people to continue having economic relations with a country that avowedly uses mass murder to solve its economic problems.[2]

In the week following *Kristallnacht* the British offered to give up most of the 65,000 quota for British citizens to emigrate to the United States to increase places for Jewish refugees. Under Secretary of State Sumner Welles responded:

---

[1]Davis, *Into the Storm,* op. cit., p. 367.

[2]Ibid., p. 654 (footnote).

I reminded the Ambassador that the President had officially stated once more only two days ago that there was no intention on the part of this Government to increase the quota already established for German nationals. I added that it was my strong impression that the *responsible leaders* among American Jews would be the first to urge that no change in the present quota for German Jews be made. [Italics added].[1]

Was Welles right? True, American Jewish leaders had already gone on record against increasing immigration quotas, but would they continue such a posture in the face of *Kristallnacht?*

Samuel Margoshes, a former officer of the American Jewish Congress who had resigned from that organization, used his position as editor of *The Day* to exhort Jewish leaders to action:

We have been quiet for some time, hoping that the Nazis would tire of their murderous ways, believing in quiet diplomacy and being dubious about the efficacy of our own protests....We can no longer be silent. We cannot rely on private intercessions on our behalf....Let our leaders lead! Let them not delay and postpone...those that do not deal immediately with this crisis forfeit their right to leadership....The General Jewish Council has an opportunity right now to make Jewish history....Will it rise to this historic occasion?[2]

The General Jewish Council met the following day and, after hours of debate on an agenda that had nothing to do with *Kristallnacht,* the leaders of the American Jewish Congress, American Jewish Committee, B'nai B'rith and Jewish Labor Council finally addressed the issue by adopting a resolution giving the following advice to their constituents across the country:

---

[1]Ibid., p. 367.

[2]Letter dated 11/18/38, CZA, Wise papers, Reel 89.

Resolved that it is the present sense of the General Jewish
Council that there should be no parades, public demonstrations,
or protests by Jews.[1]

Stephen Wise, on American Jewish Congress stationary sent
out a report to his members labeled: "CONFIDENTIAL. NOT FOR
PUBLICATION IN ANY FORM WHATSOEVER."

In behalf of the American Jewish Congress, I send you this
strictly confidential report clarifying our policy in our work in
meeting the present crisis in the life of our fellow-Jews in
Germany. The silence of the American Jewish Congress...must
not be regarded either as a lack of activity or vigor on our part.
Both are the result of well considered policy.[2]

Despite the advice of the General Jewish Council, *The Day*
called for public protest, arguing that "our enforced silence
has lulled us into a deep lethargy that has undermined our
sense of responsibility to our own flesh and blood."[3]

The Pro-Palestine Federation pressed for vigorous action
bolstered by a telegram from a prominent member of
Cleveland's Jewish community which pleaded for help:

What can be done to break open the apparent conspiracy of
silence on part of British, and even on part of American
government leaders, in their completely ignoring Palestine as
the self-evident, already existing...Jewish National Home....Why
does not an American Jewish or non-Jewish leader publicly
challenge Great Britain immediately to...facilitate large mass
colonization of refugee Jews in Palestine.[4]

---

[1]Lookstein, Haskel, *Were We Our Brothers' Keepers?: The Public Response of American Jews to the Holocaust* (New York: Random House,1985), p. 59.

[2]Letter dated 11/18/38, CZA, Wise papers, Reel 89.

[3]Lookstein, op. cit., p. 65.

[4]Letter dated 11/20/38, CZA, PPF papers, F42, 36.

But the influential Sam Rosenman, one of the "responsible" Jewish leaders Sumner Welles referred to, sent Roosevelt a memorandum telling him that an "Increase of quotas is wholly inadvisable...it will merely produce a 'Jewish problem' in the countries increasing the quota."[1]

In contrast, Secretary of the Interior, Ickes publicly suggested a plan to bring Jewish refugees to a safe haven in Alaska. He was contemptuous of the American Jewish leadership and spoke to Brandeis, recording in his diary of December 3, 1938:

I spoke to him of the cowardice on the part of the rich Jews of America. I said that I would like to get two or three hundred of them together in a room and tell them that they couldn't hope to save their money by meekly accepting whatever humiliations others chose to impose upon them.[2]

On December 18, Ickes addressed the Cleveland Zionist Society in what his biographer says "may have been the best speech he ever made:"

The intelligence and culture of a humane people, by a sudden, swift revulsion, has been sunk without trace in the thick darkness of pre-primitive times. Tolerance and sympathetic understanding have given way to brutal deed. The milk of human kindness has become a corroding acid. Today the Jew in certain areas is a political eunuch, a social outcast, to be dragged down like a mad dog. Deprived of their property without even a pretense of equitable right or legal form.[3]

In New York, Mayor Fiorello La Guardia held a protest meeting in Carnegie Hall and received support at least from the Yiddish press.[4]

---

[1]Cited by Lookstein, op. cit., pp. 79-80.

[2]Watkins, op. cit., p. 670.

[3]Document dated 12/18/38, Abba Hillel Silver papers, Series I, Folder 541.

[4]Lookstein, op. cit., p. 63.

In searching the Wise papers for his private response to friends and family, one finds that the first two letters he wrote to Mack after *Kristallnacht* were approximately five weeks after that tragic event. There was no mention either directly or obliquely to *Kristallnacht* in particular, or the plight of European Jewry in general.[1]

Writing to his cousin, Rosemary Krensky, also in December, he wrote of his medical problems and was silent on Jewish suffering.[2] This was also the case in his correspondence with Lawrence, "Dutch" Berenson, a New York attorney who was a member of the Joint Distribution Committee (the JDC).[3]

In writing to Frankfurter, Wise made a cryptic, but telling reference to *Kristallnacht*, indicating he was doing as the Roosevelt administration wanted: "...I need not tell you, do I, Felix, that I have had 'to sit upon the lie' until I was almost blown skyward."[4]

Arriving in the United States at the time was Mr. Chaim Lubinsky. His arrival was little noted, but would begin a process that would completely transform the debate within the American Jewish community.

---

[1]Letters dated 11/10/38 and 12/16/38, CZA, Wise papers, Reel 115.

[2]Letter dated 12/29/38, ibid., Reel 4.

[3]Letters dated 1/10/39 and 4/5/39, ibid., Reel 90.

[4]Letter dated 11/17/38, ibid., Reel 109.

PART II

THE WAR YEARS

CHAPTER VI

ON THE HIGH SEAS

Chaim Lubinsky was the first member of the *Irgun* to come to the United States. The *Irgun* was made up of young men who had in common that they were inspired by the vision of Vladimir Ze'ev Jabotinsky. Thus, they were anathema to the Labor-Socialist establishment in Palestine and to those in the rest of the world who followed the lead of the Weizmann-Ben-Gurion coalition.

After some initial spadework, Lubinsky returned to Israel, leaving the fledgling United States organization to Yitshaq Ben-Ami. The year was 1939. Ben-Ami was born in the new Jewish city of Tel Aviv in 1913. His maternal grandfather, Zeev Leib, born in Brest-Litovsk, was influenced by pogroms in Russia and the writing of Leon Pinsker whose *Auto-Emancipation* became a rallying cry for many Russian Jews. Zeev Leib learned that Jews from Grodno had bought land in Palestine and established a settlement called Petah-Tikva. He landed in Jaffa in 1882 and took his family to join the pioneer farmers there. His daughter, the mother of Yitshaq Ben-Ami, was ten years old.

A year earlier, in 1891, Ben-Ami's paternal grandfather left Russia and moved into the Old City of Jerusalem. He lived in what later became known as the Moslem quarter. There he established a distillary which made brandy and vodka. He was killed in an explosion of a defective valve of one of his boilers. His son Shmuel, Ben-Ami's father, moved to Jaffa. He met and married Ben-Ami's mother in the early 1890s and they moved to the new suburb of Jaffa - Tel Aviv.

Ben-Ami had a typical indoctrination into the Zionist Socialist youth movement.

We went deeply into the essays of Achad Ha'am....His amalgam of lofty spiritual values and pride in the uniqueness of Jewish ethical heritage appealed to our young idealism....Children of the middle class, we condemned our parents' "indifference" to the growing social problems. Quoting Achad Ha'am, and our Socialist leaders, we vowed that the injustices and inequalities of the diaspora would never be repeated here....Like Achad Ha'am, we felt that all of this had to be a gradual process. The last thing we wanted was to revive the philosopher Max Nordau's ideas about "dumping" half a million Jews in Palestine. And, as for the "Arab problem" we would not solve it by creating a Jewish majority, but by forging links to the Arab worker who was exploited by the Arab effendi class....[1]

Ben-Ami was also influenced by the writing of A.D. Gordon who wrote that manual labor in a Jewish spiritual center in Palestine would lift the Jews of the Russian Pale out of their misery and make them strong Jews. Ben-Ami determined to become a farmer. In 1928 he worked on Kibbutz Na'an, a settlement of Hanoar Haoved - "working youth." Living in primitive conditions, "we city kids got an excellent taste of the demands of commmunal farm life."[2]

Ben-Ami first began to question his Socialist training in August 1929 when Arab gangs assaulted Jews thoroughout Palestine, killing 133. His uncle Shraga, one of those beaten, was in critical condition. Visiting him in the hospital, Ben-Ami heard from his uncle that this was the second time he had directly experienced pogroms, the first being in Kishinev in 1903. His uncle Shraga, like Ben-Ami's father, had been deeply influenced in Russia by the teachings of Habad Chassidism. Now Hebron's Jewish community, the oldest Habad community in Palestine, had been destroyed.

In Italy, where he studied agriculture, Ben-Ami had his Socialist teachings challenged by a member of Betar, the Jabotinsky youth movement. He returned to Palestine after a year and made the decision to join Betar. Showing exceptional leadership abilities, he was asked to join the Irgun, the underground Jewish defense movement which broke off from

---

[1]Ben-Ami, op. cit., pp. 52-54.

[2]Ibid., p. 56.

the Haganah. When asked by his indoctrinators what he wanted to join the Irgun, Ben-Ami answered:

> I believe that we, the youth, have to serve our nation and our homeland, like the youth of all other nations. Military service is what every country, if it hopes to survive, requires of its people. We are a nation on the way to independence and statehood, and I'm willing to serve like young men everywhere else.[1]

Ben-Ami began his work with underground immigration in 1937. It was at his suggestion that a decision was made to send a delegation to the United States to raise money. Chaim Lubinsky, Robert Briscoe, and Colonel John Patterson left immediately while Ben-Ami returned to Palestine to acquire the proper visa.

Upon his arrival in the United States, Ben Ami threw himself with great vigor into the task of raising Jewish consciousness and raising money for bringing Jewish refugees from Europe to Palestine. The process of bringing refugees into Palestine in excess of the certificate quota system established by the British divided organizations and individuals within those organizations. The British branded this immigration "illegal."

In the early 1930s, Ben-Gurion was firmly against any policy of clandestine immigration for fear it would upset relations with the British. However, the other two partners in the Socialist troika of leadership, Katznelson and Yitzhak Tabenkin, ignored the proscriptions and actively supported what the Laborites called *Aliyah Bet*. In 1934, when the *Velos*, a small craft leased by the Socialist activists, successfully landed Jewish refugees from Europe, Katznelson was on the shore and recorded in his diary: "All night on the beach. Greeting the first boat. Splendid and horrific. The capsized boat: two drowned...."[2]

In 1937, the worsening crisis in Europe and the disillusionment with British policy led to increased efforts. Jabotinsky, like Ben-Gurion, believed in achieving a homeland

---

[1] Ibid., p. 89.

[2] Cited by Shapira, op. cit. p. 274. Also see Offer, Dalia, *Escaping the Holocaust: Illegal Immigration to the Land of Israel, 1939-1944* (Oxford: Oxford U. Press, 1990), p. 10.

through cooperation with the British, but believed in more direct pressure to influence British opinion. There was complete agreement among the Revisionists about clandestine immigration into Palestine which they called *Af Al Pi* - "in spite of everything."

Moshe Galili, not directly affiliated either with the Socialists or with the Revisionists, was an activist in the underground immigration. In 1937 he approached Willy Perl, co-chairman of Vienna's Revisionists, and proposed joint action. Perl was impressed by Galili and took him to Paul Haller, a Viennese journalist who had founded the group *Die Aktion* to which Perl belonged. A partnership was formed and plans went forward. Perl, an intrepid attorney, gives a fascinating account of his face-to-face encounter in Vienna with Adolf Eichmann at a time before the Nazis closed the door to Jewish emigration. Eichmann held a gun to his head and threatened to shoot him unless Perl told him where a certain man could be found. Perl managed to talk himself out of the situation by telling Eichmann he was essential to the effort to get Jews out of Europe.[1]

The group was motivated by the desire to get as many members of Betar, the Revisionist youth movement, as possible into Palestine to prepare for what they saw as the inevitable conflict with the Arabs and the British, and to save Jews fleeing the Nazis. The latter motive took on more and more significance as the events of 1937-1938 unfolded.

In March of 1937, the *Kosta*, whose voyage was the first planned jointly by Galili and Perl, landed 16 young men on a beach near Haifa. There was no organization in Palestine at that point to receive them, but soon the underground organization, the Irgun Zvai Leumi (often designated the Irgun or Etzel which is an acronym of the full name) agreed to help disperse the refugees to safe havens. The *Artemiesia I* brought another 68 people in August of 1937.

It was the Nazi march into Austria on March 11, 1938, that brought Eichmann to Vienna. Perl describes that "blackest Friday" in Vienna. He was at the home of a friend awaiting the radio address of Austrian Chancellor Schuschnigg:

---

[1]See Perl, William R., *Operation Action: Rescue from the Holocaust* (New York: Ungar Pub. Co., 1983), pp. 10-13. Perl's account was originally published as *The Four Front War* and first republished as *Operation Action* in 1978. The citations in this book are from the revised and enlarged edition of *Operation Action* published in 1983. For the cooperation between Galili and Perl, also see Offer, op. cit., pp. 12-17.

The chancellor had received an ultimatum from Hitler demanding his country's surrender. Many Austrians were outright Nazis, and the Nazi program of anti-Semitism appealed to many more. Austrian Jews therefore greatly feared Schuschnigg's answer to the threat of an invasion by the Nazi army. When Schuschnigg concluded his radio speech, announcing his country's surrender with the words, "God save Austria," a death sentence was handed down against the community of approximately 200,000 Austrian Jews.[1]

Perl and several of his colleagues were arrested in a general roundup of Jewish leaders, but again won their release when they insisted they played important roles in helping the Nazis make Austria *Judenrein*.[2]

The clandestine Socialist immigration was also feuled by youth groups. Hechalutz, a youth movement within the Socialist camp, was affiliated primarily with the kibbutz movement. Immigration within the British certificate system could not even accomodate all the Hechalutz members who trained in Europe let alone members of Betar who were discriminated against in the allotment of precious *aliyah* certificates.

After *Kristallnacht*, the Haganah, the underground movement associated with the Socialists, established the *Aliyah Bet* Agency, the Mossad, which ultimately became the famous intelligence organization after the establishment of the State of Israel. The Mossad was based in Paris as was their counterpart organization, the Center for Aliyah, set up by followers of Jabotinsky.

The pressure on the clandestine *aliyah* effort was multiplied by the swell of Jewish refugees in 1938-1939. Dalia Offer provides some specific figures. From 1938 until September 1, 1939 (the date of the Nazi invasion of Poland), 257,878 Jews left Germany, Austria, and Czechoslovakia. Of these, only 40,147 made it to Palestine, approximately half through the certificate system and half by running the British blockade of "illegal" immigrants. The Mossad and Hechalutz cooperated to

---

[1] Perl, op. cit., p. 18.

[2] Ibid., pp. 32-52.

bring 5,500 to the shores of Palestine, while the Revisionists in conjunction with Galili saved 12,000.[1]

The lower figure for the Socialists was due in great part to the ambivalence of their leadership. Many practical economic reasons were given by Eliezer Kaplan, treasurer of the Jewish Agency, for opposing massive *aliyah*. Ben-Gurion, went from opposition to *Aliyah Bet*, to a brief period of supporting the Mossad in their efforts, then back again in 1939 to opposition. His "conscience," Berl Katznelson, consistently and vigorously argued in favor of the maximum number of immigrants. His position that *aliyah* was important as an historic movement of Jews and should not be weighed against practical considerations was close to the view of Jabotinsky.

In the United States, personal rivals Abba Hillel Silver and Stephen Wise were united in opposing clandestine immigration despite the fact that in May, the British had issued the infamous White Paper. The White Paper stated there could be no Jewish state for 10 years and then only with the consent of the Arabs, and that there would be only 15,000 immigration certificates each year for the next five years. After that there would be no immigration without Arab approval.

At the Zionist Congress in Geneva in August, 1939, Silver spoke in open opposition to "illegal" immigration. The following day, in what would be his final Zionist Congress, Berl Katznelson ascended the podium. An introspective, compassionate man not given to personality duels, he nonetheless aimed pointed criticism at Silver:

>...From this podium remarks were made yesterday by Rabbi Silver which I cannot permit myself to ignore. It was as if he cast a stone at our refugees on the high seas, and stabbed Zionist policy in the back. There is immigration which is denoted "illegal." Everything in this legal world is legal. Legitimate governments, legitimate conquest, legitimate documents, even legitimate violations of promises. Only the immigration of Jews, on the basis of the ancient mandate of the exodus from Egypt, is not legal.

In the darkness of the Nazi shadow which oppressed the Jewish people, Katznelson spoke eloquently:

---

[1]Offer, op. cit., pp. 14-16.

We do not determine the course of history, and neither can we foresee what it will bring. We may ask why it is that history did not choose free, wealthy, well-behaved Jews to be the bearers of its mission, but preferred instead the Jewish refugees, the most wretched of mankind, cast adrift on the seas. But this is a fact we cannot change. This is what history has determined, and it is left to us to accept its choice and to follow the refugee.

Katznelson explicitly rejected the Socialist adherence to the concept of "selective" *aliyah,* insisting that, "in the midst of the great catastrophe," all refugees should be brought to Palestine by whatever means. "What, after all, is Zionism all about? Summer camps? Sabbath eve gatherings? Has not its aim always been, since Pinsker and Herzl, to provide a true salvation for the Jewish people?"

Yes, there were great difficulties, Katznelson conceded, but there was also hope:

I know that sometimes even a great nation may be helpless in the face of the troubles and suffering of masses of people...at least now there is the basic foundation of a nation in its own land, the vanguard of a nation that is ready to fight for its freedom and its homeland and stands with open arms to welcome its brethren....if you will it or not, if you help or hinder, the afflictions of the Jewish people will drive the boats out to sea.[1]

Jabotinsky contacted Katznelson and the two met briefly in Paris. Jabotinsky had to return to London and prevailed on Katznelson to travel there for further discussion. Katznelson did so and they met for a series of talks. Although they agreed on the approach to the refugee crisis, the two Zionist leaders looked at each other across an ideological gulf. There was a spark of agreement when Katznelson asked if, after the war, the Revisionists would consent to return to the World Zionist Organization under certain conditions of compromise, and Jabotinsky said that they would.

By war's end, however, both leaders were dead, each death a tragic loss to world Jewish leadership.

---

[1] Quotes taken from the accounts of Offer, op. cit., pp. 19-20, and Shapira, op. cit., pp. 278-279.

While Jewish leaders hesitated to bring direct pressure on the American and British goverments to aid Jewish refugees, the Catholic Church had no such compunction where its agenda was concerned. As documented in Chapter IV, the Church did not hesitate to involve itself in lobbying on political issues. This phenomenon became even more obvious as the Spanish Civil War heated up.

On the eve of his second inauguration, Roosevelt, along with the European democracies, was faced with the news that the Germans had seized a Spanish ship. This was reported to be in reprisal for the Spanish government's confiscation of a German shipload of arms that had landed in Spain, intended for anti-government rebels. It was also reported that Hitler was sending two divisions of troops to join Italian fascist volunteers in the war on Spanish democracy.

The Bourbon dynasty had ended in Spain in 1930 when the last king vacated the throne. A constitution was established which gave all citizens the right to vote, separated Church and State, and even barred clergy from ministerial office. Much Church land had been nationalized.

The first elections reflected the traditional Spanish conservatism as right wing parties won 44% of the vote. Many of the consitutional reforms were rolled back, allaying the fears of the Church and others who prospered under the Bourbons. When, in 1936, a moderate-left coalition, including the small Spanish Communist Party, captured a majority, there was great consternation within the Church, other large land holders and big business. The Communist Party had captured only four per cent of the vote, but this was enough to clothe the revolt against Spanish democracy with an "anti-communist" patina.

Fascist Italy and Nazi Germany cynically pointed to the non-Intervention pledge they had signed with Britain and France while they rallied to the anti-Communist banner, sending arms and troops. Britain and France gave no help to the legal Spanish government, but the rebels, headed by General Francisco Franco who previously had been removed from the army General Staff, received massive aid from Musollini and Hitler. From Berlin came news that 27 Catholic cardinals and bishops had signed a pastoral letter supporting Hitler in his "war on the Reds."[1]

---

[1] Davis, *Into the Storm*, op. cit., p. 13.

The ideological underpinning of Spanish fascism was imported from Italy and drew on the notion that Spain, with Italy, stood as the guardian of the Holy Roman Empire. In point 24 of the 26 points of the Phalanx - the Spanish Fascists, this was made explicit:

> Our movement will incorporate the Catholic spirit of glorious tradition and predominant in Spain in the national reconstruction. The Church and the State will arrange a Concordat defining their respective spheres....[1]

In the United States in 1936, an arms embargo was imposed on both sides as if there were no legal government involved. Though this was opposed to what the Roosevelt administration stood for, Roosevelt stared political reality in the face and did not take a positive position in favor of the Loyalists.

And what was that political reality? Interior Secretary Ickes, who challenged Roosevelt on his silence in the face of the attack on the Spanish government, was told that the President had been advised by congressional leaders that "... to raise the embargo would mean the loss of every Catholic vote next fall." Ickes disdainfully wrote in his diary that "the Catholic minorities in Great Britain and America have been dictating international policy with respect to Spain."[2]

The Jewish stake in Spain was outlined in the Chicago *Jewish Chronicle* by a Dr. Baruch Braunstein. He wrote that anti-Semitism was endemic in Spain and that prior to the new consitution in 1930, "not more that 7,000 Jews lived in all of Spain." From the setting up of the constitutional Republic in 1930 until 1936, the year the article was written, the author estimated that 15,000 to 20,000 Jews had "returned home", mostly from Turkey, Greece, the Balkans, and North Africa. He predicted that if Franco were victorious, Spain would become "*Judenrein*"....the hatred of the Jew is so overwhelming a fact

---

[1] Hamilton, Thomas J, *Appeasment's Child: The Franco Regime in Spain* (New York: Alfred A. Knopf, 1943), p. 75.

[2] Ickes, Harold, *Secret Diary of Harold Ickes,* Vol II, p. 390, cited in Thomas, Hugh, *The Spanish Civil War* (New York: Simon & Schuster, 1986), p. 698, and p. 825.

in Spanish history that great masses of Spaniards can always be united - against the Jews."[1]

As Franco's forces made progress in the war, Senator Gerald Nye from North Dakota, though a leader of the isolationist bloc in Congress, introduced legislation that would lift the arms embargo against the Spanish government. The American Catholic leadership mobilized a campaign that delivered petitions with over one million signatures to the Congress in opposition to Nye's initiative. Roosevelt opposed the legislation that would have given arms support to the Spanish government "on a cash and carry basis" to Spain.[2]

In 1939, Franco was victorious and Roosevelt extended *de jure* recognition. John Gunther, in *Roosevelt in Retrospect*, recounts an evening when Eleanor Roosevelt, who strongly supported help to the Loyalists, said to a dinner guest as she nodded toward her husband, "[we]...will someday learn a lesson from this tragic error over Spain. We were morally right, but too weak. We should have pushed him harder."[3]

Spain fell to Franco in April, 1939, and his execution squads went into high gear. While there were tensions between the Fascists and the Church, the Church got everything it wanted. Divorce and civil marriage were abolished and all properties that had belonged to the Church prior to 1930 were restored as was the previous level of funding by the State.[4]

While the Catholics in the United States were successfully pushing their particularist interests that directly impacted major foreign policy issues and had nothing to do with saving Catholic lives, the situation among Jewish leadership was quite different. In the wake of *Kristallnacht*, Senator Wagner of New York introduced legislation to allow 20,000 German Jewish children into the United States over a two year period. Stephen Wise agreed to testify before the committee conducting hearings on the bill and was something less than a strong advocate for the special legislation that would gain their admission to the United States:

---

[1] *Chicaco Jewish Chronicle*, 8/7/36.

[2] Davis. *Into the Storm*, op. cit., pp. 398-399.

[3] Cited, by Davis, ibid.

[4] Hamilton, op. cit., p. 96.

...so far as I am concerned, there is no intention whatsoever to depart from the immigration laws which at present obtain...If there is any conflict between our duty to those children and our duty to our country, speaking for myself as a citizen, I should say, of course, that our country comes first; and if children cannot be helped, they cannot be helped....[1]

Ten days after his testimony, and with no reference to it, so the timing may have been coincidental, Wise wrote to Missy LeHand, presidential secretary requesting "...a really good picture of the Chief. I know that he cannot send his picture to all his friends. But if you will let me know where the very, very best picture is to be had...I will send for it and then have it sent to you for autographing."[2]

In contrast to Wise's testimony was that of writer Quentin Reynolds who had been in Germany for two extended visits. Congressman Samuel Dickstein, who had previously supported legislation that would loosen the restrictive U.S. immigration laws, asked Reynolds if he thought there would be more pogroms like *Kristallnacht*. Reynolds answered: "I am confident the complete pogrom is not far away." Dickstein asked if he meant "annihilation," and he responded: "Yes, a complete pogrom." Reynolds and Dickstein saw no difficulty in accommodating the refugee children in the United States. The legislation, without vigorous support from Jewish leadership, got nowhere.[3]

How desperate were German Jews to get out of Germany in 1939? By the end of 1939, approximately 200,000 had already left, and concerning those remaining, we have this entry into the diary of William Shirer who was a foreign correspondent in Germany:

Though the quota of Germans allowed entry into America annually is 27,000, Marvin [a fellow journalist] found a waiting list of 248,000 names at the American consulate. Ninety-eight per cent were Jews - or about half the Jewish population of

---

[1]Medoff, op. cit., p. 58.

[2]Letter dated 5/1/39, CZA, Wise papers, Reel 108.

[3]Medoff, op. cit., pp. 266-267.

Germany." [Actually, 248,000 was considerably more than half of the Jews remaining in Germany at the time of this diary entry].[1]

While desperate refugees were trying to get to Palestine in Hechalutz and Revisionist ships, another ship laden with Jews steamed toward Cuba, having been promised refuge there.

The fate of the *St. Louis* was decided in the months of May and June, 1939. In the previous six months *Kristallnacht* had shocked the world, the British had issued the infamous White Paper slamming shut the gates of Palestine, and a Fascist government with Italian and German troops fighting at their side had won the civil war in Spain.

Stephen Wise's papers reflect that he knew in advance of the British decision to issue the White Paper. He sent a telegram to Roosevelt asking him to pressure the British to call off the pronouncement of the deadly policy. When no such help was forthcoming, he wrote to a friend: "I suppose I resent it a little that, while the President has done much, he ought to have been successful in preventing Chamberlain from doing this idiotic as well as dastardly thing."[2]

Wise also knew in advance of the arrival in Cuba of the *St. Louis* that the Cuban authorities were balking at allowing the refugees into Cuba. On May 5, 1939, Frederico Laredo Bru, the head of the Cuban government, had issued decree 937 forbidding entry into Cuba of the refugees. A Cuban Nazi party had recently been given legal status. This was part of a power play between Bru and Manuel Benitez, the Cuban director of immigration, and in a larger sphere between Bru and military strongman, Fulgencio Batista.[3] In a May 13 letter, "Dutch" Berenson, who negotiated with the Cuban government on behalf of the JDC, wrote to Wise: "I must leave for Cuba in a few days on the refugee mess."[4]

---

[1]Shirer, William, *Berlin Diary: The Journal of a Foreign Correspondent* (New York: Alfred A. Knopf, 1941), p. 292.

[2]Letter dated 5/4/39, CZA, Wise papers, Reel 5.

[3]see discussion in: Thomas, Gordon and Max Morgan Witts, *The Voyage of the Damned* (Greenwich: Fawcett Publications, 1974), pp. 78-86.

[4]CZA, Wise papers, Reel 90.

Less than two weeks later, after the White Paper had been publicly issued and the Jews aboard the *St. Louis* were desperately seeking help, Wise swallowed his resentment and wrote to Roosevelt:

In this hour of sorrow over the betrayal of Jewish faith and hope by the Chamberlain government, we feel impelled to say to you that we are mindful of all you have sought to do on behalf of our cause in recent years....World Jewry and particularly the Jews of Palestine will not, dear Mr. President, forget all that you have done or sought to do on our behalf. We shall remember and be grateful always.[1]

There was no mention of the Jewish refugees adrift on the high seas. The day before the *St. Louis* docked in Cuba, Wise wrote to his cousin:

What with the tragic Palestine situation and the really rising tide of anti-Semitism everywhere, I do not know what to do!....Last night, after Carnegie Hall was refused to the so-called Christain Front, made up of Coughlinites, they marched up and down 57th Street, shouting: "Hang Rabbi Wise to a flagpole! Lynch Rabbi Wise."[2]

As this letter was penned, the latest issue of Wise's *Opinion* went to press, issuing the call: "Let us not fear accusations of international intrigue from the Coughlinites, et al. Our actions must be determined not by fear of libel but by the courage of men and the heart of the Jews."[3]

Although most Jewish publications were silent on the fate of the *St. Louis*, there were notable exceptions. *The Day* called for pressure on Cuba to allow the refugees to disembark and denounced the silence of Jewish leaders. "The Jewish leadership owes us an immediate explanation. If they cannot do

---

[1] Letter dated 5/17/30, Voss, op. cit., pp. 232-233.

[2] Letter dated 5/26/39, CZA, Wise papers, Reel 4.

[3] Letter dated 5/26/39, ibid.

anything, let them make room for new, energetic Jewish leadership." *The New Palestine* asked: "Why have not the eminent leaders and spokesmen been heard from?"[1]

Wise was kept informed by the JDC's "Dutch" Berenson who traveled to Cuba to try to negotiate a solution to the stalemate. He reported to Wise that "the President made three definite promises to me on three different occasions to admit them."[2] After steaming northward off the coast of South Carolina and finding the doors to the United States as barred as those of Cuba, the passengers on the *St. Louis* were ultimately returned to Europe. France accepted 224 passengers, Belgium 214, Holland 181 and Britain 288. While they were not returned to Germany, many of them fell victim to the Nazi conquest of previously free areas and were killed in the Holocaust. [3]

Just as Wise blamed the British instead of the Roosevelt administration in the wake of both the fruitless Evian Conference and the White Paper which closed the gates of Palestine, he now cast blame for the hopelessness of Jewish refugees on his rivals in American Jewish politics:

> The tragedy of the *St. Louis* and other boats tells the world of today and the generations of tomorrow a shameful story of Jewish disintegration and division in the face of disasters, parts of which could have been forestalled. The leaders of the nationalist camp will not carry the brunt of the blame. For years they have been sounding the warning and calling for unification of effort and centralization of guidance. It is those whose fear of nationalism makes them resist any centralization who will answer for what was humanly possible to do but was not attempted.[4]

A more honest assessment was given in the publication of the American Jewish Congress:

---

[1] See Lookstein, op. cit., p. 88.

[2] Letter dated 6/14/39, CZA, Wise papers, Reel 90.

[3] Thomas, Gordon and Max Morgan Witts, op. cit., pp. 305-306.

[4] Cited by Medoff, op. cit., 61.

It did not even occur to Jews to appeal to the American government to find a way of saving the hapless passengers of the *St. Louis*. Our own depression and demoralization are immeasurably more dangerous to ourselves than the blows of our enemies.[1]

Wise also opposed another attempt from within the Roosevelt administration to help Jewish refugees. Interior Secretary Harold Ickes' idea of settling Jewish refugees in Alaska was not merely an idle, empathic gesture. Ickes' staff drafted a detailed plan which was issued as "The Problem of Alaskan Development" in August of 1939. The report outlined a cooperative effort between government and private entities to develop Alaska. This would at the same time provide work for thousands of unemployed Americans and a revision of immigration quotas to bring in "skilled labor from the four corners of the earth."[2]

When Sumner Welles at the State Department scotched the idea within the administration, Ickes persisted and turned to the legislative process. The King-Havener Bill met the same legislative fate as other congressional attempts to alleviate the misery of the Jewish people in Europe. Again, as opposed to his thunderous denunciations of the American Jewish Committee for their timidity and fearfulness of what non-Jewish Americans would think, the actions of Stephen Wise continued to be identical to and in concert with those of the rival organization to his American Jewish Congress. Wise rationalized his opposition to Ickes' Alaska plan by his concern about "a wrong and hurtful impression to have it appear that Jews are taking over some part of the country for settlement."[3]

While these debates took place in the United States, heroic action on the high seas continued. The Mossad ran the British blockade when the *Tiger Hill* rammed the beaches of Tel Aviv with over 1400 refugees on board.

On September 1, 1939, British appeasement policy went up in flames as German planes attacked Poland from the skies and German tanks and troops poured across the Polish border. The

---

[1]Cited by Lookstein, op. cit., p. 102.

[2]Watkins, op. cit. pp. 673-674.

[3]See Medoff, op. cit., p. 68.

British navy was active that day against helpless Jewish refugees. The *Lorna*, on duty off the coast of Palestine, fired on the *Tiger Hill*, killing two Jewish refugees.[1]

The architect of British policy, Prime Minister Neville Chamberlain, told his country England was at war, admitting that "everything I have believed in in my public life has crashed in ruins."[2]

On that infamous Sept 1, 1939, Willy Perl was in Greece. Frustrated by the small size of the boats he had managed to enlist in clandestine immigration to Palestine, he set his sights higher. At the end of August, he received news that he might be able to get a Turkish or Iranian ship that could carry over 2,000 refugees. Anticipating the outbreak of a general war, he made reservations on the Orient Express every day for a week ahead. On Sept 1, he went to the Athens depot:

No description of the Athens railroad station on that day can do justice to the bedlam there. Everyone who could afford to flee to the West tried to catch a train out. The environs of the railroad station were clogged with automobiles loaded to the brim inside and with boxes on the rooftops...and in between goats and donkeys that had become caught in the stream of automobiles and horse-drawn vehicles converging on the railroad station.[3]

Perl was able to get a ticket for Zurich where it had been agreed his group would gather if war broke out. His freedom to travel had been facilitated by a trick he played on the British. In May, 1939, he had gone to the British Consulate in Bucharest to apply for a visa to England. Perl's role in "illegal" immigration was known to British officials. The British knew, and Perl knew, that if they could get him onto British soil, they could arrest him. While this was unspoken, they closely questioned his reasons for wanting to go to England. He brazenly told them he wanted to go there to raise money to get Jews to Palestine.

---

[1]Perl, op. cit., p. 178.

[2]See Davis, *Into the Storm*, op. cit., pp. 488-489.

[3]Perl, op. cit., p. 273.

After a delay of a week, he was granted a visa that, in red handwritten letters, stipulated "pleasure visit only." Perl assumed that, knowing he was going to Britain for business reasons, the British were using this subterfuge to arrest him once he had arrived.

In fact, Perl had no intention of going to England. The British visa served two key purposes: When dealing with ship owners worried about the opposition of the British to Jewish immigration into Palestine, he showed his papers to "prove" that the British were actually secretly working with him, and secondly, with the British visa, he was able to get transit visas for other European countries.

Arriving safely in Zurich, Perl went to 14 Schuetzengasse, a small street off the Bahnhofstrasse, Zurich's main artery. There, at the Swiss immigration headquarters of the Revisionists, he met Rudi Hecht, who as Reuven Hecht ultimately became one of the State of Israel's most successful industrialists as the owner of the huge Dagon building in Haifa, Israel's largest grain operation.

Hecht was the son of a wealthy shipping family which cut him off when he joined the Irgun. The head of the Irgun, David Raziel, saw Hecht as ideal for the *Af Al Pi* (clandestine immigration) work. His Swiss passport was a valuable asset in moving freely in Europe and in helping ease transactions with Swiss officials. Most importantly, Hecht had in common with Perl the brazen *chutzpah* necessary to rescue work carried out in the heart of a hostile Europe.

One evening when Perl and Hecht were in Budapest working with the Orthodox *Agudas Yisrael* to arrange a large transport, they went into a cafe where an American singer they assumed to be Jewish was singing. At one table was a boisterous group of German officers who induced the singer to sing some German songs with them. At the end of one song, Hecht shouted: "You should be ashamed of yourself, that you, a Jewish woman, are catering to the Germans in times like these." Perl describes the scene:

For a moment there was dead silence. Some people moved in their chairs, ready to flee from the expected brawl, when the singer switched her entertainer's smile from the Germans to Hecht and me and started singing a Yiddish song, "A Yiddishe Mama." There were other Jews in the cafe, but Rudi and I were the only ones who applauded; in fact we rose doing so. Hecht and

I rarely have a drink. We may have had a glass of wine with our meal that night, but I believe that our behavior resulted simply from indignation and youthful impulse.

The Germans, apparently fearing they would be disciplined if caught being entertained by a Jewish singer, hastily left. The singer apologized to Perl and Hecht for making them uncomfortable. It turns out she in fact was not Jewish.[1]

Perl and Hecht, working with Orthodox groups were able to secure the large ship they sought - the *Sakarya* which could hold over 2,000 people.

Just as the common understanding of the urgency of rescue brought together Revisionists and Orthodox Jews in Bucharest, so too did the same groups find a common bond in the United States.

Rabbi Eliezer Silver had travelled a long road on the way to becoming one of the most revered of American Orthodox leaders. He was born in Lithuania in 1881. His earliest education was provided by his father, but soon hedeparted for Vilna whose population in 1902 was approximately fifty per cent Jewish. Silver was ordained by the senior rabbi of the Vilna *Bet Din*, Rabbi Shlomo ha-Kohen. One of his mentors was Rav Chaim Ozer Grodenski.

With the increase in pogroms, Rabbi Silver moved with his wife, the former Bassia Aranowitz, to the United States in 1907 and settled in Harrisburg, Pennyslvania. He became treasurer of the *Agudas HaRabonim* in 1917 and a member of its presidium in 1923. He served as a spiritual leader in Springfield, Massachusetts, from 1925-1931, at which time he began a long career of service in Cincinnati.

Silver kept in close correspondence with Rav Grodenski as Jewish persecution reached its height. The responsa of Rabbi Grodzenski published in 1939 painted a dark picture:

How desperate is the plight of our people. Even during the Middle Ages, persecution of the Jews did not reach the current level. The entire diaspora is aflame, and houses of study and Torah scrolls are daily burned on every street. New decrees are promulgated by our enemies which seek to completely destroy the Jewish religion. Entire, important and large Jewish

---

[1]Ibid., pp. 308-309. See Perl's entire account of this period, pp. 271-340.

communities are uprooted and they cannot find a new haven. Families wander throughout Europe attempting to flee from the ever increasing waves of hatred. We have become an object of derision for our neighbors.[1]

In November, 1939, American Orthodox rabbis came together to address the desperate conditions in Europe. On September 14, *Rosh HaShanah*, Silver had received a telegram from Rav Grodinski, telling him of the ever increasing desperation, and the national meeting was the result. Some championed the existing institutions like the Joint Distribution Committee and the Orthodox *Ezras Torah*. The primary advocate of an entirely new organization was Eliezer Silver. It was pointed out that *Ezras Torah* had raised less than $35,000 in all of 1938 and that a whole new way of thinking was required.[2]

After a great deal of debate a new organization was born - the *Vaad Hatzala*, (Rescue Committee). Although it sprang from the *Agudas HaRabbonim*, it was an independent body with Rabbi Silver as president. Representatives of other Orthodox bodies actively joined in the *Vaad Hatzala*, including Rabbi Herbert Goldstein of the Rabbinical Council of America and Irving Bunim, one of the founders of Young Israel. Bunim and Rabbi Avraham Kalminowitz, the Rosh Yeshiva of America's Mirrer Community, were two of the driving activists on the Vaad.[3]

The difference between pleading for Jewish lives and demanding that Jewish lives be saved is illustrated by Bunim's efforts to rescue the family of a Polish rabbi. To circumvent the rules of the British, Bunim set up a dummy bank account for the rabbi. With this accomplished he ran headlong into the bureaucracy of the Jewish Agency which informed him that since he had broken British law, the requisite papers could not be issued by the Jewish Agency.

Bunim called a meeting with leading Jewish personalities in New York who had influence with the Jewish Agency. He told them:

---

[1]For the early background of Silver, see Rakeffet-Rothkoff, Aaron, *The Silver Era: Rabbi Eliezer Silver and His Generation* (New York: Feldheim, 1981), pp. 43-65

[2]Ibid., pp. 186-187.

[3]Ibid., pp. 188-189. For the formation of the *Vaad Hatzalah*, also see Bunim, op. cit., pp. 72ff.

I have a very large stone in the bottom drawer of my desk. Tomorrow, at noon, I am going down to the Jewish Agency headquarters on Fifth Avenue. Do you know that big show window on the first floor? If Rabbi Farber's family isn't granted visas for Palestine by noon tomorrow, I'm going to smash that window to bits.

His pronouncement was met with some degree of skepticism by the others who asked what he thought he would accomplish. Bunim gave them an answer:

The police will come. Irving Bunim smashed a window! Arrest him! The *New York Times* will come and the nice young reporter will ask, "Mr. Bunim, why did you break the window?" Then I'll tell them the whole story. You guys will be drummed out of America.[1]

Within 24 hours Rabbi Farber's family had their visas.

The desperate-acts-for-desperate-times approach of the *Vaad Hatzala* and the Revisionists contrasted sharply with the legalistic approach of the established Jewish organizations in the United States. While divided on personal questions and battles for leadership, men like Wise, Mack, Abba Hillel Silver, and Louis Lipsky, all affiliated with the American Jewish Congress and the ZOA, and leaders like Rabbi Jonah B. Wise, Cyrus Adler and others affiliated with the American Jewish Committee and the Joint Distribution Committee all favored a more cautious, "legal" approach.

On stationary of the United Jewish Appeal, which bears the names of all of these men, went out a letter condemning Revisionist rescue actions. Berl Katznelson's emphatic appeal at the Zionist Congress a few months before had made no impact on American leaders. The letter to American Jews continued to support the limited, "selected" immigration of Jews to Palestine, despite *Kristallnacht*, despite the fate of the *St. Louis,* and despite the fact that over 3,000,000 Jews were now trapped in Nazi occupied Poland. The letter said, in part:

---

[1]Bunim, op. cit., pp. xiii-xvi.

Selectivity is an inescapable factor in dealing with the problem of immigration to Palestine. By "selectivity" is meant the choice of young men and women who are trained in Europe for purposes either in agriculture or industry or who are in other ways trained for life in Palestine....Sentimental considerations are, of course, vital and everyone would wish to save every single Jew who could be rescued out of the cauldron of Europe...but when one is dealing with so delicate a program as unregistered immigration, it is obviously essential that those people sent to Palestine shall be able to endure harsh conditions.

The letter then turned to the efforts of Perl, Hecht and others to get the *Sakarya* safely to Palestine.

When the Revisionist-sponsored transport on the Danube became a public issue two weeks ago, a responsible individual indicated to the American Friends of Jewish Palestine that this particular affair could be satisfactorily liquidated if the American Friends of a Jewish Palestine would cease its separate fund-raising activities...and if it were to agree to "selectivity" in immigration....The American Friends of a Jewish Palestine refused to meet these conditions.[1]

What was the American Friends of a Jewish Palestine? How was the group of people affiliated with this group and with other groups that would follow in its wake able to unite against them such long standing rivals as the American Jewish Congress and the American Jewish Committee?

It is to this group that we now turn.

---

[1]Letter dated 2/1/40, CZA, Wise papers, Reel 1.

CHAPTER VII

WHO WAS PETER BERGSON?

Peter Bergson was "one of the most controversial figures in the country."[1] Bergson was in his late twenties when he came to the United States in 1940. Diminutive, with a high, squeaky voice, he came with a mission, a purpose, but with no experience in dealing with the vast, slow-moving bureaucracy in Washington. How, in less than five years, did he arouse strong passions, enlist hundreds of senators and congressmen in his work, and play an important role in the establishment of a United States government agency that would do what no government agency had done before - save Jewish lives?

Bergson was born Hillel Kook in Latvia in 1914 or 1915. As a pre-school child in Russia, he experienced violence; his brother Nachum was shot in a pogrom but survived the attack. His father, Dov Ber Kook, moved his wife and eight children across a Europe torn by revolutions and world war and finally sailed for Palestine, arriving in 1920.

The brother of Dov Ber was the beloved Yitshaq HaCohen Kook, the chief rabbi of Palestine. Young Hillel attended *Mercaz HaRav*, the yeshiva of his illustrious uncle but, in his teens, he left formal religion behind. At age nineteen he was again exposed to violence against Jews, this time in their ancient homeland. The Arab riots of 1929 made a deep impression on Kook as they did on Yitshaq Ben-Ami. With his good friend, David Raziel, Kook joined Haganah *Bet*, a splinter group within the Haganah that believed in direct counteraction against the Arabs.

---

[1]Article in *New York Post*, by Victor Riesel, 6/1/44.

In 1937, the leader of Haganah Bet, Avraham Tahomi, led a large number of young men back into the central Haganah fold; those who did not follow him established the Irgun Tzvai Leumi. David Raziel became head of the Irgun, and appointed Hillel Kook chief Irgun representative to the Diaspora. Kook traveled to Europe to involve himself in *Af Al Pi*, clandestine immigration. Just as the Mossad, though associated with the Labor Socialists, was an independent organization, so too was the Irgun, though associated with the Revisionists Zionists, an independent organization. This was a sticking point for some in Jabotinsky's New Zionist Organization who thought the Irgun should be subordinate to the political organization.

Jabotinsky called a meeting in Paris in 1939 to mediate the quarrel. Hillel Kook attended along with David Raziel and the charismatic Avraham Stern. Jabotinsky recognized Raziel as the head of an independent Irgun. While the men of the Irgun considered Jabotinsky their supreme commander, Jabotinsky was barred from Palestine by the British and was limited to helping guide the Irgun from a distance.

Hillel Kook was a member of Betar, the Revisionist youth group, but was never a member of the New Zionist Organization, the Revisionist party. He was in Europe as a member of the Irgun, and it was in that capacity that he was Raziel's personal representative to provide education and military training for young members of Betar and to endeavor to get them to Palestine.

Kook used more than one name in the underground. As he was the son of Dov Baer, one name he took was Berson, but when he met a Zionist named Berson in Geneva in 1939, he inserted the "g" to become Bergson. The first name "Peter" was chosen because one of his Irgun comrades had a son named Peter.[1]

When Bergson arrived in the United States in July, 1940, he assumed direction of the organization Chaim Lubinsky had started and turned over to Yitshaq Ben-Ami. News arrived that Avraham Stern had formally split with Jabotinsky. Stern was a dreamer, a poet, and a self-styled revolutionary. Jabotinsky's belief in the politics of pressuring the British was to him folly. Kook wrote to Stern, telling him that such a split was unthinkable. But Stern persisted on his independent course and formed Lochemai Herut Israel often called by the acroynym Lechi. His underground group, smaller than the Irgun, was

---

[1] Oral interview with Hillel Kook, tape #1316, Hebrew University Institute of Contemporary Jewry, Division of Oral Documents.

known to many as "the Stern gang" and, unlike the Irgun, practiced acts of individual terror and assassination.

On August 4, 1940, less than a month after Bergson arrived in the United States, Jabotinsky was struck by a heart attack and died while visiting a Betar camp in New York. Kook, Ben-Ami and many Jews all over the world felt an irreparable loss. Ben-Ami describes the angst:

> Losing him was, for all of us, like losing a father. We were intellectually and emotionally tied to him as our leader and teacher, and his death created a vacuum in our hearts that we knew could not be filled. He had died when we needed him more than ever, and we felt a kind of desperate abandonment.[1]

In Palestine, Schneur Zalman Shazar, a labor leader who would later be the third President of Israel, paid tribute to the fallen leader of the rival Zionist group: "The full-toned violin that once seemed destined to play the leading role in the orchestra of Jewish revival has suddenly broken."[2]

Peter Bergson was Raziel's appointed leader in the United States and their work lobbying for a Jewish Army and raising money for clandestine *aliyah* went on. There was a New Zionist Organization in the United States, but "the Bergson Boys" or "Bergson Group" as they came to be known were independent. Though they thought of themselves as *Irgun* members, they wore no uniforms and did not salute nor use other military symbols.[3]

Ben-Ami did a great deal of work before Bergson arrived, and found a receptive audience in Irving Bunim, leader of Young Israel and a member of the *Vaad Hatzala*, the Orthodox rescue committee. Bunim was impressed with the intellectual honesty of Jabotinsky and the fact that, while not himself religious, he and his followers had profound respect for Torah learning. This contrasted to his contempt for the Socialist Zionists who he saw as despising religion and discriminating against Orthodox Jews in the allocation of *aliyah* certificates.

---

[1]Ben-Ami, op. cit., p. 244.

[2]Katz, Shmuel, *Days of Fire* (Jerusalem: Steimatzky's Agency Ltd., 1968), p. 51.

[3]Oral History interview, op. cit., tape #1316.

When some of Bunim's associates questioned his cooperation with a Jewish organization that did not strictly follow the Torah, Bunim told them the story of Reb Chaim of Brisk who ordered his followers to eat on Yom Kippur when they were ravaged by the plague. When some of his zealous supporters questioned his "leniency," Reb Chaim replied that he was not lenient about Yom Kippur, but was very strict about *pekuach nefesh* - the saving of lives.

Ben-Ami drew much of his early financial support from members of Young Israel. In a talk at Brooklyn College he openly acknowledged Bunim's help.[1]

Ben-Ami was in contact with Perl and Rudi Hecht in aiding their attempts to get the 2,000 Jews aboard the *Sakarya* out of Europe. When he received a desperate wire asking for $10,000 to facilitate the voyage of the *Sakarya*, Ben-Ami went to work. Illustrating that Jewish rescue was an issue independent of whether one was or was not a Zionist, Ben-Ami approached two "anti-Zionists," Lucius Littauer and David Donneger. After contacting Rabbi Louis I. Newman and having him vouch for Ben-Ami, they contributed $10,000, and in January, 1940, Ben-Ami was able to wire the money to Reuven Hecht.[2] The *Sakarya* ultimately landed its human cargo safely on the shores of Palestine.

Another early source of support was Frances Gunther, the Jewish wife of John Gunther, noted journalist and author who was not Jewish. John Gunther familiarized Ben-Ami with the Arabist orientation of the State Department and the indifference to Jewish issues in the White House. He advised that the most effective route of action would be through the Congress.

At the end of 1939, Frances Gunther, a frail, but determined woman, persuaded her internationally known husband to broadcast on a national hookup an appeal for Jewish refugees fleeing Europe. On December 26, 1939, he told listeners that on the night after Christmas "it is quite fitting to talk about Palestine...the greatest Jew in history was born there some nineteen hundred and forty years ago." He made a strong appeal

---

[1] Bunim, op. cit., pp.9ff.

[2] Ben-Ami, op. cit., pp. 263-264.

for the refugees headed for Palestine "because it was the only place to go - all the other places were closed."[1]

William Ziff, the author of *The Rape of Palestine,* was drawn to the young Palestinian Jews as was Harry Selden, another Jewish writer. Selden read Ziff's *The Rape of Palestine* and it changed his life. Ziff agreed to a Selden-edited digest of *The Rape of Palestine* and donated the income to the American Friends of a Jewish Palestine. In an epilogue he wrote for the digest of Ziff's book Selden writes: "Palestine until a year ago was a meaningless symbol to me. It was an old-man's dream - a vague ideal, somehow unrealistic in its approach to modern problems." He explains that while he had been "growing away from any consciousness of Judaism...the news of anti-Semitic excesses in Germany and elsewhere made a contemplation of...the problem unavoidable." Selden continues:

> It was in this sober frame of mind that I read *The Rape of Palestine*...in putting over its message it had to overcome a formidable handicap, compounded of apathy, skepticism, a far drift from my Jewish origins, and an ardent Anglophilism engendered of an early diet of Kipling, Jerome and Galsworthy.

Selden's view of the British goverment was irrevocably altered. Pointing out the distinction between the government and the people, he writes that "leading in this fight for justice and decency are the noblest figures in England itself." Selden issued a ringing call to conscience:

> If ever there was a time when the conscience of civilization must assert itself it would appear to be here and now. It is a question which every Jew must regard with indignation and rising anger; so too must every true Christian who believes in the spirit of the Bible and the letter of its Prophecy.[2]

---

[1]Ibid., pp. 255-256.

[2]Selden, Harry L., *A Digest of The Rape of Palestine by William B. Ziff* (New York: American Friends of a Jewish Palestine, 1940), pp. 209-210.

Selden often took pen in hand to write letters to the leading New York newspapers. To the *Herald Tribune* he wrote that "if the British government must choose between Arab and Jew, the Jews must offer at least as aggressive resistance as the Arabs." He quoted extensively from British Member of Parliament, Josiah Wedgewood:

> The Arabs stand up and fight, and massacre....On the other hand the Jews are always complaining and begging for justice. That, of course, is the result of 1,800 years of servitude. For 1,800 years they have been dependent on the good graces of governments and never on their own right arm.

Wedgewood addressed the issue of Jewish regard for legality and respectability:

> We must realize that laws to prevent people from doing something which they have a God-given right to do...cannot be insisted upon. Very often the Jews feel that they must be respectable at all costs, and the idea of doing anything illegal sounds to them disreputable. They have got to get over that feeling, and to realize that the really great thing is to make a sacrifice of their respectability and even of their lives in order to secure justice.

Wedgewood believed that the world would respond positively if Jews stood up:

> The only way the Jews in Palestine and in the world have of securing justice is by using those forces which we have blamed in other people, although we have always exercised them ourselves. If they will resist now - and with their backs to the wall they must resist unless they are to lie down forever - they will realize that the sympathy and the respect of the entire Anglo-Saxon world goes to those who stand up.[1]

---

[1]See Selden letter to *New York Herald Tribune*, 3/9/40.

While Ben-Ami had made a credible beginning, he realized his group had to reach more people. He explains why Peter Bergson was the man to do it, writing of Bergson: "A master public relations man in the American mold, he had unlimited *chutzpah*. He had an ability to accept defeats with little emotion. He would retreat and lick his wounds, and the next day he would be ready for the next round."[1]

One of the most important Bergson recruits was Ben Hecht. Hecht was an accomplished and immensely successful writer for both stage and screen. *The Front Page, The Moonshooter*, and *Twentieth Century* were three plays he wrote with his close friend Charles MacArthur, the husband of Helen Hayes. Hecht was lured to Hollywood in 1925 by a telegram from Herman Mankiewicz: "Will you accept three hundred per week to work for Paramount Pictures....Millions are to be grabbed out here and your only competition is idiots."[2]

Although he wrote scripts for over 60 movies, Hecht viewed movies as "an eruption of trash that has lamed the American mind and retarded Americans from becoming a cultured people."[3] Mankiewicz instructed Hecht that while the hero in a novel can "lay ten girls and marry a virgin for a finish," in a movie both the hero and the heroine had to be virgins.[4]

In order to be able to write truthfully, he decided to write about gangsters instead of heroes and heroines and in one week wrote the script of Hollywood's first gangster movie, *Underworld*. Paramount loved it and Hecht received a $10,000 bonus check.[5]

In Hollywood, what writers create is often more famous than the creators themselves, and this was true for Hecht. At a time when he was working for Metro-Goldwyn-Mayer, he was borrowed by David O. Selznick of Paramount in the middle of the shooting of the most famous movie in the history of film, *Gone With the Wind*. Three weeks into the shooting of the classic, Selznick decided he did not like the script and promised Hecht fifteen thousand dollars a week to rewrite it.

---

[1]Ben-Ami, op. cit., 295.

[2]Hecht, Ben, *A Child of the Century* (New York: Simon and Schuster, 1954), p. 466.

[3]Ibid., p. 468.

[4]Ibid., p. 479.

[5]Ibid., p. 480.

Hecht had not read the book so Selznick and an associate read aloud, playing out the scenes. Hecht agreed the screen play was terrible, and, borrowing from a draft written three years before by Sidney Howard who died in the interim, Hecht went to work. In a week of 18-20 hour days, Hecht finished the first nine reels of *Gone With the Wind.*[1]

Hecht saw no contradiction between being an American and being a Jew; before 1939 he did not identify as either, but after 1939, he aggressively affirmed both as important components of his identity. "I had before then been only related to Jews. In that year I became a Jew and looked on the world with Jewish eyes."[2]

For the first time in his life, Hecht joined an organization. "Fight for Freedom" was formed to help bring the United States into the war against Germany. He collaborated with MacArthur on a pageant called "Fun to Be Free" and wrote shows for the Red Cross and for War Bond drives. "I had been no partisan of democracy in my earlier years. Its sins had seemed to me more prominent than its virtues. But now...I was its uncarping disciple."[3]

Hecht felt shamed by his fellow professionals. "The Americanized Jews who ran newspapers and movie studios who wrote plays and novels, who were high in government and powerful in the financial, industrial and even social life of the nation were silent."[4] Hecht, who had commanded the highest writing fees in Hollywood, began writing a column for *P.M.*, a New York newspaper, for $75 a week. He wrote about the city and about Jews. In 1941, in a column called "My Tribe is Called Israel," he speaks to his assimilated past:

> I write of Jews today, I who never knew himself as one before, because that part of me which is Jewish is under a violent and apelike attack. My way of defending myself is to answer as a Jew....My angry critics all write that they are proud of being Americans and of wearing carnations, and that they are sick to

---

[1] Ibid, pp. 488-489.

[2] Ibid, p. 517.

[3] Ibid.

[4] Ibid., p. 519-520.

death of such efforts as mine to Judaize them and increase generally the Jew-consciousness of the world.

Speaking directly to these critics, he suggested:

Good Jews with carnations, it is not I who am bringing this Jew-consciousness back into the world. It is back on all the radios of the world. I don't advise you to take off your carnations. I only suggest that you don't hide behind them too much. They conceal very little.[1]

In his autobiography, Hecht tells of his days as a young reporter when he hung around the Harrison Street police station in Chicago to pick up stories. He saw drunks brought before the bar of justice who, when asked to speak up on their own behalf, would give an answer that began with: "Well, your honor I was walking down the street, mindin' my own business...." Hecht felt the same way as he approached the Twenty One Club to have drinks with Peter Bergson and Jeremiah Halpern, two "strangers." In telling about the encounter, as the defendents in Chicago told of theirs, he writes: "I offer my evidence neither as a Jew nor propagandist but as an honest writer who was walking down the street one day when he bumped into history."[2]

Jeremiah Halpern was a Jew who captained Jewish ships on the high seas. One day he would captain a vessel called the *Ben Hecht*, but this day he and Bergson were trying to educate Hecht about Palestine. Hecht responded that he cared little about Palestine, that the problems there only confused the issue of the massacre of Jews in Europe. The meeting was brief, but ended with Hecht agreeing to meet again with Bergson and two others.

At the second meeting Hecht faced the three who for the next seven years were for Hecht "the committee." Bergson, Ben-Ami, and Samuel Merlin, the three young Palestinians who formed the backbone of the "Bergson group," were asking Hecht to send out letters inviting New York Jews to join him in

[1]Ibid., pp. 520-521.

[2]Ibid., p. 516.

working for The Committee for a Jewish Army. He protested to them that they had the wrong person; he never went to meetings and certainly knew nothing about raising money. "My arguments as to who and what I was only made them smile. They continued to look at me knowingly, as if I were a mystery only they understood."[1]

Ben-Ami describes the meeting from his own perspective:

Ben Hecht was rough to tangle with. He had a compassionate heart, covered up by a short temper, a brutal frankness and an acid tongue...unlike many other creative Jews who lost their roots...[Hecht] felt viscerally disturbed by the silence of the successful Jews among whom he lived and worked.[2]

Ben Hecht, the cynic, the "assimilated" Jew, gave the next seven years of his life to Jewish survival despite the sacrifice of time and money it entailed. His works were banned from England, and his literary friends often shunned him. How was this worldly, independent writer drawn into the realm of a young, "squeaky-voiced" Palestinian Jew who knew nothing of America. What was it in the character of Peter Bergson that drew him?

His calm and seeming cheeriness, as if he were some school-tie British diplomat, made him a rather unexpected representative of Jews. Neither violence nor hysteria were in him. But there was a quality a hundredfold more effective. He was as persistent as a force of nature. He was somewhat un-Jewish in another regard. He had no respect for the great men whom he bagged with his persistence. He respected only his cause.[3]

Stephen Wise was now, in the summer of 1940, absorbed in Roosevelt's reelection. In June, the Republicans had a tense contest at their convention. Thomas Dewey led at the end of the

---

[1] Ibid., pp. 521-522.

[2] Ben-Ami, op. cit., Ibid., p. 284.

[3] Hecht, op. cit., p. 577.

first ballot with 360 votes, to 189 for Robert Taft, and 105 for Wendell Wilkie. The balloting went on into the early morning when Wilkie turned the tide, eventually winning the nomination on the sixth ballot. The following month in Chicago, the Democrats nominated Roosevelt to run for an unprecedented third term.

Wise was no longer president of the ZOA, but was still the head of the American Jewish Congress. The status of this organization was described to Wise in an internal memo from his trusted associate who ran the day-to-day activities of the Congress, Lillie Shultz. She told Wise the Congress was solvent, but "has made and continues to make a very serious mistake in the sense that it has been ignoring what is known as the "provinces." While it had been a strength of the Congress to sell the American Jewish Committee and the Anti-Defamation League on the importance of local community organizations, Shultz warned Wise: "These community organizations are in danger of being taken out of our hands because we have been neglecting the country."[1]

Wise, like many important leaders, was not absorbed by the details of organization, but by other issues. He was acutely aware not only of the refugee crisis, but also the State Department foot dragging on Jewish issues. He wrote to a friend: "The State Department makes all sorts of promises, and takes all our lists; and then we hear that the consuls do nothing." Wise identified politics as the reason for the inattention to Jewish suffering, then revealed his own priorities:

What I am afraid lies back of the whole thing is the fear of the Skipper's friends in the State Department that any large admission of radicals to the United States might be used effectively against him in the campaign. Cruel as it may seem, as I have said to you before, his re-election is much more important for everything that is worthwhile and that counts than the admission of a few people, however imminent be their peril.[2]

---

[1]Memo date 8/2/40, CZA, Wise papers, Reel 87.

[2]Letter dated 9/17/40, Voss, op. cit., pp. 241-242.

Roosevelt was elected to his third term on November 3, 1940. Two weeks later the Warsaw Ghetto was bricked off from the rest of the city. As early as February, 1940, Richard Lichtheim, a German Jewish Zionist who spent the war years in Switzerland and was in frequent contact with Jewish leaders around the world, wrote to the United States to warn of conditions in Poland. He told of 1300 people "dragged from their homes in the night... [who] had to leave the town [Stettin] and all their possessions within a few hours."[1] With the Warsaw Ghetto sealed off, he alerted Jerusalem, London, and New York to the deteriorating situation, and made an important distinction between not knowing and not wanting to know:

> Life in Europe is indeed not very pleasant today, but it cannot be bettered by those who do not wish to be disturbed by the aspect of ugly things and turn away from it.[2]

Stephen Wise contined to gather information and pass it along, hoping, it appears, on the one hand that it would get to Roosevelt, while saying on the other hand that he knew Roosevelt should not be bothered. Writing in March, 1941, to Felix Frankfurter who two years earlier had been appointed by Roosevelt to the Supreme Court, he comments on a report about the fate of Bulgarian Jewry:

> Isn't this pathetic! It comes from Bulgarian Jewry. Note what happened to the Bulgarian Jewish subjects as a result of the threat of the incoming Nazi hordes, and note, particularly, the pathos of their confidence in the redemptive power of the Skipper. I wish he might see this, but I know he cannot be burdened with all this material.[3]

Wise's dependence on his relationship with people he saw as men of high authority is illustrated by the feelings which came

---

[1]CZA, Emergency Committee for Zionist Affairs papers, F39, 13.

[2]Gilbert, Martin, *Auschwitz and the Allies* (New York: Holt, Rinehart and Winston, 1981), p. 28.

[3]Letter dated 3/5/41, CZA, Wise papers, op. cit., Reel 109.

to the surface when Brandeis died in October, 1941. The ZOA put out a release noting his death and stressing Brandeis' role in American Zionism. Wise was quick to take offense that his name had not been mentioned in connection with Brandeis. Rabbi Isadore Breslau, an official of ZOA wrote Wise trying to calm him:

I confess I am still disturbed...by the interpretation you put on the Brandeis release....It simply refers to the record of Brandeis' relationship to the official ZOA....I may be taking too great liberty with you but I do it on the basis of a long relationship of disciple and teacher...Please do not misunderstand me, therefore, when I say that you too are often ill-advised. I...look to you to lead us in the direction of high objectives without involvemment in the petty clash of personalities.[1]

A clearer idea of what Wise was objecting to emerges from a letter he wrote to Frankfurter on the subject:

There came to me the other day a statement issued from the office of the Zionist Organization of America....You will notice at the foot of the first page, "In July 1938, with the beginning of the administration of Dr. Solomon Goldman, Justice Brandeis re-established contact the the Zionist Organization of America."

Many old wounds were opening and Wise's feelings poured out:

Need I tell you, Felix, that throughout the years, I worked as faithfully at Brandeis' side as any man in Zionism....I wanted nothing for myself, excepting, of course, that I did cherish the joy and honor or meeting with and dealing with a man of Brandeis' lofty stature...Need I tell you that we worked together, that I did his will, whatever it was, going to Europe again and again, toiling with all my might against Partition,

---

[1] Letter dated 10/8/41, ibid., Reel 107.

fighting Chaim [Weizmann] and getting rid of him, in large part because LDB [Brandeis] had come to distrust him....[1]

Nor did Wise let Rabbi Breslau off the hook, writing to the ZOA official:

> It is painful for you to fail to find the vicious misrepresentation in the article written by Dr. Goldman....Among circles in which I move it is considered one of the most dastardly things that has ever come out of any office. If you do not see that, there is no discussing it with you.

Wise pointed to the statement that Brandeis reestablished contact with the ZOA in July, 1938, during the presidency of Dr. Solomon Goldman. "That is a foul and slanderous lie, and you know it is, or else you know nothing about Zionism in America," Wise exploded, then continued:

> Now I am going to say something very intimate and personal to you. Relations with Mr. Brandeis had been less friendly and intimate...in the last three years. Dr. Goldman succeeded in achieving this less friendly relation on Mr. Brandeis' part toward me....I found Mr. Brandeis...poisoned by Dr. Goldman not only against Mr. Lipsky and Weizmann, but even against me, who had been the most steadfast of Mr. Brandeis' Zionist friends.[2]

While it is possible there was some ZOA politics involved in the wording of the release of Brandeis' death, the near hysterical nature of Wise's response adds to the pattern of similar responses cited in earlier chapters, and gives some insight into the degree to which Wise's self image was tied to his perception (often exaggerated) of his relationship with men like Brandeis and Roosevelt.

---

[1] Letter dated 10/10/41, ibid., Reel 109.

[2] Letter dated 10/14/41, ibid., Reel 107.

Meanwhile the Orthodox *Vaad Hatzala*, like the Bergson group, was focused on rescue. On the Saturday before Roosevelt's election to a third term the *Shabbas* rest of Irving Bunim was interrupted by the unexpected visit of Rabbi Boruch Kaplan and Rabbi Alexander Linchner. They told Bunim of a telegram from Vilna concerning a plan to get approximately 1000 Chassidim out of that war-torn city. While an escape plan existed, money was urgently needed for visas and passage on available ships.

Just as the Brisk Rebbe had put *pekuach nefesh* above fasting on Yom Kippur, so too did the saving of lives take precedence over the laws governing *Shabbas*. The three men jumped into a taxi and made the rounds. By the end of the day they had $45,000 in pledges and loans and the money was turned over to the Joint Distribution Committee which added some funds of its own and released the money in Vilna for the rescue plan.[1]

But the cooperation between the *Vaad Hatzala* and the JDC was often difficult. In March, 1942, Rabbi Eliezer Silver complained to the JDC about criticism of his group which had been leveled in a letter from a JDC representative to a Jewish Federation in the midwest. Silver noted that each side had complaints about the other, but that the *Vaad* refrained from public criticism "because we value greatly the work of the JDC....It seems to us that this form of destructive criticism is destructive to both organizations." Silver pointed out that the *Vaad* was able to reach Jews in places the JDC "cannot or will not go." This was a reference to the JDC's strict interpretation of United States trading-with-the enemy laws.

Though the Japanese were safeguarding the lives of Jews who had managed to get from Europe to Shanghai, the JDC objected to the *Vaad* sending these isolated Jews financial support, as evidenced by this letter from a JDC official in May, 1942:

As you are doubtless aware, such remittances [to Shanghai] are prohibited by our own Government under war laws, and we, as an American organization cannot be involved in anything that has the remotest color of trading with the enemy. [2]

---

[1] Bunim, op. cit., pp. 85-87.

[2] See Rakeffet-Rothkoff, op. cit., pp. 207-210 for an excellent discussion of this tension between the *Vaad Hatzala* and the JDC.

While the Irgun members in the United States were not religious Jews, their commander in Palestine was. This further illustrates the danger inherent in generalizing about Jewish leaders as Zionist vs. anti-Zionist or assimilationist vs. religious. David Raziel, the commander of the Irgun and a longtime friend of Hillel Kook who was now working in the United States as Peter Bergson, took his *talit* and *tefillin* with him to Iraq on a mission for which he was recruited by the very people who had imprisoned him - the British. With Bergson he had attended yeshiva, but unlike Bergson, he remained a religious Jew when he joined the underground.[1]

When Rashid Ali toppled the pro-British leadership in Iraq in April, 1941, key resources came into the hands of local Arabs working with Nazi Germany. The British called on the knowledge and experience of Raziel and the Irgun to blow up fuel depots in Baghdad. Yaakov Meridor, an Irgun field commander experienced in the use of explosives, was called in.

Meridor tried in vain to convince Raziel to leave the mission to him and not risk his own life in such a dangerous undertaking. The two men landed at a British airbase in Iraq on May 17, 1941. Three days later, Meridor and Raziel went in different directions in an attempt to make contact with friendly Indian units who could help identify their target. Raziel, accompanied by a British major, was unsuccessful in reaching the friendly forces and headed back toward the British base at Habanya. The military vehicle in which they were riding was strafed by German planes. Raziel and the British officer were killed. Ben-Ami describes the loss:

> Thus, on that dusty road to Baghdad, an era in the history of the Irgun ended. David Raziel, our most effective military leader...he had authored together with Abraham Stern the first Hebrew literature on weapons and military concepts for our youth to follow...he would not send men to battle unless he shared their dangers. This was why we loved "Razi" and this was why he fell...it was most fitting that he died in the old land of the Euphrates and the Tigris.[2]

---

[1]The following account of Raziel's mission is based on that of Ben-Ami, op. cit., pp. 244-247.

[2]Ibid, pp. 246-247.

Within one year, Ben-Ami and his small group lost both Jabotinsky and Raziel, their two most experienced and beloved leaders. In Palestine, the Irgun fell into a period of disorganization which was to continue until the end of 1943 when Menachem Begin became the new commander. In the United States, the "commander" was Peter Bergson.

Bergson stressed to Abba Hillel Silver and other Jewish leaders their common purpose and urged cooperation.[1] Though he initially met with some success in this mission he soon ran into the familiar demand that all activities go through "proper" Zionist channels. Bergson wrote to Abba Hillel Silver a few months after their initial contact: "Hasn't the time arrived yet when things have to be dealt with by their merits and not by the fact that they are represented by people who don't belong to this or that political party?"[2]

Bergson persisted in his efforts for unity, but received this response from Stephen Wise:

> I want formally to acknowledge your two letters which I have discussed with my colleagues....For reasons which should be well known to you, they cannot give their support to the activities of a body like the "Irgun" which refuses to recognize the authority of the duly constituted national bodies and is responsible to no one but itself.[3]

Pierre Van Paassen, a non-Jewish writer long associated with Jewish causes, was an early supporter of Bergson. Years before he had worked closely with Stephen Wise whom he admired. He wrote to Wise urging cooperation on the issue of a Jewish Army, but made little headway. At the same time Bergson contacted Nahum Goldmann, an international leader in the World Jewish Congress now living in the United States, asking for cooperation.[4]

---

[1] Letter dated 2/12/41, PSCP, Reel 1.

[2] Letter dated 5/25/41, ibid.

[3] Letter dated 6/4/41, ibid.

[4] Letters dated, 12/3/41, ibid.

The bombing of Pearl Harbor and the American entrance into the war brought many Jews into the uniform of the American armed forces. Desiring to make clear that he did not intend for American Jews to enlist in the Jewish Army for which he was lobbying, Bergson changed the name of the committee from Committee for a Jewish Army to Committee for a Jewish Army of Stateless and Palestinian Jews.

The lobbying efforts of the Bergson group began to yield results. The first full-page advertisement of the group was placed in the *New York Times*, January 5, 1942. It was headlined "Jews Fight for the Right to Fight" and was signed by a long list of well-known personalities including Louis Bromfield, Ben Hecht, Francis Gunther, Melvyn Douglas and Max Lerner as well as leading Christian thinkers Paul Tillich and Lowell Thomas.[1]

The same month, Senator Guy M. Gillette, a Senator from Iowa began what would be a long and fruitful period of cooperation with Bergson when he became a member of the Committee for a Jewish Army. And in its January edition *Esquire* magazine printed an article by Ben Hecht with the following editorial comment:

Ben Hecht, famous author, journalist, play-writer and producer, became one of the first champions of the Jewish Army....We are reproducing his "Champion in Chains" as the conclusive article of this publication.[2]

Meantime, Richard Lichtheim, from his Jewish Agency post in Geneva, continued to inform Jewish officials around the world of the fate of European Jews. In a letter to Arthur Lourie of the Emergency Committee for Zionist Affairs in New York, he sent some of the earliest news of the extent of the unfolding tragedy, mentioning that a common acquaintance of Lourie and Lichtheim had been sent "to the concentration camp of Buchenwald, where he died." He continued with a report on Balkan Jews:

---

[1] *New York Times*, 1/5/42; a copy can be found in Reel 1 of PSCP.

[2] *Esquire*, 1/10/42, copy in Reel 1 of PSCP.

8,000 Serbian Jews are dead or have fled or are now in labour-camps...30,000 Croat Jews are being worked to death under the supervision of the Ustachi, the gangster organization of the Croat Chief of State.

Lichtheim closed his letter on a prophetic note: "The number of our dead after this war will have to be counted not in thousands or hundreds of thousands, but in several millions."[1]

About this time, Secretary of War Henry Stimson endorsed the drive for a Jewish army. This led Lieutenant-Colonel Julius Klein to pledge 10 dollars a month to the committee.[2] William Green, the President of the American Federation of Labor also joined the committee.[3]

Was it this growing public support for the activities of the Bergson group that prompted Arthur Lourie, representing the "official" Zionists, to write saying he was breaking off the negotiations for united action between the two groups? This was the same Arthur Lurie who had received the drastic news from Richard Lichtheim cited above. The incredulous response of the Bergson group to Lourie indicates the significant extent of the contacts that had been established between leaders of the two groups:

The Committee for a Jewish Army cannot bring itself to believe that your letter represents the considered views of the Zionist leadership in this country. In the light of the various conversations which our representatives have had with Mr. Emanual Neumann, Dr. Nahum Goldmann, Mr. Louis Lipsky, Dr. Abba Hiller Silver, Judge Louis Levinthal and Mrs. Rose Halperin, your conclusions appear quite inexplicable. They stand in direct contradiction to the views expressed by them in the course of our conversations, which gave us the impression that we are on the road to a friendly understanding.[4]

---

[1]Lichtheim to Lourie, 2/11/42, cited by Gilbert, *Auschwitz and the Allies*, op. cit., p. 30.

[2]Letter dated 1/12/42, PSCP, Reel 1.

[3]Letter dated 1/13/42, ibid.

[4]Letters dated 1/26/42 and 2/9/42, ibid.

Maurice Winograd, editor of the *Daily Forward*, pressed Wise to cooperate with Bergson:

> The writer has been one of your great admirers for some time. He was therefore pained to read your statement about the Committee for a Jewish Army. Not that he is a member of this committee or belongs to the Revisionist movement...I am merely a deeply concerned member of the world's most dispersed and most unhappy race....Why continue to fight the Revisionists who have been maligned so cruelly all these years....No, dear Dr. Wise, this isn't the way...to act - cetainly not in the present crisis.[1]

Unfortunately such appeals fell on deaf ears.

Speculation that the successes of the Bergson group were contributing to the negative reaction from established Jewish groups is supported by this letter written from a Philadelphia Zionist to Secretary of State, Cordell Hull:

> I would like to bring to the attention of the Department the agitation that is being aroused among Jewish circles by a small band of Palestinian Jews, urging the creation of a Jewish Army. This demand does not even have the support of the Zionist organization and certainly not of the educated classes of Jews in America. Nevertheless this movement is gaining support from the masses, and it is a flareback against the British Government.

The letter went on to raise the possibility of the State Department bringing deportation proceedings against Ben-Ami as an "undesirable alien."[2]

Ben-Ami, Bergson, and the growing number of Jewish and non-Jewish supporters of their committee continued their efforts. In April, 1942, Senator Gillette made an address covered by the *New York Times* which headlined: "Jewish Army Urged for Protecting Syria - Senator Gillette Pleads for

---

[1]Letter dated 2/28/42, CZA, Wise papers, Reel 102.

[2]Ben-Ami, op. cit., p. 323.

Checkmating of Vichy."[1] In May a gathering of 800 people at a Waldorf Astoria dinner organized by Bergson heard a call for a Jewish army from Senator James M. Mead of New York. Supportive messages came from Secretary of the Navy, Frank Knox, Eleanor Roosevelt and a number of British Members of Parliament.

The need for these activities was punctuated by reports from Europe. In March, 1942, a Joint Distribution Committee representative, back in the United States after two years service in relief activities, estimated in a New York press conference that the Nazis had already murdered over a quarter of a million Jews.[2] The same month, an issue of the American Jewish Congress' *Congress Weekly* reported an eye-witness report by a JDC representative who brought news from the city of Borisov where 7,000 Jews were forced to dig a mass grave before being murdered. The same JDC representative reported that in Kiev 240,000 Jews were buried in a common grave.[3]

In May, the *New York Times* reported on page four the estimate of a United Press correspondent that 100,000 Jews had been killed in the Baltic States, 100,00 in Poland, and 20,000 in western Russia.[4]

Pressed by the emerging facts and the activism of the Bergson group, organized Jewry took up the cause of a Jewish army. Judge Louis E. Levinthal president of the ZOA, demanded that "recognition should be given to the right of the Jews of Palestine to play their full part in the war effort and in the defense of their country, through a military force fighting under its own flag and under the high command of the United Nations." In response, Chaim Weizmann stated his minimalist demands. The phrase "Jewish Army," he said, is "somewhat pretentious....I will be satisfied if not an 'army' but a Jewish contingent."[5]

---

[1] *New York Times*, 4/27/42. Copy in Reel 4, PSCP.

[2] See Wyman, David S., *The Abandonment of the Jews: America and the Holocaust, 1941-1945* (New York: Pantheon Books, 1984), p. 20.

[3] *Congress Weekly*, March 20, 1942, cited by Medoff, op. cit., pp. 75-76.

[4] *New York Times*, 5/18/42, cited by Wyman, p. 21.

[5] *Jewish Telegraphic Agency*, 5/13/42.

Bergson's group spread their activity to Canada and England. In May the *Montreal Gazette* reported "Intensification in Canada of a campaign now being waged throughout the United States for the creation of a Jewish Army in the Middle East..."[1] In London, Captain Jeremiah Halpern opened a branch of the committee and immediately attracted the support of a number of Members of Parliament as well as that of Mr. William Greenberg, Editor-in-Chief of the independent *London Jewish Chronicle.* Greenberg joined the Committee for a Jewish Army as head of public relations.[2]

Convening in London at the same time was the meeting of the World Jewish Congress where the delegates heard estimates that over one million Jews had already been killed by Hitler's war machine. Szmul Zygielbojm of the Polish Labor Bund had just released a report detailing murders by the use of gas vans: "On the average, 1,000 people were gassed every day." In the United States, the *Boston Globe* headlined this story across three columns on page twelve.[3]

In Palestine, the Jewish community read about the reports in *Davar*, the newspaper of the Socialist labor movement:

None of those taken away are ever heard of again. The able-bodied are slowly worked to death in labor camps. The infirm are left to die of exposure and starvation, or are deliberately massacred in mass executions...the numbers of victims of these bloody cruelties is reckoned in many hundreds of thousands.[4]

In Pittsburg, the Committee for a Jewish Army was embraced by the president of the Carnegie Institute, Colonel Samuel Harden Church.[5] The same month, the *Philadelphia Record* and the *New York Mirror* gave editorial support for a Jewish Army.[6]

---

[1] *Montreal Gazette*, 5/18/42.

[2] Bulletin of London Committee for a Jewish Army, 6/19/42, PSCP, Reel 1.

[3] See Wyman, op. cit., pp. 21-22.

[4] *Davar*, 7/1/42.

[5] *Pittsburgh Post Gazette*, 6/29/42.

[6] *Philadelphia Record*, 7/7/42, and *New York Mirror*, 7/11/42.

In contrast to these efforts for a change in administration policy, at a Madison Square Garden Rally cosponsored by the American Jewish Conference, the Jewish Labor Committee, and B'nai B'rith, Stephen Wise gave voice to the Roosevelt administration line, saying the fate of Europe's Jews depended on "a victory speedy and complete of the United Nations."[1]

During the summer of 1942, a cable from Gerhart Riegner was sent to the State Department detailing the Nazi plan for exterminating European Jewry. This cable gave further confirmation to the previously published reports of mass murder. At the behest of Under Secretary of State Sumner Welles, Wise kept the report secret. While Wise sat on the report, Jacob Rosenheim of the Orthodox *Agudas Yisrael* received a telegram from Isaac Sternbuch detailing mass murders and the use of corpses for soap and fertilizer.[2]

During the time that the report from Reigner was being suppressed, similar information was flowing from Richard Lichtheim to Palestine, London and New York. Realizing, as he had in 1940, that some people receiving the news did not believe it or did not want to believe it, he tried to break through the denial:

Maybe this man is exaggerating, but we have heard the same things from other sources, especially with regard to the large number of Jews from Warsaw who have been killed after being sent to other places. Putting all these pieces of evidence together, there can be little doubt that the deliberate destruction of Jewish communities in Poland is not only contemplated but already on its way.[3]

Lichtheim continued to press reality on those receiving his reports, writing, in October, 1942, to a Jewish Agency Executive:

---

[1] See Wyman, op. cit., p. 25, and report dated 7/21/42, Taminent Institute, Robert F. Wagner Labor Archives, JLC, Reel MN 2040.

[2] The best reports of this period are those of Wyman, op. cit., pp. 42-58, and Gilbert, op. cit., 55-92.

[3] Letter dated 9/12/42, cited by Gilbert, p. 82.

I have the impression that my previous reports have not always found the necessary understanding. Some of our friends do not want to believe that something like this can happen....It is pointless to deal now with the motives which have caused this. Events speak an inexorable language....[1]

A month later he wrote to an official in Jerusalem:

I am sure you will not be deluded - as so many of our friends in Palestine - by wishful thinking. There is a great difference between being an optimist and living in a fool's paradise, and that is exactly what a considerable number of our friends are now doing.[2]

In December, 1943, Lichtheim wrote to a friend who informed him of revelations in the *Palestine Post* of the Nazi brutality: "The facts now published in Palestine are not new to me. You cannot divert a tiger from devouring his prey by adopting resolutions or sending cables. You have to take your gun and shoot him."[3]

---

[1]Letter dated 10/8/42, ibid.

[2]Letter dateed 11/9/42, ibid., p. 87.

[3]Letter dated 12/9/42, ibid., p. 90.

Chapter VIII

The Moral Rights of Stateless and Palestinian Jews

The fight for a Jewish army was motivated by the desire to give the Jews of Palestine and the refugees from Europe a means to fight back as Jews. It was to a great extent a question of pride and morale as had been the persistence of Jabotinsky in forming a Jewish Legion during World War I. The idea received widespread support, including support from David Ben Gurion. The following letter from Weizmann to Wise documents this support as well as the back-biting that went on among Zionist leaders:

I have never feared that Ben-Gurion's antics would make any serious impression on Zionist opinion in this country. He has behaved so foolishly....As to his views about the role of the Jewish Army, of which I heard so much recently, he seems to have gone much further than Jabotinsky ever dared to go.

It is entirely possible that Weizmann was misrepresenting Ben-Gurion's position as Wise had reason to know. Wise was made aware of the feud between the two leaders earlier in 1942 when he received Ben-Gurion's assessment of Weizmann:

Dr. Weizmann...has been acting in a way which, in my view, jeopardizes the political objectives of Zionism....Unless this disastrous situation can immediately be remedied, no other course will be left for me than to ask the Executive and the Actions Committee in Palestine to call for his resignation.[1]

Whatever Ben-Gurion's real position on a Jewish army, the followers of Jabotinsky began to question their primary focus on this issue.

The entire executive of the Committee for a Jewish Army of Stateless and Palestinian Jews met in New York in November, 1942, and reviewed its efforts. While there were some differences of opinion, Bergson was firm in his insistence that the rescue of Jews had to be the top priority. The result was a proclamation entitled: "A Proclamation on the Moral Rights of the Stateless and Palestinian Jews." The proclamation said, in part:

> We shall no longer witness with pity alone, and with passive sympathy, the calculated extermination of the anicent Jewish people by the barbarous Nazis....We recognize the right of these Jews to return to their place among the free peoples of the earth, so that the remnants of tortured Israel...may take up life as a free people...to fight as fellow partners in this war...in their own army, to which the United Nations High Command will assign them.[2]

In December, the new Proclamation was spread across a two-page advertisement in the *New York Times.* Among the hundreds of signatures were those of 20 senators, 109 congressmen, and 14 governors. The advertisement was also placed in key newspapers across the country, carrying the signatures of over 3,000 people, including Herbert Hoover, Clare Booth Luce, Eugene O'Neil, and Taylor Caldwell.

Paid advertisements were the only reliable way the *New York Times'* readers were able to learn of the Nazi extermination plan. As David Wyman points out, of the five Sunday editions following Wise's press conference announcing the details of the Reigner information, in the paper's extensive News-of-the-

[1]Letters dated 10/2/42 and 6/19/42, CZA, Wise papers, op. cit., Reel 122.

[2]See Ben-Ami, p. 282 and PSCP, Reel 4, undated report.

Week section, four issues ignored the issue completely and the fifth carried only a minor story.[1]

Senator Edwin Johnson spoke to the Senate about the press silence:

> Unfortunately close association with misery often breeds callousness. One may anticipate, therefore, in a world at war a dulling of sensibility toward blood and carnage. Sordid report follows sordid report, and we proceed with our knitting as each soggy blood-soaked head falls with a dull thud into the basket. Mass murder in another continent seems far removed. But even so, America views with far too much unconcern for her own good the current cold-blooded deliberate premeditated extermination of 5,000,000 Jews.

Senator Johnson contrasted the press treatment of unprecedented mass murder with its focus on titilating news of the day:

> A few weeks ago, I noticed a front page story in one of America's leading newspapers whose glaring headlines announced "Lovesick Woman Kills Self"....I glanced through other pages. On page 17 of that particularly well known, widely read metropolitan newspaper, I noted a short story, this time in small headlines; in fact it was inserted in the bottom left hand corner of page 17. Substantiated by our own State Department it reported therein very causally that since 1939 in central Europe 2,000,000 human beings have already been mowed down by machine-gun fire, choked to death in poison gas chambers, and buried alive.[2]

Despite the growing bitterness over the passivity of the "official" Jewish leadership, Bergson continued to press ahead for efforts to unify all groups on the crucial issue of rescue. He obtained a meeting with ZOA officials and afterward expressed his hope that coordination of effort could be achieved:

---

[1]Wyman, *Abandonment of the Jews*, op. cit., p. 62.

[2]Congressional Record, 1/14/43.

It was gratifying indeed for my colleagues on the Executive Board and myself to meet with you, Mr. Lipsky and Mr. Konivitz last Saturday in such a cordial atmosphere of understanding and appreciation of the heavy burden....Our Executive Board ...welcomes most heartily the possibility of an "entente cordiale" between the Zionist organization of America and this Committee.[1]

The hopes for such a rapproachment was appealing both to those among Bergson's supporters who saw the Zionist establishment as important and by "regular" Zionists who admired what Bergson was accomplishing. A Metro-Goldwyn-Mayer executive who supported Bergson wrote to him: "I do not believe we can arrive at a completely successful conclusion of our work without the important Jews of the Emergency Committee and the ZOA."[2] Rabbi Aaron Decter of Congregation Beth Israel in Philadelphia wrote:

I write to you hesitantly though unequivocally about my desire to formally join the Committee for a Jewish Army. My hesitation is not due to the possible repercussions of my action, but to a feeling of guilt in not adding my voice to yours much earlier. As you know, I have been sympathetic to the Committee for a Jewish Army since its inception. I have defended and championed it against all attack. At the same time, I determined to work as a disciplined Zionist through the "proper" channels in behalf of our great cause. Needless to say, I am disappointed in the work that we Zionists have so far accomplished....[3]

Historians often write of the limited ability of ethnic groups to influence public policy, especially during the 1940s. However, the fact that it was possible to do so was well known to Jewish leaders from the actions of an ethnic group far weaker than the American Jewish community.

---

[1] Bergson to Levinthal, letter dated 12/7/42, PSCP, Reel 1.

[2] B.P. Fineman to Bergson, 1/8/43, PSCP, Reel 1.

[3] Letter dated 1/11/43, ibid.

In the spring of 1941, long before Martin Luther King set new standards for ethnic protest, and at a time when African-Americans were known as Negroes, leaders of this ethnic group rose up to protest discrimination against them in defense industries. Roosevelt had campaigned on a policy of equality of opportunity and had made promises to Negro groups; now they wanted action on those promises.

Leaders of the National Negro Council asked Roosevelt for an executive order to end discrimination in hiring in the defense industries which were working around the clock to produce war material for the Allies. When Roosevelt was not responsive, A. Phillip Randolph, leader of the Brotherhood of Sleeping Car Porters, threatened a massive march on Washington. Randolph was subjected to great pressure not to pursue the idea. Eleanor Rooosevelt told him she feared such a march would set back efforts for improvement in civil rights for Negroes.

When Randolph remained resolute, Roosevelt himself, along with leaders of the Defense Department, met with Randolph to pressure him to call off the march on Washington. They told him that the American people would resent such coercion. Randolph was not moved.

As the time for the march approached, Roosevelt gave in and issued Executive Order 8802 banning descrimination in defense industry hiring.[1]

This militant approach by Negro leaders contrasted sharply with the approach of "official" Jewish leaders. On December 8, 1942, Roosevelt met with leaders of Jewish organizations.

Present were Stephen Wise representing the American Jewish Congress, Rabbi Israel Rosenbert of the Union of Orthodox Rabbis, Maurice Wertheim of the American Jewish Committee, and Adolph Held of the Jewish Labor Committee. While the leaders presented to Roosevelt a resolution which spoke to Nazi atrocities, the meeting was perfunctory and produced no changes in Roosevelt's policy.

Adolph Held of the Jewish Labor Committee, in a lengthy report on the meeting, describes the scene:

We were taken into the President's office in the White House by General Watson, the President's personal military aide, exactly

---

[1]Burns, James MacGregor, *Roosevelt, 1940-1945: The Soldier of Freedom* (New York: Harcourt Brace Javanovich, 1970), pp. 123-124.

at 12 o'clock...The President sat behind the desk smoking a cigaret in a long cigaret-holder. The desk was full of all sorts of trinkets - ash trays, brass and porcelain figures, etc. There was not an empty spot on his desk.

After Wise summarized the report on Nazi atrocities, Roosevelt replied:

The government of the United States is very well acquainted with most of the facts you are now bringing to our attention. Unfortunately we have received confirmation from many sources....There must be in Germany elements, now thoroughly subdued, but who at the proper time, I am sure, will rise and protest against the atrocities, against the whole Hitler system. It is too early to make pronouncements....[1]

Wise's cousin, Milton Krensky, wrote of the positive public relations value of the meeting:

Your visit with President Roosevelt this week has had a great amount of publicity and certainly has been helpful to the entire Congress Movement. I assume that you realize that the stock of the American and World Jewish Congress has gone up in value considerably in the past few months....[2]

Wise responded in kind, emphasizing the primary role of his organization in obtaining the meeting:

Yes, I have been under a terrible strain and I am very happy that you write that our meeting with the President, which was arranged solely by us, we really doing the whole job, including the preparation of the material for the President - that all this has helped. I think the Madison Square Garden meeting and our

---

[1]Report dated 12/8/42, Taminent Institute, Robert F. Wagner Labor Archives, JLC, Reel MN.

[2]Letter dated 12/1//42, CZA, Wise papers, Reel 4.

leadership in the matter of going to the White House ought to help the Congress a great deal.[1]

Further evidence for the absence of rescue on the agenda of the American Jewish Congress comes from the February, 1943, issue of Wise's publication *Opinion*. There is an extensive review of the Hitler era to date with articles contributed by fifty-two people in various fields. While one participant called for a change in the immigration quota system and an active plan of rescue, as Lookstein documents: "No one else mentioned the word 'rescue.' "[2]

Did all American Jewish leaders believe they were doing everything that could be done? Was everyone on the Roosevelt "win-the-war-first" bandwagon? A postal telegraph from Jacob Pat to Stephen Wise the same month as the above mentioned review in *Opinon* suggests otherwise:

> The Office Committee of the Jewish Labor Committee instructed me to express their extreme dissatisfaction that the Emergency Committee was not assembled this week. The Jewish situation is so horrible that the Emergency Committee is duty-bound to act without delay.[3]

Pat's own sense of urgency is highlighted by the fact that he waited only a week to prod Wise again:

> Several days ago, I sent you a telegram transmitting the request of our Office Committee, that the Emergency Committee should hold meetings more frequently and become more activized. Thus far we have received no reply to our telegram, although two weeks have already passed since the last meeting

---

[1] Letter dated 12/14/42, CZA, Wise papers, Reel 4.

[2] Lookstein, op. cit., p. 106.

[3] Telepraph dated 2/26/43, Taminent Institute, Robert F. Wagner Labor Archives, JLC, Reel MN 2024.

of the Emergency Committee was held, nor has a new meeting as yet been called. Frankly we are displeased at this inaction.[1]

Nine days later, Pat received a notice of the next meeting of the Emergency Committee.

Two articles, both published in Yiddish in early 1943, make it clear that some Jewish leaders understood there were choices for American Jewry and were bitterly disappointed in the choices being made by the Jewish organizations. *Agudas Yisrael* leader Rabbi Isaac Lewin, who was aware of the Sternbuch cable and the suppression of the Reigner cable, asked:

> Where was the storm of protest from Jewish leadership over atrocities which had no parallel in our history? The alarm must be sounded. The "voice of Jacob" must be heard. We ask the leaders of American Jewish organizations: What will you answer on the day of judgement? What will you say when you will some day be called to account for what you have done while the blood of your brothers was flowing like a river?[2]

From the depths of the soul of Chaim Greenberg welled up a cry of protest which he poured onto the pages of the *Yiddisher Kemfer* in February, 1943. Lookstein points out that the article did not appear in English until 1964 and wonders if Greenberg consciously wanted to confine his remarks to a Jewish audience. Greenberg wrote pointedly:

> If moral bankruptcy deserves pity, and if this pity is seven-fold for one who is not even aware how shocking his bankruptcy is, then no Jewish community in the world today (not even the Jews who are now in the claws of the Nazi devourer) deserves more compassion from Heaven than does American Jewry...we

---

[1] Telegraph dated 3/3/43, ibid.

[2] Lookstein, op. cit., p.123.

have become so dulled that we have even lost the capacity for madness.[1]

He attacked directly those who spoke of a future for Jews after the war, those who talked of a Jewish home in Palestine, asking: "A home for whom? For the millions of dead in their temporary cemeteries in Europe?"[2]

The task was to awaken American Jews to the necessity of abandoning business-as-usual and to concentrate with a unity of purpose on the rescue of Jews. The Bergson group met to plan strategy early in 1943. They knew they had to move on all fronts with attempts to mobilize public attention, initiatives for legislation in Congress and pressure for action within the administration.

Was it realistic to expect an administration busy with a world war to deal with anything other than the single-minded purpose of winning the war? American labor, which had a major role in providing the materiel needed to win the war, did not hesitate to press its domestic agenda, and Roosevelt had no choice but to attend to their demands.

Early in 1943, there was a strike of 15,000 coal miners. Roosevelt ordered them back to work, and union members in several other industries went on strike. Roosevelt ordered a circumvention of the age-deferment provisions of the draft law, directing that striking miners be drafted. This brought only a temporary pause in the demands and by the end of 1943 Roosevelt was spending many hours every day mediating the labor disputes.[3]

While American labor pressed its agenda, Ben Hecht pressed the Jewish agenda. In February, 1943, he met with Chaim Greenberg, whose appeal to the conscience of the American Jewish leadership was just cited. Hecht sought out the editor of the *Jewish Frontier* because he was told that Greenberg was one of the most well informed people on the details of the Nazi atrocities. The two journalists met for lunch and Greenberg brought documents for Hecht to read. "Dr. Greenberg sat silent as I read," Hecht reports:

---

[1]Ibid., p. 109.

[2]Ibid., pp. 129-130.

[3]Burns, op. cit., pp. 335ff.

I read of the freight cars lined with tons of quicklime into which five thousand live Jews were jammed, and out of which five thousand partially consumed corpses were removed at the end of the trip....I read of the twenty thousand Jews herded together in a field in Silesia and used as practice targets for the *Luftwaffe* gunners....I read of the burning alive of the Jewish population of Cologne, of five thousand Jews burned alive in Bavarian towns....I read of the hanging of rabbis, of the rape and torture of Jewish women, of German exterminators forcing old Jews to rub excrement over their heads and faces while they prayed.[1]

Greenberg asked what Hecht was planning to write, cautioning him to keep in mind that Jews had to rise above their bitterness and not attack only out of pain. He asked him to remember that Jews cannot become like the Germans. Hecht says: "I thanked this man whose kindness I understood. But his way was not my way. I was unable to answer his philosophical words. My head was full of faraway screams."[2]

Hecht decided to meet with his fellow writers, to convince them that they could awaken the conscience of the nation. "Thirty famous writers (and one composer) were assembled at George Kaufman's house by my friend, his wife Beatrice. All had written hit plays or successful novels."

Hecht told them of all that he had learned about the murders. "I said I felt certain that if we banded together and let loose our talents and our moral passion against the Germans we might halt the massacre." Hecht, who wrote many plays but hated being on stage, talked on and on about the possibilities. "There was no applause when I stopped talking...the authors of hit plays and novels are more interested in receiving applause than giving it." He recalls the angry voice of Edna Ferber asking him: "Who is paying you to do this wretched propoganda? Mister Hitler? Or is it Mister Goebbels?"

After most of the collected talent filed out, Hecht admitted to his hostess, Beatrice Kaufman that he had failed. "I'm sorry it turned out like this," she replied, "but I didn't expect anything much different. You asked them to throw away the most valuable thing they own - the fact that they are Americans."

---

[1]Hecht, *Child of the Century*, op. cit., pp. 549-550.

[2]For an account of this meeting, see Hecht, pp. 551-553.

Hecht wondered how to convince his friend, "a fine woman with as bright a mind and as soft a heart as anyone I knew," that her guests "had not behaved like Americans but like frightened Jews."[1]

Two men waited until the others left and approached Hecht. Moss Hart and Kurt Weill asked that they be counted in on any project that Hecht undertook.

Hecht, Moss, and Weill met in the Beekman place home of Billy Rose. Of Rose's joining the group, Hecht writes: "He needed no briefing. He came under his own steam, which was considerable."[2] It was decided that Hecht would write a pageant, Kurt Weill would write the music, Moss Hart would direct it and Billy Rose would produce it. Hecht had the collection of talent he had sought. Weill, married to the actress Lottie Lenya, had a number of hit musical comedies to his credit. Moss Hart with George Kaufmann had already written *You Can't Take it With You,* which won a Pulitzer Prize, and *The Man Who Came to Dinner.* Billy Rose was a legend in the entertainment world. In his 20s he was one of the most sought after and highly paid songwriters in the country. In the 1930s he was the most successful producer on Broadway.

These men decided it would be more effective to produce a pageant that would have the backing of all elements of the Jewish community, not only the Committee for a Jewish Army. Hecht asked Bergson to arrange a meeting of the various Jewish organizations and the letters went out. The result was a bitter disappointment to Hecht.[3]

In the archives of the American Jewish Committee is a memorandum of the meeting. The memorandum documents the broad range of organizations represented at the meeting:

The meeting was attended by approximately 25 people including Jacob Pat and Leo Dennen of the Jewish Labor Committee, Kaplan who is one of the editors of the *Congress Weekly* [publication of the American Jewish Congress] whom I know; no one for the ADL; several representatives from the Committee

---

[1] Ibid.

[2] Ibid., p. 553.

[3] Ibid., 557-558.

for a Jewish Army; several representatives from various community organizations.

The memorandum, written by Frank N. Trager of the American Jewish Committee, not only mentions Bergson's offer of cooperation, but the fact that there was a positive response from some of the Jewish leaders present:

Bergson...spoke up and declared that although he and his group had instigated [the Hecht pageant], in the interests of harmony he would be glad to withdraw the sponsorship of his organization if that would elicit the sponsorship of a united Jewry....Dennen and Pat for the Labor Committee, and Kaplan for the Congress, said they thought it was a good idea but they would have to report back to their organizations. I indicated for the American Jewish Committee "No comment" but would transmit results of the meeting.

Though the writer of the memorandum acknowledged that the Hecht pageant "may have literary merit" and had praise for a recent article by Hecht ("his article in the current issue of the *American Mercury* is excellent"), he concluded: "Obviously, we as a Committee should have nothing to do with this venture."[1]

If Kaplan of the American Jewish Congress thought Bergson's offer was "a good idea," he failed to convince his president. Hecht reports his phone conversation with Wise:

Rabbi Wise said he would like to see me immediately in his rectory. His voice, which was sonorous and impressive, irritated me. I had never known a man with a sonorous and impressive voice who wasn't either a con man or a bad actor.

Hecht told Wise that he was busy with his production and did not have time to see him. He recalls Wise's reply:

---

[1]Memorandum dated 2/1/43, YIVO, AJC, Waldman papers, Box 43, War and Peace file.

Then I shall tell you now, over the telephone, what I had hoped to tell you in my study. I have read your pageant script and I disapprove of it. I must ask you to cancel this pageant and discontinue all your further activities in behalf of the Jews. It you wish hereafter to work for the Jewish Cause, you will please consult me and let me advise you.[1]

William Ziff, author of *The Rape of Palestine*, consistently prodded the Bergson group to redouble their efforts at cooperation with Jewish organizations. Samuel Merlin informed him of further efforts to seek cooperation on the Hecht pageant:

When we learned that the American Jewish Congress contemplated running a mass meeting at Madison Square Garden on March 1st, we ignored the fact that this meeting was scheduled for that date on two weeks notice in order to "get there first" and called upon Mr. Louis Lipsky of that group in order to avoid the duplication. Mr. Bergson, our National Director, and Mr. Wechsler, our National Secretary, offered the Congress joint sponsorship...a script was delivered to Mr. Lipsky, who seemed favorably inclined and promised to bring the matter to the attention of the Executive of the Congress....It is our understanding that these proposals were hooted down at the meeting and that it was decided as a matter of policy to hamper and destroy any activities of our Committee no matter how worthwhile.[2]

Wise's Congress was not only at odds with the Bergson group. In a letter written in February, 1943, Wise documents the failed negotiations with the American Jewish Committee and reveals that the subject of the negotiations was not rescue, but postwar planning:

It is significant that the statement of principles adopted and made public by the American Jewish Committee last Sunday

---

[1] Hecht, *Child of the Century*, op. cit., p. 564.

[2] Letter dated 4/23/43, PSCP, Reel 1.

marks the termination of it's discussions with Zionist and Congress representatives, which, it was hoped, would in the end produce a joint program of action on postwar problems. After months of protracted meetings it became evident that agreement was impossible.[1]

On the congressional front, the Bergson group continued to lobby senators and congressmen. Senator Edwin Johnson of Colorado agreed to accept the title of national chairman of the Committee for a Jewish Army for Stateless and Palestinian Jews. Senator Johnson was not from a state with a large Jewish constituency. He had been raised on a cattle ranch in Western Nebraska before moving to Colorado. He served as Lieutenant Governor of Colorado for four terms, and Governor for two terms before becoming a senator.[2] Upon joining the Committe for a Jewish Army, Johnson issued a formal statement:

I refuse to believe that this world has grown so callous, so inured to the diabolical actions of the Nazi murderers that we can sit back and do nothing while four million human beings in Europe face the same fate that the two million of their brethren have already experienced....I cannot sit idly by while millions of my fellow-humans are slain. I must take my place in the ranks of those who refuse to believe that nothing can and will be done.

Johnson outlined a three-part plan for specific action for rescue.

1. The immediate appointment of an inter-governmental commission of military experts to determine a realistic and stern policy of action, to stop the wholesale slaughter of European Jewry.

[1]Memorandum dated 2/5/43, YIVO, AJC, Waldman papers, Z- non Z 1943 file.

[2]See profile in *Answer* 4/43.

2. The immediate formation of a Jewish Army of Stateless and Palestinian Jews, including Commando squads which will raid deep into Germany, and Eagle Air Squadrons for retaliatory bombing of Germany.

3. To initiate any possible transfer of European Jews from Hitler dominated countries to Palestine and to temporary refuges in the territory of any of the United Nations.[1]

A real possibility of rescue arose in February, 1943. The *New York Times* published a dispatch from Arthur Sulzberger in London reporting a Rumanian offer to move 70,000 Jews from their territory, asking that they be paid for expenses.[2] Kurt Weill read of the offer in a Swiss-German newspaper and brought it to the attention of Hecht. Hecht received confirmation from Bergson that there may be something to it.[3]

Hecht wrote an advertisement that appeared three days later in the *New York Times.* It was vintage Hecht: "Roumania is tired of killing Jews...Seventy Thousand Jews Are Waiting Death In Roumanian Concentration Camps....Act Now."[4] Hecht acknowledged that he wrote the ad "in bitter phrases. Its object was to shock Jews, infuriate Jews and set them to screaming."[5]

Some Jewish leaders screamed, but not at the Roosevelt administration. They concentrated their fire on the Bergson group and accepted Undersecretary Welles' contention that there was nothing to the Rumanian report. As Wyman points out:

The main issue is not whether the plan might have worked. The crucial point is that, against a backdrop of full knowledge of the ongoing extermination program, the American and British

---

[1]Statement dated 2/24/43, PSCP, Reel 5.

[2]*New York Times*, 2/13/43, cited by Wyman, *Abandonment of the Jews*, op. cit., p. 82.

[3]Hecht, *Child of the Century*, op, cit., p. 577-578.

[4]See Wyman, op. cit., p. 86.

[5]Hecht, *Child of the Century*, op. cit., p. 578.

governments almost cursorily dismissed this first major potential rescue opportunity.[1]

Minutes of a ZOA executive committee meeting in February, 1943, document that the Jewish officials had extensive information about the activity inside the Roosevelt administration. Henry Morgenthau, Jr., Secretary of the Treasury, had approached Roosevelt, who shunted him to the State Department. Undersecretary Welles obtained information about contacts between a Dutchman doing business in Rumania and Jewish officials. The Dutchman brought the offer to an official of the Jewish Agency.[2]

However, given the choice of attacking the State Department's cursory dismissal of the offer or attacking the Hecht advertisements, many Jewish leaders chose the latter.

Leaders of Orthodox Jewry took the Rumanian offer very seriously, as can be seen from this letter sent to the Jewish Labor Committee:

A special urgent conference of the representatives of the Union of Orthodox Rabbis, *Mizrachi...Agudas Yisrael,* Young Israel... held today considered the information regarding the possibility of saving seventy thousand Rumanian Jews. The unanimous opinion of the meeting was that the problem is the most important in Jewish activities at the present moment and has to be put ahead of all other matters.[3]

Other Jewish leaders declined to join in the attack on the Bergson group, instead targeting the passivity of the Jewish organizations. Judah Piltch, in the American Hebrew language *Hadoar* left this ringing statement for future historians to ponder:

---

[1]Wyman, op. cit., pp. 83-84.

[2]Ibid., pp. 82-83.

[3]Letter dated 2/18/43, Taminent Institute, Robert F. Wagner Labor Archives, JLC, Reel MN.

And what will happen when my son asks me tomorrow: "What did you do while your brothers were being exterminated and tortured by the Nazi murderers?" What will I say and what will I be able to tell him? Shall I tell him that I lived in a generation of weaklings and cowards who were neither moved nor shocked when they heard of hundreds of thousands of their brothers being led to the slaughter hour by hour, day by day, year by year? Shall I describe this chapter in the annals of American Jewry and admit that our people did not meet the test of history?[1]

In the independent *Jewish Spectator*. The editor, Trude Weiss Rosmarin, wrote:

It is therefore, shocking, and - why mince words - revolting that at a time like this our organizations, large and small, national and local, continue "business as usual" and sponsor gala affairs, such as sumptuous banquets, luncheons, fashion teas, and what not....It would require the fiery pen of Jeremiah or of a Bialik to find adequate expression of condemnation for the abysmal indifference and heartlessness flaunted by those who can bring themselves to sit down at banquet tables, resplendent in evening clothes, while on the very same evening hundreds of Jews expire in the agonies of hunger, gas poisoning....[2]

Ben Hecht was providing the fiery pen, but meeting much the same response from his fellow Jews as did Jeremiah in his day.

Hecht tried unsuccessfully to get a statement from Roosevelt condemning Nazi atrocities in conjunction with the pageant scheduled for New York March 9 and Washington April 12. Billy Rose turned to Governor Thomas Dewey of New York to issue such a statement. Despite pressure from Wise not to do so,[3] Dewey declared the day of March 9, 1943 a "Day of Mourning."

---

[1]*Hadoar*, 1/15/43, cited by Lookstein, op. cit., p. 214-215 and Watkins, op. cit. pp. 799-800.

[2]*Jewish Spectator*, 3/43, cited by Lookstein, op. cit., p. 121.

[3]See Hecht, op. cit., pp. 575-576, Ben-Ami, op. cit., pp. 325-326, and Wyman, op. cit., p. 90.

The Wise rally March 1, and the Hecht pageant March 9, both at Madison Square Garden, demonstrate two important points: (1) there was a hunger for outlets for people to express their anguish and (2) the difference between an approach that *pleads* for action as opposed to one that *demands* action and condemns inaction in the face of mass murder as criminal.

The Wise sponsored March 1 rally was attended by 20,000 people and an estimated 50,000 more were outside. There were speeches by Wise, Chaim Weizmann, Mayor Fiorello La Guardia and other notables. An 11-point plan for action was presented. Not involved in the planning of the March 1 rally was the Jewish Labor Committee and Orthodox Jewry.

The activism of the Orthodox community and the Bergson group brought them together now as it had done before. The script for Hecht's pageant called for a praying scene, but his casting assistant, Rose Keane, informed him that the Orthodox rabbis she had contacted were unwilling to pray on a theatre stage. A meeting was arranged at Schwartz's Kosher Restaurant in New York. Hecht faced the group of bearded rabbis with trepidation. "What could anyone say to such holy men, and how could I ever persuade them to commit a sin?"[1]

One rabbi noticed Hecht's hesitancy and offered to speak to his friends for Hecht. He was "over six feet tall," Hecht recounts, "with a long white beard riding on his chest....He looked a little like Michelangelo's Moses...."[2]

Rabbi Levin of Czechoslovakia spoke to his peers in Yiddish and succeeded in convincing them that the times called for their participation.

On May 9, 1943, in Madison Square Garden, and April 12 in Constitution Hall in Washington, the rabbis were part of a large cast which took the stage. Two performances in New York brought the pageant before 40,000 people in one day. In Washington, six Supreme Court justices and many administration officials were in the audience. Two huge tablets inscribed with the ten commandments formed the backdrop of the stage. A roll call of Jews who had made major contributions to the world brought forward Moses, Rabbi Akiba, Maimonides and many others. The rabbis sang *kaddish* for their people and the narrator said:

---

[1] Hecht, op. cit., p. 559.

[2] Ibid., p. 560.

The corpse of a people lies on the steps of civilization. Behold it. Here it is! And no voice is heard to cry halt to the slaughter, no government speaks to bid the murder of human millions end.[1]

For the Washington performance Hecht added to the narration:

We the actors who have performed for you tonight, are nearly done. But there is another cast of actors whose performance is not done. This cast is our audience...a notable cast, playing vital roles on the stage of history. It is to this audience more than to any group of human beings in the world, that the dead and dying innocents of Europe raise their cry "Remember us!"[2]

In the forward to a published copy of the script of "We Will Never Die," Hecht wrote that "The silence of our governments makes us all part of the massacre. We who could halt a crime and do not are not its witnesses but its participants." He went on to speak to American Jews:

There is no one as bold and certain as the American Jew when he is asked to think as an American on American problems. Asked to consider any Jewish problem the American Jew becomes immediately full of alarms and illogic....But I offer no arguments to them. If they are timorous of raising their voice as Jews, let them raise it then as Americans.[3]

Hecht abandoned this restraint a few paragraphs later:

Yet for Jews to keep silent for any reason, however politic or logical, is as craven a policy as the human mind can conceive. The silence of the world toward the slaughter of six million

---

[1]Wyman, op. cit., p. 91.

[2]Ben-Ami, op. cit., p. 286.

[3]Undated document, PSCP, Reel 8.

Jews is part of a spiritual lethargy that must be blasted out of being. The silence of American Jews toward the crime of Europe is not lethargy. It is a species of criminal cowardice and shabby inferiority that calls for as great a human contempt as does the murder policy of the Germans.[1]

In April "We Will Never Die" was performed before a capacity crowd of 15,000 people in Philadelphia, 18,000 in Chicago, and in July to 10,000 in the Hollywood Bowl, "the limit permitted in an outdoor assemblage under wartime regulations."[2]

That the Bergson group was effective far beyond Washington is indicated by a memorandum which came from the Minnesota Jewish Council to the American Jewish Committee:

An organizer for the Committee for a Jewish Army was recently in town and has succeeded in setting up an organization....Some of the more reputable Jewish Zionists are becoming parties to this movement. They certainly will get the support they are after in our communities unless something is immediately done by the reputable national organizations....[3]

The "reputable national organizations" tried and were successful in keeping the Hecht pageant out of many cities.[4] They even approached J. Edgar Hoover with sinister suggestions of criminal wrongdoing by the Bergson group. In a letter Hoover sent to the Justice Department, an individual identified only as "an executive of the American Jewish Congress" was quoted as saying the Committee for a Jewish Army "was sponsored by a group of thoroughly disreputable Communist Zionists." Hoover learned through his informant that:

---

[1]Ibid.

[2]*Los Angeles Examiner*, 7/22/43.

[3]Memorandum dated 3/8/43, YIVO, AJC, Waldman papers, Box 43, War and Peace/Jewish Army file.

[4]See Wyman, op. cit., p. 92.

the American Jewish Committee, through its powerful Washington contacts, would see to it that all the senators and congressmen whose names appeared on advertisements would withdraw.[1]

But there was no unanimity in the American Jewish Congress and American Jewish Committee on the activities of the Bergson group, and some within each organization continued to pursue avenues of cooperation. In March, 1943, after the New York performance of the Hecht pageant, members of both organizations as well as representatives of B'nai B'rith and the Jewish Labor Committee met with Bergson and Alfred Strelsin of the Committe for a Jewish Army.

Bergson offered to drop the Jewish Army proposal from a list of possible joint projects if they could come together on rescue. One possibility raised by the others was that "the Army Committee be invited to send two representatives as observers in the next two or three meeting of the Joint Committee...and see how we get along together."[2]

At this time, pressure in England and the United States brought the two governments together for the Bermuda Conference in April, 1943. Just as at Evian in 1938, the process was intended to placate public opinion while making no changes in policy. Congressman Sol Bloom, who could be counted on to stay within the confines of administration policy, was named a representative to the Bermuda Conference.

No one in the Jewish community expected results from Bermuda. Anthony Eden was in Washington prior to the conference and met with Wise and Judge Joseph Proskauer and told them that nothing could be done.

Correspondence in the spring of 1942, between Proskauer and the executive director of the American Jewish Committee, Morris Waldman, and the President, Maurice Wertheim, point to a power struggle within the organization. Proskauer, who in 1943 became the first president of the American Jewish Committee to ascend to that office other than by the death of the previous president, opposed the compromise his group was

---

[1]Letter dated 4/13/43, Dept. of Justice; Division of Records: No. 149-178 and F4173, cited by Ben-Ami, op. cit., p. 325.

[2]Rosenblum to Waldman, 3/11/43, YIVO, AJC, Waldman papers, Box 43, War and Peace/Jewish Army file.

fashioning with the Zionists. It is interesting that this correspondence is found in the Waldman files, but none of it is to be found among Proskauer's papers.

Proskauer wrote a "confidential memorandum" to Wertheim in which he put pressure on Wertheim and Waldman, using as a lever the threat by Morris Lazaron to split from the American Jewish Committee and form a rival organization on the issue of open opposition to Zionism [Lazaron subsequently made good on his threat, forming, with others, the American Council of Judaism]. Proskauer wrote to Wertheim:

> I have before me this morning two documents: 1) a statement of principles by Morris Lazaron and (2) a pronunciamento from the American Jewish Congress....I am approaching the following conclusion....the American Jewish Committee must adopt an affirmative platform essentially similar to Lazaron's...or a new organization must be formed that will affirmatively voice these principles.[1]

Several exchanges of letters ensued but did little to close the gap between them. Six weeks later comes this letter from Proskauer to Wertheim concerning an impending compromise with the Zionists:

> I think it right to record my conviction, as expressed on Sunday and which remains unchanged, that the project to make this agreement with the Zionists is to my mind a tragedy for American Jewry. I am so deeply opposed to it, that at the moment I don't see how I can remain a member of the American Jewish Committee.[2]

By early 1943, Wertheim was out and Proskauer was in as President. Despite a polite announcement of the change that tried to conceal the friction within the organization, Jacob

---

[1]Letter dated, 4/23/43, YIVO, AJC, Waldman papers, Box 49, Zionism-non Zionism, April-June 1942 file.

[2]Letter dated 6/11/42, ibid.

Fishman, a respected Jewish editor, was not fooled, writing for the Independent Jewish Press Service:

> An inglorious chapter in the history of the American Jewish Committee reached its climax at the recent thirty-sixth annual meeting of that body....The American Jewish Committee is now headed by Joseph H. Proskauer. His election was preceded by a formal statement by Wertheim to the effect that the "war effort" in Washington necessitated his withdrawal....Regardless of the surface proprieties, there can be no misreading...of the election of Mr. Proskauer. Former Judge Proskauer is a symbol of the extreme anti-Zionist group in the American Jewish Committee.[1]

Neither Proskauer, the symbol of anti-Zionism, nor Wise, the symbol of aggressive Zionism, raised an alarm in the light of Anthony Eden's negative response to their suggestions for alleviating the plight of European Jewry.

In a meeting with Roosevelt, Eden was equally blunt in saying that if the Allies started taking Jews out of some countries "the Jews of the world will be wanting us to make similar efforts in Poland and Germany. Hitler might well take us up on any such offer and there simply are not enough ships...to handle them."[2]

As to the shipping, Martin Gilbert writes:

> Between 1942 and the end of the war, shipping was found to transport a total of 371,683 German prisoners-of-war, and 50,273 Italian prisoners-of-war, across the Atlantic to the United States.[3]

And what of Eden's attitude toward easing the restrictions on Jews coming to Palestine? His private secretary, Oliver

---

[1] Article dated 2/19/43, ibid, Box 50.

[2] See Gilbert, op. cit., p. 127.

[3] Gilbert, ibid.

Harvey, noted in his diary: "Unfortunately A.E. is immovable on the subject of Palestine. He loves Arabs and hates Jews."[1]

But the British did not have to worry about pressure from the American government. Paul Alling of the State Department, while noting in a memo that "Immigration into Palestine has not taken place even at the reduced rate permitted by the White Paper," concluded: "It is our view that the British should not be asked to enlarge their commitments respecting refugees in so far as Palestine is concerned."[2]

During the Bermuda Conference Wise wrote to his cousin Milton: "We are not very happy about the outlook in Bermuda....American Jewry is represented by a contemptible little squirt [Sol Bloom] who...has been foisted upon us in order to cover things up, if it should be agreed by both governments that nothing is to be done."[3]

Whether or not she was aware of the Jewish dictum that "he who saves a single life, it is as if he saved the whole world," Eleanor Rathbone thundered in the British Parliament:

...let no one say we are not responsible. We are responsible if a single man, woman, or child perishes whom we could and should have saved.[4]

In the American Congress, Emanuel Celler protested:

Two million Jews dead already, but we are told to wait, wait until Nazi *blutbaden* liquidate the refugee problem for us. Yes, soothe with words those awaiting the end and murmur consolingly, "death will release you."[5]

---

[1]Ibid., p. 132.

[2]Memorandum dated 4/2/43, PSCP, Reel 3.

[3]Letter dated 4/19/43, CZA, Wise papers, Reel 4.

[4]See Gilbert, op. cit., p. 139.

[5]Document dated 5/3/43, PSCP, Reel 4.

Pressing for effective action from American Jews, Celler wrote to Wise:

You may recall that a few months ago I made a suggestion that there be held in Washington an unofficial conclave of Representatives and Senators sympathetic to active and genuine rescue of refugees. At first blush, you thought well of it, and...subsequently...frowned on the idea. In view of what has happened at Bermuda, I renew the suggestion. I ask you again to discuss it with interested persons.[1]

The level of urgency that Wise gave Celler's call to action is indicated by the following letter Wise wrote to Proskauer:

Here's a note from Celler...If we could get the right Senators and the right House members to think and act upon the question, it would be well worthwhile, but can we? Perhaps we will meet in the next day or two and talk things over.[2]

Proskauer responded to Wise the following day:

Very tentatively I venture to suggest the possibility of just saying to him that we do not desire to influence his judgement in the matter, that he was better placed than we are to form a judgement, and that he should do whatever he thinks is right.[3]

Wise and Proskauer were united in the low priority they assigned to rescue. By contrast, Jacob Pat, president of the American Labor Committee, continued to protest to Wise about the inactivity. It was Passover time and the final liquidation of the Warsaw Ghetto was underway:

---

[1]Letter dated 5/14/43, AJC, Proskauer papers, Emergency Committee 1943 file.

[2] Letter dated 5/18/43, Proskauer papers, AJC, Emergency Committee, 1943 file.

[3]Letter dated 5/19/43, ibid.

Can't understand why the Emergency Committee is silent in the face of the horrifying news coming from the Warsaw Ghetto....Under the circumstances the silence...is strange indeed. What happened to the two press conferences one in Washington and one in New York that were supposed to be called? The last call of anguish from our brothers in the ghettos has reached us here. We can no longer delay action.[1]

Action was forthcoming, but form a different direction.

---

[1] Letter dated 4/23/43, ibid.

Chapter IX

The Emergency Committee to Save
the Jewish People of Europe

Action continued to come from the Bergson group which paid
for a two-page advertisement in the *New York Times* which
headlined: "To five million Jews in the Nazi death-trap,
Bermuda was a cruel mockery."[1] The ad touched a nerve in the
White House, as did "My Uncle Abraham Reports" later in
1943:

My Uncle Abraham was a ghost delegated by the millions of
murdered Jews to represent all their ghosts at the conferences
working "to make the world a better place to live." He would sit
on the windowsill and take notes, then report back to his
departed friends. He told them that for some unknown reason,
their names were never mentioned - not in Moscow, not at 10
Downing Street, London, not at the White House. When we were
killed, we were changed from Nobodies to Nobodies. Today on
our Jewish tomb, there is not the Star of David but an
asterisk.[2]

Hecht received a call from Bernard Baruch, an influential
Jewish Democrat. "I knew Baruch slightly and had once done
him the favor of removing his name from some movie

---

[1] *New York Times*, 5/4/43.

[2] see Ben-Ami, pp. 327-328.

dialogue." Baruch reported that Roosevelt was very upset by Hecht's advertisements. He promised that Roosevelt would address Jewish problems "to my satisfaction - and yours."

Hecht had a favorable impression of Baruch and sought out Bergson, Ben-Ami and Merlin to tell them his "top secret." They disagreed on the significance of the phone call, but acceded to Hecht's request that the attacking ads stop. After a month and no change in Roosevelt's policy, Hecht phoned Baruch to tell him the amnesty was over. He reports Baruch's response:

> I have had a two-hour talk with President Roosevelt about the Jews and the Jewish problem. I have spoken also to Governor Dewey on the same subject. I can only tell you...despite my having been a lifelong Democrat, I would rather trust my American Jewishness in Mr. Dewey's hands than in Mr. Roosevelt's.[1]

Even more "militant" than the Bergson group was Szmul Zygielbojm, a Jewish Socialist member of the Polish National Council who committed suicide in London, leaving this note:

> The responsibility for this crime of murdering the entire Jewish population of Poland falls in the first instance on the perpetrators, but indirectly it is also a burden on the whole of humanity, the people and the governments of the Allied States which thus far have made no effort toward concrete action for the purpose of curtailing this crime. By the passive observation of the murder of defenseless millions and of the maltreatment of children, women, and old men, these countries have become the criminals' accomplices....As I was unable to do anything during my life, perhaps by my death I shall contribute to breaking down that indifference.[2]

The Bergson group was not alone in making appeals to the administration. Proskauer and Wise also sent messages and proposals to the State Department. The wording of the messages

---

[1] Hecht, op. cit., pp. 580-582.

[2] see Wyman, p. 123.

make it clear they did not believe the administration's claim that nothing could be done before the final victory of the Allies or that efforts to save the Jews would detract from the war effort.[1] What then was the difference in the dynamics of what Proskauer and Wise were doing and what the Bergson group was doing?

From the time that the Committee for a Jewish Army changed its emphasis to rescuing European Jewry, each activity was part of an overall, day-in and day-out strategy of all members of the organization which was growing in numbers of supporters and money raised for lobbying efforts. They understood political pressure and did not hesitate to use it.

By contrast, Proskauer and Wise headed organizations that were primarily fighting turf wars among themselves and whose activities were poorly coordinated with no pretense of follow-up nor strategy of pressure. The Independent Jewish Press Service took American Jewish leaders to task for their approach:

> Now let's be frank about this, our dear Leaders. Isn't it a fact that for ten years you have been trooping up to the State Department with bated breath and hat in hand, getting the run-around. Politely of course. Then why didn't you report back to us, the Jewish people of America, so that we could try to do something about it before it was too late? What could we have done? We could have done what other Americans do when their kinsmen are threatened....We could have brought pressure to bear on Congress, on the President, on the State Department - *mass* pressure, not just backstairs "diplomacy"....

The article closed by pointing squarely to the reason none of this worked: *"It is too easy for a government official to say no when he knows it isn't going any further....*[2] [italics added].

This article speaks in the past tense as if it is too late for effective action. An internal memorandum from an executive committee meeting of the Bergson group one month after this article demonstrates that the group still saw plenty of

---

[1]For example see memoranda dated 4/13/43 and 5/13/43, AJC, Proskauer papers, Emergency Committee, memoranda, material file.

[2]Independent Jewish Press Service, 3/12/43, city by Medoff, op. cit., p. 110.

opportunity for rescue. After discussing his lobbying plan, Bergson said emphatically:

> It has a good chance of changing the attitude of the leading Jews of America such as Lehman, Morgenthau and their contemporaries who do not take the initiative in these Jewish matters not because they are cruel or don't feel it, but because they are confused and think it will be un-American to take action themselves on a Jewish issue. We will have to sell them this formula and put their minds at ease, by saying they are Americans of Jewish descent; if we sell them this point, we will get action on their part.

And what was the plan for approaching the non-Jewish community?

> The other problem is even easier, that of explaining to the non-Jews the factual situation and informing them that no initiative is coming from their Jewish colleagues and therefore, their duty is not to wait, but to go ahead themselves. To explain to them that psychologically, the Jews of the country can do nothing because of their confused status today....Otherwise, it will never occur to any of say, the President's executive assistants that they should go to the President and ask why nothing is being done about the Jewish problem....They think that Rosenman and Lehman have the thing at heart and are doing everything possible.

Bergson referred to Hecht's pageant:

> The five or six Supreme Court Justices that attended the performance of "We Will Never Die" in Washington were very deeply impressed but it never crossed their mind that it was up to them to do something the next morning about it. They figured that if Frankfurter, the Jew so close to the problem hasn't done anything, there is little to do. It never occurred either to Knox or Jesse Jones [administration officials], who attended that

evening that they should do something, because Morgenthau and Baruch were probably doing all that could be done.[1]

There was no lack of specific information available from Europe. The Director of the Royal Yugoslav Information Center sent the following eye-witness report to the World Jewish Congress with a specific request that it be sent to "Dr. Wise."

In Broko the Ustashis [Bosnian Croats] brought 30 Serb and Jewish children to the bridge of the Sava River and killed them one by one by hammer blows on the head and threw them into the river. The ages of these children were 5 to 10 years. The scene was a horrible one to watch; the children cried but the *Ustashis* killed them mercilessly....In the same town the *Ustashis* entered the home of Dr. Bukvica and in spite of all his resistance dragged out two Jewish girls 10 and 15 years old, the playmates of his daughters, killed them with a hammer on the bridge and threw their bodies into the Sava River.[2]

Two weeks after receiving this memorandum, the same Jewish official wrote to Wise not about rescue plans but how to prevent the Bergson group from "stealing the thunder" of their organization.[3] The "official" Jewish leadership was busy planning yet another umbrella organization, the American Jewish Conference, drawing this response from one of their own in the *Congress Weekly*, the publication of the American Jewish Congress:

It is not difficult to understand the initial reaction of distrust...regarding the entire idea of the Conference. Jews, ordinary Jews with sound national instincts, asked apprehensively when they first heard of the Conference. "What!

---

[1]PSCP, Reel 4. undated.

[2]Gavrilovic to Perlzweig, 5/31/43, CZA, Wise papers, Reel 92.

[3]Perlzweig to Wise, Goldman and Shultz, 6/16/43, ibid.

Another organization! Is this the solution for a people that stands on the brink of annihilation?"[1]

The new American Jewish Conference was being proposed to replace the Joint Emergency Committee, the subject of the charges of inaction by Jacob Pat mentioned above. In June, 1943, Pat fired another, more bitter accusation at the leaders of the Emergency Committee which he comments "died...without the benefit either of doctors or witnesses." The letter was addressed to Lillie Schultz, one of Wise's colleagues at the American Jewish Congress:

> I am quite aware that the guilt for the failure of the Emergency Committee is shared by all organizations comprising the Committee but you will agree with me that it is the leadership - those who have the reins of the organization in their hands - that is most to blame. And the leadership until today, for obvious reasons - were you, Mr. Shulman, Dr. Wise and Judge Proskauer.[2]

The Emergency Committee was indeed dead. Now, in the summer of 1943, comes the unfolding of major organizational efforts of the "official" Jewish organizations on the one hand and of the Bergson group on the other hand.

In the election of delegates to the American Jewish Conference, elections which took place all across the United States, there was a significant split between the Zionists and non-Zionists. As the election of delegates to the American Jewish Conference was proceeding, Proskauer wrote to Wise in June, 1943:

> I am sorry to inform you that at the election last Sunday the most capable, the most popular and the best known national leader of Minneapolis was defeated....The repetitive steamroller tactics is stirring up bitter resentment against the Zionist

---

[1] *Congress Weekly*, 6/18/43, cited by Medoff, op. cit., pp. 119-120.

[2] Letter dated 6/24/43, AJC, Proskauer papers, Emergency Committee, 1943 file.

Organizations all over the country. This I deeply deplore. I think the Zionist Organization should do something to stop it.[1]

The following day, Proskauer wrote again:

My morning mail brings me a letter...saying that the cumulative system of voting in LA resulted in the election of what was in effect nothing but a Zionist group....I have a letter from...Madison, Wisconsin [whose report] convinces me that it [the American Jewish Conference] is nothing more or less that a Zionist convention.[2]

The very next day, Proskauer was again in communication with Wise:

I am greatly troubled by the formal declaration issued both by the ZOA and the American Jewish Congress declaring for the extreme position re Palestine as their platform for the Conference. I am assuming - and I hope not foolishly - that these are not ultimate, but intended as bases for discussion, because if this isn't so, there isn't much use in having a Conference.[3]

In an internal communication, the executive director of the American Jewish Committee wrote to his president, Proskauer, suggesting that the Zionist tactics could redound to the benefit of their organization:

If a break comes the Conference then will become strictly a "political party." If that should happen, we would naturally then become the spearhead of an opposing "political party"...if that would happen, we would be doing an "institutional promotion" job at one fell blow that otherwise might take us years to do. If

---

[1] Letter dated 6/22/43, ibid., Proskauer papers, American Jewish Conference, 1943 file.

[2] Letter dated 6/23/43, ibid.

[3] Letter dated 6/24/43, ibid.

this would happen, we would be afforded a grand opportunity to assert the leadership in Jewish life.[1]

While this organizational maneuvering was going on as if there were no crisis for world Jewry, a conference of a different kind was being planned by the Bergson group. The conference was planned for New York at the end of July. The activity was noted also at the other end of the American continent. The *San Francisco Examiner* reported on July 1, 1943:

Necessity for speed in adopting a plan of action to save the lives of 4,000,000 Jews in Europe was stressed by Rear Admiral Yates Stirling, Jr., and other speakers at a meeting here today. Announcement was also made...that Secretary of the Interior Harold L. Ickes will formally open the Emergency Conference to save the Jews of Europe.[2]

The conference in New York coincided with the efforts in Congress to pass legislation to establish a rescue agency. The *Washington Times Herald* reported that "five members of the Senate have issued a statement of welcome to the Emergency Conference to Save the Jews of Europe."[3]

The same day, Jacob Pat, one member of the "official" Jewish community who *was* focused on rescue instead of Jewish politics sent his latest protest:

There was an appeal from Italy recently which stated, that an appeal to the Pope would perhaps stop the deportation of Jews

---

[1] Letter dated 6/30/43,ibid.

[2] *San Francisco Examiner*, 7/1/43.

[3] *Washington Times Herald*, 7/14/43.

from Italy...the [Zionist] Emergency Committee did nothing about this matter. A meeting wasn't even called.[1]

In the meantime an important letter came from Secretary of the Treasury Morgenthau to the Bergson group. "It is my earnest hope that out of your Emergency Conference will come a specific plan to relieve the critical situation which exists among the Jewish people." Morgenthau took note of the significant support developing for the conference: "With so substantial a group of outstanding people backing your efforts, I feel confident that some plan and some action will certainly result."[2]

The New York conference was not a rally called for public personalities to give speeches. It was pointed toward the specific plans for which Morgenthau hoped. A background paper prepared for the July conference was detailed and targeted specific areas where rescue was possible.

The report reviewed the "illegal immigration" during the time the Nazis were allowing emigration, noting that over 400,000 Jews escaped from Germany, Austria and Czechoslovakia before 1940. Noting that this exodus from Nazi controlled territory slowed in 1941, the report quoted the Joint Distribution Committee's review of 1941 to show that Jews were still able to get out: "at the beginning of 1941 emigration proceeded normally via Portugal and Spain from the countries of Greater Germany, as well as from unoccupied France."[3]

Turning to the efforts of the United States, the Bergson report noted that under the quota system, 150,000 immigrants per year were allowed entry into the United States, but that only 70,000 were admitted for the two year period of 1939-1940, and only a little more than 50,000 in 1940-1941.

The report gave a country by country evaluation of rescue opportunities, beginning with Hungary:

---

[1]Letter dated 7/14/43, Pat to Shultz, Taminent Institute, Robert F. Wagner Labor Archives, JLC, Reel MN.

[2]Morgenthau to Lerner, 7/15/43, PSCP, Reel 4.

[3]Report dated 7/20/43, ibid.

Let us begin with Hungary where more Jews are concentrated now than in any other country under Nazi domination, with the one exception of Poland. In Hungary and its annexed territories, there are at least 800,000 Jews....In a speech delivered at a meeting of the Hungarian Government Party in Budapest on May 29, 1943, the prime-Minister, Von Kallay, said that the Jewish problem in Hungary could be settled only by emigration. This, however, he added, was not possible as long as there was no place where the Jews could have been resettled.[1]

The failure to respond seriously to the Roumanian offer to release Jews was reviewed in the report. "Roumania, like Germany, wishes to get rid of her Jews....Why not take it for granted that the Roumanian Goverment really wanted ro release the 70,000 Jews...why was there no attempt to establish...negotiations with those who made the offer?"[2]

The Emergency Conference to Save the Jewish People of Europe opened July 20, 1943, to wide press coverage. The *Herald Tribune* reported a proposal for special officials in the administration who would focus on rescue. "The request was made in proposals adopted by a panel on international relations at the second session of the Emergency Conference to Save the Jewish People of Europe being held at the Commodore Hotel."[3]

The same day the *New York Journal American*, carried a large picture of Eri Jabotinsky, Vladimir Jabotinsky's son, with two military experts with the headline: "Rescue of Jews Demanded Now."[4]

Max Lerner, a writer who was involved in the planning of the conference, kept up the drumbeat of pressure on Roosevelt in an article in *P.M.*, the New York newspaper Hecht was writing for when he joined forces with the Bergson group:

What about the Jews, FDR. I address you with great reluctance, President Roosevelt. You are a man harried by every group in the country....You carry the massive weight of the war on your

---

[1] Ibid.

[2] Ibid.

[3] *New York Herald Tribune*, 7/22/43.

[4] *New York Journal American*, 7/22/43.

shoulders...but I think that the fate of 4,000,000 Jews is not a trifling matter....Hitler has made out of Europe a charnel-house of the Jews. But the State Department and Downing Street avert their eyes from the slaughter.[1]

On July 23, 1943, the *New York Times* carried the story of a relief expert who "pointed out that the problem of providing food for a harassed minority had been successfully met in the case of Greece," and added: "It was also reported at the meeting that there are adequate transportation facilities to rescue European Jews without interfering in any way with the war program."[2]

The White House was unable to ignore the gathering of 1,500 people in New York and Roosevelt and Secretary of State Hull sent messages to the conference "promising that this Government would not cease its efforts to save those who could be saved."[3]

In its July issue, the *New Republic* pointed out in an editorial that other conferences, like the Bermuda Conference, had failed, because "they refused to consider the actual problem of how to get the Jews out of Europe." Turning to the specific proposals of the current conference, the writer concluded:

If the present conference fails it will not be through fault of its own. The Emergency Conference worked out a nine-point program calling for removal of the Jews from Europe by road, rail and steamship into neutral countries for temporary asylum, while the Allies provide food and shelter and undertake to conduct them into their own territories.

While acknowledging that the United States could not be expected to take in 4,000,000 Jews, the *New Republic* countered:

---

[1] *P.M.*, 7/22/43.

[2] *New York Times*, 7/23/43.

[3] Ibid., 7/26/43.

We can at least insist that it [the U.S. government] at least allow temporary immigration within the European quota. The law allows a total of about 150,000 European immigrants a year. Within the last five years immigration has dwindled to a mere 20 percent of quota. We could thus save some 750,000 Jews merely by fulfilling our quota of the last five years.[1]

There was a perception inside the American Jewish Congress that Henry Montor, Executive Director of the United Jewish Appeal, was a proponent of the Bergson group. An internal memorandum written at the end of the Bergson conference in New York complained that "he [Montor] has consistently been in favor of the operations of the Jewish Army Committee." Montor was informed of the complaints about his use of the Independent Press Service to write editorials that "seem to express your personal opinions and not the opinions either of the Editorial Board or of the organizations which have created at least the financial basis on which the Service depends."[2]

More editorial support for the Bergson group came from *The Nation's* July issue:

Two million Jews out of Europe's six million have already been slaughtered by the Nazis; this is the most colossal and atrocious crime in history, and it is a crime to which the democracies are accessories before the fact. Now the Emergency Conference to Save the Jews of Europe is making one more effort to arouse the sympathies of the world. It has a number of concrete proposals to make....[3]

The New York conference was followed by a national lobbying campaign to bring pressure for rescue of European Jews. William Randolph Hearst was convinced to order editorials written in all of his newspapers supporting the Bergson committee, and an approach was made to Secretary of the

---

[1] *New Republic*, July 1943.

[2] Letter dated 7/30/43, Shultz to Montor, CZA, Wise papers, Reel 93.

[3] *The Nation*, July 1943.

Treasury, Henry Morgenthau asking him to use his influence inside the administration to urge rescue.[1]

The *New Republic* followed their strong editorial of July with a special section : "The Jews of Europe: How to Help Them."

The failure of the democratic powers to make any sustained and determined effort to stay the tide of slaughter constitutes one of the major tragedies in the history of civilization, and the moral weakness which has palsied the hands of our statesmen is nowhere more vividly disclosed than in the now conventional formula, so often on their lips, that only victory will save the Jews of Europe. Will any of these Jews survive to celebrate victory?[2]

The emerging American Jewish Conference set its first meeting for August, 1943, amid ongoing disagreements on the issue of political Zionism. Internal memoranda make it clear that there was sentiment inside the "official" organizations for exerting more direct pressure on behalf of European Jews. One memo noted that the Canadian government was "susceptible to pressure...but only if a sufficient pressure be exerted."[3] Lillie Schultz, Wise's top aide, exerted her independence. The minutes of an August meeting record the following:

Miss Shultz expressed the view that, under the pressure of circumstances, we have put all our eggs in one basket, and that on the assumption that there is a friendly administration in Washington, our proposals for action were couched in terms of appeal. The time has come, she said, to be critical of lack of action and in view of the fact that this is the eve of a presidential election year, ways can be found to indicate to the administration...that the large and influential Jewish communities will find a way of registering at the polls its

---

[1]See Wyman, op. cit., p. 148.

[2]*New Republic*, 8/43, cited by Wyman, p. 150.

[3]Letter dated 3/8/43, Waldman to Proskauer, AJC, Proskauer papers, Emergency Committee, 1943 file.

dissatisfaction over the failure of the administration to take any effective steps to save the Jews of Europe.[1]

The degree of pressure Proskauer was willing to exert on the administration is demonstrated by a letter dated one day after Schultz expressed the above views. Proskauer wrote to Roosevelt:

Knowing your deep interest in the Jewish situation...I had in mind to ask you for an appointment to discuss certain phases of the situation. It seems to me however a patriotic duty, when you are engaged in matters of transcendent importance, not to urge this request on you at this time.[2]

Stephen Wise signalled his continued support for the Roosevelt administration in his speech to the American Jewish Conference. Wise, who throughout his career had admonished what he called "the assimilationists" of the American Jewish Committee for stressing their American identity at the expense of their Jewish identity, now declared:

This is an American Conference. We are Americans first, last, and all the time. Nothing else that we are, whether by faith or race or fate, qualifies our Americanism. Everything else we are and have deepens, enriches and strengthens, if that can be, our Americanism.[3]

In an apparent attempt to counter the publicity generated by Bergson's rescue conference, Wise gave a statement to the press. Taking note that former President Hoover, and William Randolph Hearst, both Republicans, were supporting the Bergson efforts, he cast the Jewish issues of the day in terms of partisan American politics. The headline suggests that

---

[1] Minutes of 8/10/43 meeting of JEC, YIVO, AJC, Waldman papers, Box 23, JEC, 1942-43 file.

[2] Letter dated 8/11/43, AJC, Proskauer papers, Emergency Committee, 1943 file.

[3] See Lookstein, op. cit., p. 31.

"collaboration" with Hoover and Hearst would "betray Jews." Wise instructed that "the way to save the Jews is to unite the Jewish people and all Americans firmly behind the victory program of President Roosevelt."

Rescue was given a very minor role at the conference. One lone delegate registered his perception that the Jews of America demanded more leadership on this issue than they were getting:

We are told that nothing has to be done, that everything is being done....If we leave this Conference...satisfied merely with a paper resolution about rescue, we will be condemned by the Jews of America.[1]

Approaches to the State Department in the summer of 1943 also point to the difference in the agendas of the Bergson group and that of "official" Jewish groups. In a letter marked "personal" Proskauer wrote to Sam Rosenman, now retired from the New York Supreme Court and serving full-time as a White House aide to Roosevelt with daily access to the President. The subject of the letter was Jewish politics, not rescue. Proskauer's close relationship to Rosenman, who was also a member of the American Jewish Committee, is illustrated by this personal request: "Will you call me sometime tomorrow morning or afternoon at the office when you get a minute."[2]

Secretary of State Hull, in the meantime, responded positively to an appeal by the Bergson group. He wrote to a State Department representative in Ankara, Turkey:

The Department has been informed of the desire of the Emergency Conference to Save the Jewish People of Europe that a representative should be sent to Turkey and that other representatives should be sent to several other places for the purpose of inquiring about practicable steps which might be

---

[1]Cited by Wyman, op. cit., p. 165.

[2]Letter dated 9/16/43, AJC, Proskauer papers, American Jewish Conference, 1943-48 file.

taken in regard to obtaining releases, from Nazi dominated countries.

Hull then passed along the name of a man that had been suggested to him by the Bergson group:

> Representatives of this Conference [to Save the Jewish People of Europe]...requested that an inquiry be directed to you, to which the Department has given its consent, for the purpose of requesting your advice on the question whether a temporary representative would in any way contribute to the extrication of persons in the category mentioned from Balkan countries. The name of Mr. Ira Hirschmann...has been mentioned in this connection.[1]

Hirschmann, the vice-president of Bloomingdale's who wandered into a Hitler rally in Germany in 1933, risked his career by supporting a boycott of German goods by major retailers, and fought on a matter of principle with his friend Fiorello La Guardia, writes that his pent-up emotions "erupted" as news of Nazi atrocities accummulated:

> It was clear that Hitler's unholy crusade against the Jews had been permitted to gain in fury with little or no effort at opposition from the outside world....In our concentration and zeal for killing the enemy, we had lost sight of our obligation to try at least to save the innocent. Where was the heart that had beat for the Belgians, the Chinese, the Armenians. Had it stopped where the Jews were the victims - or was it just broken.

And where did Hirschmann find an outlet for his desire to make a contribution to Jewish rescue?

> Restlessly I searched for advice on the best place to establish a base for the rescue of refugees. Then, in the summer of 1943,

---

[1] Cable dated 9/4/43, PSCP, Reel 2.

someone took me to a meeting of a group called the Emergency Committee to Save the Jewish People of Europe. There I met Mrs. John Gunther and Peter Bergson, who gave me advice on where I could be most effective....Bergson, a resourceful organizer well versed in the ways of the Middle East, told me that Turkey, a neutral country in the confluence of the waterways and rail systems leading toward Palestine, would be the ideal base for rescue operations.[1]

Hirschmann began meeting with State Department personnel and Jewish leaders to prepare himself to be of service.

Yom Kippur, 1943, brought an extra dimension of soul searchng for American Jews. The day before the Day of Atonement, the normal comings and goings of people walking the streets of Washington was altered by the sight of over four hundred Orthodox rabbis walking solemnly toward the White House. Samuel Margoshes describes the scene in *The Day* :

...the procession of the Orthodox Rabbis as it moved through the streets of the capital...Rabbis wearing their chassidic garb of long silk and gabardines and round plush hats, moved along Pennsylvania Avenue...presented a picture which for its exotic quality was unprecedented even in such a cosmopolitan city as Washington....They watched in wonderment and respect. The traffic stopped, and here and there a burgher removed his hat. I myself saw many a soldier snap to salute....[2]

The view from the White House was quite different. A White House staffer recorded in his diary entry of the day that "The President told us in his bedroom this morning he would not see their delegation." Roosevelt's decision was reinforced by Sam Rosenman who was present:

Judge Rosenman, who with Pa Watson [Roosevelt aide] also was in the bedroom, said the group behind this petition was not representative of the most thoughtful elements in Jewry. Judge

---

[1] Hirschmann, *Caution to the Winds*, op. cit., pp. 127ff.

[2] *The Day*, 10/23/4. An English translation of the yiddish article is in PSCP, Reel 4.

Rosenman said he tried - admittedly without success - to keep the horde from storming Washington. Said the leading Jews of his acquaintance opposed this march on the Capital.[1]

When the Rabbis, who had joined forces with Bergson to organize the petition to the President, arrived at the White House, Rabbi Eliezer Silver read a rescue memorandum in Hebrew and Rabbi Aaron Burack read an english version.[2]

Rosenman's statement to Roosevelt that "leading Jews of his acquaintance" opposed the Rabbi's march, was confirmed by an editorial in Wise's *Opinion:*

> They who set out to be leaders must bear themselves with a sense of responsibility. There is such a thing as the dignity of a people. It must not be ignored. But the stuntists who arranged the orthodox rabbinical parade are not so much concerned with the results of their pilgrimage as with the stunt impression which it makes.[3]

Six leading Christian clergymen did not agree with this assessment and sent a letter to 6,000 churches asking that the Sunday following Yom Kippur be designated as a day of prayer:

> We have set aside Sunday, October 10, as a Day of Intercession, when the Christian Churches may lift up their voices to God on HIgh, beseeching Him to ameliorate the lot of these Jewish people....We have chosen a day that follows immediately upon the most solemn Holy Day of the Jewish Calender...to show our compassion for a people so sorely harassed and endlessly persecuted, and to dedicate ourselves to the task long awaiting the Christian Churches - the task of eradicating anti-Semitism....

---

[1]See Lookstein, op. cit., pp. 165-166.

[2]See the account of Rakeffet-Rothkoff, op. cit., p. 220.

[3]*Opinion*, Nov, 1943, cited by Medoff, op. cit., p. 131.

The six Christian leaders went beyond a call for prayer to ask for action:

Will not the members of your congregation form themselves into a committee to work with the Emergency Committee to Save the Jewish People.[1]

Orthodox Jewish leaders tried to get Proskauer to join them in rescue efforts after he withdrew his American Jewish Committee from the American Jewish Conference in the fall of 1943, shortly after it was born. Jacob Rosenheim, president of *Agudas Israel*, wrote to Proskauer:

Rumors are now spreading that the Zionists, angered by your withdrawal, wish to dissolve the Joint Emergency Council, the only remaining common platform of united work for the rescue of European Jewry...if these rumors are founded, it would perhaps be possible to organize some united rescue work....[2]

The notion that the Zionists were angry is confirmed by this letter from Proskauer to Sam Rosenman:

Our withdrawal from the conference has been followed by a good deal of intemperate abuse, not unexpected, but still not pleasant. I have the feeling that the time has come when I ought to explain to the President the Jewish picture from the point of view of our Committee....I would very much like to talk with you about the desireability of asking the President for an interview....[3]

The reason Proskauer withdrew from cooperation with Wise in the American Jewish Conference had to do with disagreement

---

[1] Document dated 10/10/43, PSCP, Reel 4.

[2] Letter dated 10/28/43, YIVO, AJC Waldman papers, Box 23, JEC 1942-43 file.

[3] Letter dated 10/27/43, AJC, Proskauer papers, Emergency Committee 1943 file.

over political Zionism, not rescue, and it was the opposition of the American Jewish Committee to a Jewish state that Proskauer wished to take up with Roosevelt.

The Bergson group kept up the pressure for rescue with a public tribute to Sweden and Denmark following their cooperation in getting eight thousand Jews out of Denmark. Advertisements in the *New York Times* and papers across the nation hailed this action as evidence that something could in fact be done. Over 3,000 people jammed Carnegie Hall and approximately twice that number were turned away. Henrik de Kauffman, an official from Denmark, addressed the gathering:

> The Danes of Jewish race form an integral part of the Danish people....Denmark would not have been what it is without them. When it became known in Copenhagen that the Nazi invaders contemplated to eliminate the Danish Jews, all Danes acted as any decent person would have done....[1]

And from Leon Henderson, a former member of the Roosevelt adminstration, came a forceful and direct condemnation of Roosevelt and the Allies:

> The Allied Governments, in the face of a clear call of moral duty, have been guilty of cowardice....I say in all earnestness that Sweden and Denmark have proven the tragedy of Allied judgement. At a time when the ideals for which we fight need illumination and fortification, these two brave countries have shown America the path of leadership.

Henderson addressed the often used excuse that rescue operations would hamper the war effort:

> We hear vague statements of "military expediency." This is an abuse of the rightful use of military expediency....I know, far better than many of you, that the Allies have engaged in many a bold, risky and concealed venture to handle special situations of high political and strategic importance. But I know of none which

---

[1] Document dated 10/31/43, PSCP, Reel 1.

are more justifiable than specific aid which the Allied Governments might extend to European Jews.[1]

On November 11, 1943, an historic resolution was introduced concurrently in the Senate and House of Representatives, the culmination of persistent efforts by the Bergson group. The Resolution reads as follows:

A RESOLUTION DEMANDING THE CREATION OF AN AGENCY TO SAVE THE JEWISH PEOPLE OF EUROPE INTRODUCED IN THE SENATE

WHEREAS the Congress of the United States adopted, on March 10th, 1943, a concurrent resolution condemning Germany's "mass murder of Jewish men, women, and children": and

WHEREAS this mass murder has already resulted in the extermination of nearly two million human beings- constituting about thirty percent of the total Jewish population in Europe; and

WHEREAS the American tradition of justice and humanity dictates that all possible means be employed to save the surviving Jews of Europe; and

WHEREAS the Nazis have uprooted the remaining four million Jews rendering them destitute and homeless; and

WHEREAS a specific plan pointing towards feasible methods of staying this mass murder and of saving the remnants of these people has been elaborated by a group of recognized experts; and

WHEREAS the fate of these people constitutes a specific and urgent problem;

NOW THEREFORE, Be it Resolved that the Senate of the United States recommmends and favors the immediate creation by the President of an Agency to Save the Jewish People of Europe, to function under the guidance of the Secretary of State. Said Agency to be composed of military, economic and diplomatic experts, and given full authority to determine and effectuate a realistic and stern policy of action to save the lives and preserve the dignity of the ancient Jewish people of Europe whom Nazi Germany has marked for extinction; and BE IT FURTHER RESOLVED that the Senate of the United States favors

---

[1] Document dated 11/1/43, PSCP, Reel 11.

the development of the Agency to Save the Jewish People of Europe into an United Nations Agency.[1]

Within a week, the Bergson group had obtained a strong endorsement from eight of the most influential leading Christian clergymen in the country: the Rt. Rev. William T. Manning, Bishop of New York, Protestant Episcopal Church; Archbishop Athenagoras, Greek Orthodox Archdiocese of North and South America; Dr. Henry Sloane Coffin, Moderator of the General Assembly, Protestant Church, and President of the Union Theological Seminary; Bishop William J. McConnell, Resident Bishop of the Methodist Church; the Rt. Rev. Thomas J. Heistand, Bishop of Harrisburg, Pa. Protestant Episcopal Church; Dr. Angus Dun, Dean of Protestant Episcopal Theological College, Cambridge, MA.; Dr. Russell Stafford, Minister of the Old South Church, Boston; and Dr. Charles E. Park, Minister of the First Church, Boston. These men urged passage of the Senate resolution:

As Christians and as Americans, we urge the passage of the Senate Resolution proposing the creation of a special governmental commission to find ways and means to save the surviving Jewish people of Europe.

The strongly worded manifesto closed with this message:

If the will be strong enough and the heart be stout enough, then efforts to rescue will be made and will succeed. If we remain feeble and complacent, then death alone will have its way. Let no possible sanctuary be closed, whether in America or elsewhere. Let each door of refuge be opened and kept open. This is the Christian way.[2]

The introduction of this legislation brought into sharp focus the different approaches to the tragic era of Nazi rule.

---

[1] Document dated 4/10/43, PSCP, Reel 4.

[2] Ibid.

Historians have differed over the impact of the Bergson group, the interest of American Jews in their activites or in any rescue activities at all, and whether or not any effective action was possible given the context of the times. Nowhere are these issues more clearly elucidated than in the months of November and December, 1943. It is to this period that we now turn.

Chapter X

The Gillette-Rogers Bill

When Proskauer withdrew the American Jewish Committee from the American Jewish Conference, in October, 1943, all pretense of cooperation between Proskauer and Wise was over. The American Jewish Committee drew up a summary of their position, stating: "There is sharp division among American Jews on the Zionist issue. The Zionists have been thoroughly organized and have used extensive propaganda. The non-Zionists are for the most part unorganized."[1]

While this split demonstrates the disunity of the two Jewish organizations on the question of Zionism, the issue of a Jewish state was a post-war issue. In November, 1943, rescue was a *now* issue.

The news that millions of Jews had already been killed and that the massacre was continuing daily was known to everyone. While Proskauer and Wise sent private memos to the State Department clearly stating they thought rescue of Jews was possible without disrupting the war effort, in public they supported the Roosevelt administration's steadfast assertion that nothing could be done except winning the war.

It has already been noted that Senator Edwin Johnson of Colorado, an early backer of the Bergson efforts did not come from a state with a significant Jewish constituency. This was also true of Senator Guy Gillette who, from the time he joined the Committee for a Jewish Army, fought consistently for Jewish rescue.

Gillette was born ih Cherokee, Iowa. He was a local prosecuting attorney from 1907-1909, and he served in the Iowa state senate from 1912-1916. The future senator

---

[1] Report dated 11/8/43, AJC, Proskauer papers, Emergency Committee, 1943 file.

experienced the realities of war as a sergeant in the Spanish-American War and as an infantry captain in World War I. In 1932, Gillette was elected to Congress and, with the death of Iowa's Senator Louis Murphy in 1936, he was elected to complete that term. In 1938, he was reelected to a full six-year term.

Gillette's counterpart in the House of Representatives was Will Rogers, Jr., the son of the famous raconteur. In contrast to Gillette's long experience, Rogers was in his first term in Congress when he joined in sponsoring a resolution to create a special agency to rescue European Jews. An article in the *Chicago Sun Times* took note of the new congressman:

> A young man worth watching is Congressman Will Rogers, Jr. Coming out of the Army into Congress where he has been more active and apparently more effective than a maiden congressman is expected to be, Will Rogers, Jr. has bright signs of being the sort of leader young men need on the home front during and after the war....

The article highlighted Rogers' own minority background as a factor in his support for rescue:

> Will Rogers. Jr. is active in trying to save the Jewish people of Europe. That also is a job which politicians of our own and other Allied countries have been none too eager to tackle boldly. It is significant that Will Rogers, Jr., with American Indian blood in his veins, gets in and pitches for another minority. His ancestors became a minority in their own land and were almost exterminated.

The fact that his efforts embroiled him in controversy did not deter Rogers, nor, as the article noted, did he hesitate to speak candidly with those American Jews he felt were missing the point:

> This job he has undertaken will keep him in hot water, but he doesn't seeem to mind. He bluntly tells American Jews that it is foolish to be quarreling about what to do with people who aren't

yet sure they'll be alive in a few months. The intra-Jewish arguments about a JEWISH ARMY and about PALESTINE makes Jews look no better than American Gentiles who wrangle among themselves....[1]

There was wide-spread coverage of the rescue resolution in both the general press and the Jewish press. The Chicago *Herald-American* editorialized:

One of the greatest calamities to the modern world, one of the greatest crimes of all times, is the attempted extermination of the Jews by Hitler and his savage hordes. This is not a Christian or a Jewish question....Peter Bergson, a co-chairman of the Emergency Committee to Save the Jewish People of Europe, declared before the House Foreign Affairs Committee that "1,000,000 additional Jews would be murdered by the Nazis before an armistice"....What is required now is action.[2]

In New York, the *Herald-Tribune* issued a "call for leadership."

A resolution with bipartisan sponsorship has been introduced in both Houses of Congress recommending that the President create a commission [for rescue]....If anything can be done to stop the Nazi murder of a people, surely the American people must be willing to take the lead in doing so. Certain it is that nothing will be accomplished to save Nazi Europe's surviving Jews from methodical extermination by doing nothing.[3]

In the nation's capital, the influential *Washington Post* also gave its editorial support:

---

[1]*Chicago Sun Times,* 11/19/43.

[2]*Chicago Herald-American,* 11/12/43.

[3]*New York Herald-Tribune,* 12/1/43.

It is a rare occurrence in legislative history for a bill or a resolution introduced in either House of Congress to have multiple sponsorship and the backing of both parties. This however is precisely what happened in the case of the resolution...urging the creation of a commission to save the surviving Jewish people of Europe....[1]

In the House, the legislation went to the House Foreign Affairs Committee headed, ironically enough, by Sol Bloom, who had represented the Roosevelt administration at the Bermuda conference on refugees. A blunt editorial was aired over a New York radio station criticizing the lack of strong support by Jewish organizations for the rescue legislation:

Large Jewish organizations are said to be identified with the attitude of Congressman Bloom in opposing any action by the United States Government to help rescue their compatriots. However, thus far no spokesman for their group has ventured to explain openly why the policy of rescue is opposed....[2]

While no open opposition to the bill had been announced by Jewish groups, the perception was widespread that it was being opposed. Wise insisted that his agenda be attached to the proposal and attacked the Bergson group who was behind the legislation. Gillette recalled a visit to his office by Wise and a few of his colleagues prior to hearings on the bill:

None of these gentlemen seemed to be enthusiastic for the passage of the resolution and the tenor of the conversation seemed to suggest their belief that the action as proposed by the resolution was not a wise step to take, although they professed very strong interest in everything that would look to the saving of the remnant of the Jewish people....[3]

---

[1] *Washington Post*, 11/24/43.

[2] See Medoff, op. cit., pp. 134-135.

[3] Ibid., p. 132.

The *Daily Jewish Courier*, a Yiddish newspaper, pointed to the problem of mixing the issues of rescue and Zionism:

Dr. Stephen Wise has declared before the House Foreign Affairs Committee that the resolution of both Houses of Congress to create an American commission to save the Jewish people of Europe is far insufficient....The Emergency Committee to Save the Jewish People of Europe has made a public statement that the resolution in Congress has nothing to do with political questions about Palestine or other territories....This is to say that Dr. Wise has confused several issues...before anything else, the Jews must be rescued from annihilation....[1]

A Cincinnati Jewish newspaper also criticized Wise's testimony:

It seems to us that Dr. Stephen S. Wise indulged in too much fault finding when he appeared last week before the House Foreign Affairs Committee....It seems to us that it was hardly the place and time for Dr. Wise to denounce "rashly written resolutions"....We think many of the statements made by Dr. Wise before that Committee were "rash."

While distancing itself somewhat from the Bergson group, the article praised their initiative:

We hold no brief for the initiators of the Committee for a Jewish Army and the Emergency Committee to Save the Jewish people of Europe, but we bless them for their energy and initiative which has made us realize how little we have actually done toward saving our brethren from Hitler's torture chambers.[2]

---

[1] *Daily Jewish Courier*, 12/7/43. An English translation of this article as well as copies of much of the press coverage of this legislation can be found in Reel 4, PSCP.

[2] *Every Friday*, 12/10/43.

From England came this observation from a column by a Phineas J. Biron released to Anglo-Jewish papers by Seven-Arts Syndicate, Dec 10, 1943:

> We still don't understand why some top-notch Zionist leaders are opposed to the resolution sponsored in Congress by the Emergency Committee to Save European Jewry....The resolution calls for a special government commission to look into the status of Jewish refugees in Europe....Even if the Zionists don't like some of the leaders of the Emergency Conference, it seems to us that it's bad policy to fight a measure that can only alleviate the plight of European Jewry.[1]

An article in *The Day*, noted that the news of Jewish mass murders had aroused "the conscience of many sincere people of the non-Jewish world." The author of the article, Dr. I. Brutskus, praised the efforts of the Bergson group, and pointed to the "deplorable dispute" in the Foreign Affairs Committee, criticizing the "many Jews who have quietly intrigued in political circles against this proposition."[2]

Support came from many parts of the country. From a B'nai B'rith publication in California - "The Jewish citizens of America look with great eagerness to our Congress for immediate action on this resolution. We see in it the only hope of saving tens of thousands of human beings..."[3] from Detroit: "write to your Congressman and Senators and ask them to vote for this bill"....[4] and from St. Louis: "What can be done for the surviving Jews of Europe...this measure in behalf of the most ferociously treated of all Hitler's victims should have an early hearing by both houses."[5]

Inside the commmittee hearing room, Jews and non-Jews were bringing pressure on Congressman Bloom and his colleagues to act. Mayor La Guardia of New York told Bloom

---

[1] Document dated 12/19/43, Reel 4, PSCP.

[2] *The Day*, 12/10/43, ibid.

[3] *B'nai B'rith Messenger*, Los Angeles, 11/12/43.

[4] *Jewish Chronicle*, 11/19/43.

[5] *St. Louis, Post-Dispatch*, 12/18/43.

pointedly that "we must be ready to do as much as we ask other countries to do. Let us be perfectly frank about that." Bloom professed not to understand: "What do you mean by that?" La Guardia responded:

> I mean this, that if we say here [to other countries], "We find it necessary that you open your doors and give asylum to a number of these oppressed peoples," whoever speaks for the Government will be able to look them in the eyes and say, "we will do as much".....An adverse vote in the House would be misconstrued and misrepresented and be fatal....[1]

Dean Alfange, of the American Labor Party testified that he thought public pressure could be brought on Britain, only to be asked by one congressman if that would "create any enthusiasm among the Arabs," Alfange responded: "I do not know. I would not care. It takes precedence over the question of politics." The congressman then wanted to know if Alfange was Jewish and was informed that Alfange was a member of the Greek Orthodox Church.[2]

William Ziff, author of *The Rape of Palestine* reminded the committee of the conclusions of the July Conference to Save the Jews of Europe:

> In July of this year a conference of experts was convened in New York City to study the technical problems involved if such an operation [rescue] were undertaken. Among them were high ranking military and naval officers, transportation executives, economic planners, statesmen and churchmen of all denominations....Their unanimous opinion was that there were many effective measures which should and could be undertaken. Moreover they stated their convictions that the steps advocated would not hinder the war effort.

---

[1]This quote and the following quotes are from the committee testimony which is reproduced in transcript form in *Problems of World War II and Its Aftermath,* part 2, pp. 147-148. (Washington: United States Government Printing Office, 1976). This is volume II of selected executive session hearings of the House Committee on International Relations, 1943-1950.

[2]Ibid., p. 23.

Ziff put moral and ethical considerations above practical ones:

> The question is not alone whether we shall be able to do anything practical in regard to saving these peope...for if we do not offer at least a gesture of moral and physical support, we shall be guilty of condoning by our silence the vilest and most despicable crime known to the pages of our history....It is hopeless to debate whether anything can be done about this situation. How does one know what can be done unless an effort is made to do it?[1]

Congressman Clark Baldwin, who with Rogers was a co-sponsor of the House bill, stressed to the committee:

> One of my purposes in introducing this resolution, along with Mr. Rogers, was to demonstrate that on this important party matter there was no party line and no religious line. It is an emergency matter. The permanent solution I do not think is the concern of thie committee at this time and should not be brought up.[2]

The latter statement was likely aimed at the attempts by Wise to attach to the resolution the issue of post-war planning in Palestine.

When Bergson was sworn in as a witness, Chairman Bloom interrupted him in the middle of his opening statement. Bloom later referred to the Intergovernmental Committee he had been influential in setting up at the Evian Conference in 1938.

> Chairman Bloom: Mr. Bergson, is it not a fact that the Intergovernmental Committee that has been functioning now [is] doing just the same work?

---

[1] Ibid., p. 45.

[2] Ibid., p. 73.

Mr. Bergson: Mr. Chairman...that is what I termed before a tragic misunderstanding. There is a difference of a full 100 percent. There is no similarity and very little connection....

Bloom interrupted to give his view of the Intergovernmental Gommittee:

Chairman Bloom: The Intergovernmental Committee, functioning today in London, with a personal representative sent over by the President...is functioning today on those things that we are trying to do here to save the Jews and other refugees throughout the world; is that not a fact?

Mr. Bergson: No, sir, very definitely no, and I want to clarify my statement.

Chairman Bloom: Please do it briefly.

Mr. Bergson: I say that not only is there no similarity, there is contradiction. The Intergovernmmental Committee on Refugees, in order to fulfill a good job, has to encourage, and rightly so, the people of Bulgaria or the people of Poland to stay in Poland....They are naturally making it very tough, and again I say rightly so, for the people of occupied Europe to leave Europe...as far as Jews are concerned, [Bloom again interrupts]

Chairman Bloom: You have answered that. Now, how many people have we taken out of Spain? Do you know?

Mr. Bergson: Mr. Chairman, I am interested in the people in Warsaw, not in Spain. As I said before, we are completely disinterested in people who are not in enemy-occupied territory, because these people are saved. But we are interested in saving the people whose lives are threatened.

Chairman Bloom: You can say the Intergovernmental Committee has not the authority to act upon that?

Mr. Bergson: I can say that the Intergovernmental Committee is interested in the Poles staying in Poland and the Czechs staying in Czechoslovakia. We are interested in having the Jews separated and taken out, because the Poles are going to live there. The Germans are not killing 30 million Poles, but they are killing 4 million Jews.[1]

Commenting on Bloom's handling of the hearings, the *Forward* remarked that "there have been moments when the hearings

---

[1]Ibid., pp. 110-111.

turned into a heated debate between Congressman Bloom and the witnesses," then added:

> It is really difficult to understand why Congressman Bloom is so vitally interested in digging up arguments against the resolution. Another of his arguments was that among the Jews themselves, among Jewish organizations there is no unanimity as to what constitutes the best plan to save the Jews. Is this then an argument why Congressman Bloom should not aid the plan which has been submitted to Congress?[1]

Paradoxically, perhaps the biggest boost the rescue legislation received was from the hostile testimony of Breckinridge Long. Long, an Assistant Secretary of State, personifies for many a bigoted resistance to rescue that emanated from the State Department. We get this profile of Long from Roosevelt biographer Kenneth Davis:

> Breckinridge Long, whose mother was of the politcally famous Breckenridge family of Kentucky and whose father was of the only somewhat less politically famous Longs of Virginia, had been Roosevelt's ambassador to Italy from 1933 to 1936. He was married to the very wealthy granddaughter of Francis Preston Blair, Jr.; the Blair family had been a major power, first in Democratic politics, then in Republican, before and during the Civil War.[2]

Long appeared before the committee and grossly distorted State Department statistics about immigration into the United States. He was called on his deceit from several quarters. On December 21, the *Washington Post* wrote:

> Assistant Secretary of State Long, in testimony before the House Foreign Affairs Committee, declared that "everything humanly possible" was being done to rescue persecuted

---

[1] *The Forward,* 11/26/43.

[2] Davis, *Into the Storm,* op. cit., p. 291.

Europeans....Long's statement was flatly contradicted by Justice Department immigration reports, which showed that in the 10 years following Hitler's accession to power in 1933, a total of 266,635 persons of German and Austrian origin could have been admitted under immigration quotas. The actual number admitted was less than half this figure - 123,573.[1]

The *New York Post,* on the same day, was just as blunt:

Suave State Department careerist Breckinridge Long appeared before the House Committee to urge that it vote against the Resolution [for a rescue agency]. Persuasive Mr. Long threw many figures at the committee and made it seem as though everything that could humanly be done was already being done. Mr. Long's figures turned out to be full of loopholes - clever, cruel loopholes.[2]

The bitterest response came from the *Jewish Times.* On December 24, 1943, it published an "Open Letter to Sol Bloom":

Dear Congressman Sol Bloom:

I hope all the *Shabbos goyim* will forgive this analogy. You probably still remember from your childhood, Congressman, that a *shabbos goy* was a non-Jew who on Saturdays and holidays would perform for a pittance such minor chores as the Jews himself is not permitted to perform on those days....It seems now, on reviewing your actions and utterances for the past few months that your entire prestige in Washington society and in administration circles rest on being a *shabbbos goy* for the State Department and performing certain duties which the administration itself finds distasteful.

---

[1] *Washington Post,* 12/20/43.

[2] *New York Post,* 12/21/43.

The letter took Bloom to task for his role in the failure of the Bermuda Conference, then attacked him for releasing Long's testimony before his commmittee:

This testimony was released by you, Congressman Bloom. You released it without an accompanying statement. Didn't you know what the intent of the statement was? Its intent was not only to kill the resolution, but to create the impression that the United States has done its share, has admitted all the refugees it can admit, that they are practically flooding the country and what more do the Jews want.

After addressing the distortion in the immigration figures that were released, the letter closed with a pointed personal attack:

The traditional *shabbos goy,* Mr. Bloom, was an amiable person, performing useful functions. Not so the *shabbos goy* who is Chairman of the House Foreign Affairs Commmittee. We would not be happy in your place, Mr. Bloom. We would have nightmares; our ears would be split by the cries of all the Jews that have perished since Bermuda; and we would feel blood, Jewish blood on our hands. Blood on YOUR hands, Mr. Bloom.[1]

Meantime, inside the Treasury Department, the activities of Breckinridge Long and the State Deparment were coming under close scrutiny. While the congressional hearings were being held, one of the most incredible dramas in the history of government was unfolding.

On December 18, 1943, Secretary of the Treasury Henry Morgenthau, Jr. met with five of his aides to discuss "this cable, which, I take it, you have all read."[2] The cable in question was from John G. Winant, United States Ambassador to Britain, to the State Department. The subject was rescue of European Jews. John Pehle briefed Morgenthau on the cable, the essence of which was that since any rescue plan might

---

[1] *Jewish Times,* 12/24/43.

[2] Morgenthau papers, Roosevelt Library, Hyde Park, Reel 200, Book 688, p. 2.

involve large numbers of Jews, "therefore, they are not going to go ahead on anything."[1]

Josiah H. DuBois, another key Morgenthau aide, brought the discussion to a head:

> Mr. Secretary, the only question we have in our mind, I think, is the bull has to be taken by the horns in dealing with this Jewish issue, and get this thing out of the State Department into some agency's hands that is willing to deal with it frontally.[2]

There was agreement that Morgenthau should go to Roosevelt, but when one aide suggested going as a private citizen because this was a humanitarian issue, Morgenthau mentioned that his department was involved in licensing currency transactions for rescue. "I want to go as Secretary of the Treasury. Just because I am a Jew, why shouldn't I look after the Jews, or the Catholics, or the Armenians?"[3] Morgenthau was doubtlessly remembering the role of his father who, as United States Ambassador to Turkey during World War I, squarely faced the issue of saving as many Armenians as possible from mass murder at the hands of the Turks.

The group decided that an approach first had to be made to Secretary of State Hull. Morgenthau said:

> I would like to say to Mr. Hull, "After all, if you were a member of the Cabinet in Germany today, you would most likely be in a prison camp, and you would be God knows where," because Mrs. Hull is a Jewess, you know. Did you peple know that?[4]

The subject turns to the possibility of Morgenthau taking with him to see Hull either Roosevelt aide Sam Rosenman or Governor of New York Lehman:

---

[1] Ibid., p. 4.

[2] Ibid., p. 5.

[3] Ibid., p. 6.

[4] Ibid., p. 7.

H.M. Jr: I wonder if it would do any good to take Judge
   Rosenman along?
Mrs. Klotz: I think so.
Mr. Paul: Well, I don't know. I have been told that he is
   generally "hands off" on the sort of question.
Mr. Luxford: How about the Governor?
Mr. Paul: Lehman might.
H.M. Jr: If I am going as Secretary of the Treasury I don't
   think we want to make a Jewish delegation out of this. I
   think we will just go as the Treasury. This is Treasury
   business. We are interested in this.
Mrs. Klotz: Mr, Morgenthau, nobody would do - none of these
   people you mention, when they are put of the spot, will do
   what you will do.[1]

When Morgenthau met with Hull and Breckinridge Long, he
told Long directly of the perception that he was anti-Semitic.
This brought the inevitable denial, but the spotlight was on the
State Department, especially with the uncovering by
Morgenthau's aide, DuBois, of the deliberate suppression by
Long of a cable relevant to the issue of Jewish rescue.[2]

In a secret memorandum, "For Secretary Morgenthau's
Information only," DuBois reported: "Breckinridge Long is
responsible for the attempt to conceal this whole situation
from this Department." He went on to say:

To put it bluntly, Mr. Secretary, it appears that certain
responsible officials of this Government were so fearful that
this Government might act to save the Jews of Europe if the
gruesome facts relating to Hitler's plans to exterminate them
became known, that they not only attempted to suppress the
facts, but, in addition, they used the powers of their official
position to secretly countermand the instructions of the acting

---

[1]Ibid., p. 8.

[2]See Wyman, op. cit., pp. 185-187.

Secretary of State [Sumner Welles] ordering such facts to be reported.[1]

In detailing Long's role in the deceit, the memorandum refers to the "completely misleading nature of the diabolical testimony which he furnished to the House Foreign Affairs Committee on the question of relief to the Jews."[2]

While DuBois was expanding this six-page memorandum into a longer, more detailed indictment of the State Department, he and his colleagues were pressing Morgenthau to go directly to Roosevelt and stop the useless dialogue with the State Department. One aide stressed the power of the President:

Roosevelt has the power to alter the complexion of this whole treatment in Europe if he feels keenly enough that he wishes to do so. England will put obstacles, and there will be other obstacles, but he can do it by himself. And he will never do it by himself - he will never pay any attention to the problem, unless he is brought to the point where he has to make a decision.[3]

A member of Morgenthau's staff met with Harry Shulman who, along with Lillie Schultz, was a key aide to Wise at the American Jewish Congress. The memorandum of the meeting makes clear that, in their efforts to put their stamp on any presidential commission that might be appointed, Shulman and Wise "felt strongly" that the Gillette-Rogers legislation did not provide for the "proper type of commission." Incredibly, with all that was widely known about the British refusal to help at all with Jewish rescue and all that was known about the obstruction in the State Department, Wise was lobbying to leave the issue in their hands:

Dr. Stephen Wise, himself [Shulman], and Dr. Goldmann [Nachum Goldmann of the World Jewish Congress] had recommended that

---

[1]Morgenthau papers, Reel 200, Book 668, pp. 223J-223K.

[2]Ibid. p. 223 "o".

[3]Morgenthau papers, Reel 201, Book 692, pp. 289-290.

the President appoint a committee...which committee would act in conjunction with the British and would implement the decisions of the Intergovernmental Committee.[1]

The memo pointed up the fact that the Gillette-Rogers commission would be "wholly independent of the Intergovernmental Committee" which had been ineffective.[2]

On January 13, 1944, at 11am, there was another meeting in the Treasury Department. In this meeting, Morgenthau's staff tied their efforts to those efforts in the Congress on behalf of the Bergson-backed Gillette-Rogers Bill to create a special government rescue agency. When told that Congressman Bloom was doing "everything he can possibly do to keep that resolution from being reported out of the House Foreign Relations Committee," Morgenthau asked: "Why shouldn't it be?"[3] He was told that Bloom

probably feels that it will be a blow to the Administration to have this thing thrown out onto the Floor of the House and debated on the basis that it will be debated. It wil not be any pleasant thing.[4]

When DuBois handed his memorandum to Morgenthau, assuring him that "this is just to the Secretary...inside the Department - Intra-Treasury report," Morgenthau sardonically remarked: "It has got a nice title, anyway."[5]

The stunning title of the Memorandum was: REPORT TO THE SECRETARY ON THE ACQUIESCENCE OF THIS GOVERNMENT IN THE MURDER OF THE JEWS.

It was decided that Morgenthau would take a few days to master the 18-page document and they would meet for a final

---

[1] Ibid., p. 235.

[2] Ibid., pp. 235-236.

[3] Ibid., p. 198.

[4] Ibid.

[5] Ibid., p. 188.

review. Morgenthau decided to invite Rosenman to the meeting and put in a call to him. The following interchange ensued:

> HM Jr: Now look Sam. Saturday morning at 9:30 the Treasury is having a meeting here in regard to this whole question of refugees.
>
> R: Uh-huh.
>
> HM Jr: And I'm inviting you to come as Assistant to the President. It will take most of the morning.
>
> MR: Uh-huh...Well, now is that wise to have the President, to have the President in it?
>
> HM Jr: Oh, yes, because the chances are the thing will have to go to the President. Don't worry whether it is wise or not until you hear it.
>
> R: Well, there won't be any publicity about that?
>
> HM Jr: There never is from the Treasury.[1]

When Rosenman asked who else would be at the meeting, Morgenthau informed him he had invited Roosevelt advisors Ben Cohen and Oscar Cox. Rosenman was clearly concerned: "Well, I have my reservations...I can see that I can be there with respect to the President. What would Ben be there? Just an individual?" Morgenthau replied pointedly: "No, he is coming from the White House, too."[2]

When Rosenman continued to express reservations, Morgenthau told him: "I don't think you have any conception of how serious this thing is."[3]

Rosenman reluctantly agreed to attend, saying that while he couldn't get there at the beginning of the meeting because he would be in Roosevelt's bedroom, he would get there as soon as he could.

"My God! Sam Rosenman," Morgenthau exclaimed to his staff when he hung up the phone. "Would there be any publicity? Would there be any leaks? He thought the choice of people coming was very bad. He said the President should be kept out of the refugee matter." Morgenthau recalled the time when

---

[1] Ibid., p. 205.

[2] Ibid., pp. 206-207.

[3] Ibid., p. 207.

Rosenman was directed by the President to "get out a joint statement, England and ourselves, causing the Jews all over the world to stop protesting against the Arabs...I finally told him it was a mistake."[1]

Morgenthau thought it added to their difficulties to have Rosenman at the meeting at the Treasury Department, "but it is much better to add to it, because fellows like Ben Cohen...will cut his throat." When Morgenthau was asked if he thought it was a good idea to give Rosenman a copy of the memorandum, he responded:

> No, I think the thing to do is to work on him while he is here, because that kind of a fellow - what you tell him in his own private boudoir merely supplies him with arguments to answer. That kind of mentality can only be pushed and shamed into a position by virtue of group activity....[2]

The report of Josiah DuBois to the Secretary of the Treasury, was a strong indictment of United States Governmmment policy. It began:

> One of the greatest crimes in history, the slaughter of the Jewish people in Europe, is continuing unabated....I am convinced on the basis of the information which is available to me that certain officials in our State Department...have been guilty not only of gross procrastination and willful failure to act, but even of willful attempts to prevent action from being taken to rescue Jews from Hitler.[3]

The report went on to deal with the congressional legislation pressed by the Bergson group:

---

[1] Ibid., p. 210.

[2] Ibid.

[3] Ibid., p. 212.

One of the best summaries of the whole situation is contained in one sentence of a report submitted on December 20, 1943, by the Committee of Foreign Relations of the Senate, recommending the passage of a Resolution (S.R. 203) favoring the appointment of a commission to formulate plans to save the Jews of Europe....The Committee stated: "We have talked; we have sympathized; we have expressed our horror; the time to act is long past due."[1]

DuBois pointed to the restrictions placed on visas as the "most glaring example of the use of the machinery of this government to <u>actually prevent the rescue of Jews</u>" [underscore is in the original document]. There follows an extensive history of the suppression of a cable by the State Department that deliberately covered up their deceit.[2]

Turning to Long's testimony before the House Foreign Relations Committee:

It is unnecessary to go beyond Long's testimony to find many examples of misstatements. His general pious remarks concerning what this Government is doing for the Jews of Europe; his statement concerning the powers and functions of the Intergovernmental Committee on Refugees...have already been publicly criticized as misrepresentations.[3]

The report closed on an emotional note:

If men of the temperament and philosophy of Long continue in control of immigration administration, we may as well take down that plaque from the Statue of Liberty and black out the "lamp beside the golden door."[4]

---

[1]Ibid., p. 216.

[2]For an excellent presentation of this issue see Wyman, op. cit., pp. 178-187.

[3]Morgenthau papers, Reel 201, Book 692, p. 227.

[4]Ibid., p. 229.

On January 15, 1944, at 9:30 a.m., the crucial meeting to review strategy took place at the Treasury Department. Rosenman did not come to the meeting, but Ben Cohen and Oscar Cox, Roosevelt advisors, were present. Cox reviewed the legislation in the Congress commenting that Sol Bloom, the House committee chairman, "feels that a large part of this is direct personal criticism of what he did as the American delegate to the Bermuda Conference."[1] Despite this, Cox pointed out that Bloom had no taste for a floor fight:

> Now Bloom, himself...feels it would be a problem to have the full debate both on the Floors of the Senate and the House, because he doesn't think he could hold the resolution in the House Committee, and it would also be a direct attack on the Administration, including the President, for having failed to act in this kind of an important situation....[2]

Cox proposed that Morgenthau take the memorandum to Secretary of State Hull first, but was opposed by the others. Morgenthau said he would go straight to Roosevelt. He saw the impending action in Congress as his strongest card:

> I personally hate to say this thing, but our strongest out is the imminence of Congress doing something. That is our strongest out. Really, when you get down to the point, there is a boiling pot on the Hill.[3]

This position was echoed by Ben Cohen, who pointed out that the President could use the same argument in dealing with Hull. When one person present suggested that the language of the DuBois memorandum be changed because of the direct charges made against the State Department, Cohen, who Morgenthau had mentioned would "cut [Rosenman's] throat" if there were

---

[1] Morgenthau papers, Reel 201, Box 664, p. 88.

[2] Ibid., pp. 88-89.

[3] Ibid., p. 97.

objections to strong action, reacted by saying: "Those charges will be made, and it is difficult to disprove them...."[1]

The debate about how to approach Roosevelt continued. Finally Morgenthau summed it up, providing an important insight into Roosevelt's decision making style which is in agreement with that given by most Roosevelt observers:

It isn't a question of the force with which you present it; it is a question of giving him the facts and his own chemical reaction. You just don't know what his own chemical reaction will be. I have been up against him on so many tough propositions, and I never know how he is going to react. Some times he has been very gentle and very considerate, and other times he just veers away. I mean, the first time I was down there I went through the most embarrassing thing of my life. He wanted to fire Miller from the Federal Reserve Board. He invited Miller in...I had to sit there for one hour while he tried to fire Miller. He kept saying, "Isn't that so, Henry? Isn't that so, Henry?" He finally fired him from the Federal Reserve.[2]

After the meeting, Morgenthau had Rosenman's office notified that the meeting was over. Rosenman phoned and asked if there was anything Morgenthau wanted to tell him. Morgenthau suggested he talk to Ben Cohen. The following uncomfortable dialogue ensued:

HM Jr: I'm sorry you weren't here.
R: Well, I - I just couldn't help it. there were a couple of things I had to see him about and we didn't get in, see?
HM Jr: Well, Ben has all the facts.
R: Yeah, he - I'm worried about the boss really because he - I think - I don't know whether the grippe leaves you as weak as he sounds, or whether - I know he is postponing doing a lot of things because he doesn't feel up to it.
HM Jr: Yeah.
R: And I don't like it. He is not seriously sick, but it leaves you damn weak.

---

[1]Ibid., p. 99.

[2]Ibid., p. 108.

HM Jr: Yeah.

R: And there are a lot of things have, have to be done.

HM Jr: Yeah - well, that's too bad. All right then.[1]

We are left to wonder if, even at this late date, Rosenman wanted Morgenthau to call off his plan to meet with Roosevelt. The meeting took place the following day, January 16, 1944, at 12:45. Present were the President, Morgenthau and two of his aides. Morgenthau told Roosevelt of the State Department deceit and asked John Pehle to provide more details. Roosevelt defended Breckinridge Long saying he had been upset when a list of Jewish people given to him by Rabbi Wise were allowed into the United States, "many of whom turned out to be bad people."[2] Morgenthau reminded Roosevelt that at a Cabinet meeting it had been indicated that only three Jews entering the United States during the war had turned out to be undesirable.

On the evening of the same day, at the home of Edward R. Stettinius, who was Undersecretary of State and would soon replace Hull as Secretary of State, Morgenthau recounted the actions of Breckinridge Long. Stettinius had no better opinion of Long:

...he said he was not surprised about Breckinridge Long since Long had fallen down just as badly and in an equally shocking way in the handling of the exchange of prisoners. Stettinius was very frank in his views on Long's failures and pointed out that in the reorganization of the State Department which he had worked out, the only remaining function assigned to Breckinridge Long is "Congressional Relations."[3]

On January 22, 1944, two days before the Gillette-Rogers Bill was scheduled to go to the Senate Floor, President Roosevelt issued an executive order creating the War Refugee Board, stating that the director would be John Pehle, Assistant to the Secretary of the Treasury.

---

[1] Ibid., p. 128.

[2] Memorandum of January 16, 1944, meeting, ibid., pp. 190-192.

[3] Ibid., pp. 191-192.

The *Washington Post* took note of "the industrious spadework done by the Emergency Committee to Save the Jewish People of Europe" and commented that "the committee is likewise entitled to credit for the President's forehanded move."[1] The *Christian Science Monitor* reported: "The Pesident's move is the outcome of pressure brought to bear by the Emergency Committee to Save the Jewish People of Europe...."[2]

Wendell Wilkie, who lost to Roosevelt in the race for the Presidency, wired Bergson:

On July 22, in a message to the Emergency Conference to Save the Jews of Europe, I urged the creation of a United Nations Agency in order to provide tangible evidence of hope and aid to the embattled victims of Hitler's ruthlessness. The justice and merit of the cause which your committee is seeking to accomplish has resulted in the formation of such a commission.[3]

A day later, Peter Bergson received a telegram from Harold Ickes, Secretary of the Interior: "I think all of the officers and members of the Emergency Committee to Save the Jewish People of Europe should feel gratified by the presidential order creating an agency with authority to inaugurate a program of action to rescue the victims of Nazi barbarism. This committee has kept itself free from collateral entanglements and has concentrated on the creation of an official agency to do this job."[4]

Ickes had fought six years earlier to establish a plan under which Jewish refugees would be brought to Alaska, a plan which could have saved thousands of lives. His efforts were unsuccessful, and he doubtlessly remembered that he had encountered the opposition of Stephen Wise and other Jewish leaders. In December, 1943, Ickes had received this letter from Wise:

---

[1] *Washington Post*, 1/25/44.

[2] *Christian Science Monitor*, 1/24/44.

[3] Letter dated 1/25/44, PSCP, Reel 4.

[4] Telegram dated 1/26/44, PSCP, Reel 4.

I was very sorry to note, as were others among your friends, that you had accepted the chairmanship of the Washington Division of the Committee to Rescue European Jews....I am under the inexorable necessity of saying to you that the time will come and come soon when you will find it necessary to withdraw from this irresponsible group which exists and obtains funds through being permitted to use the names of non-Jews like yourself....why tie up with an organization which talks about saving Jews, gets a great deal of money for saving them, but, in my judgement, has not done a thing which may result in the saving of a single Jew.[1]

There is no record of a written reply from Ickes to Wise, but we have this reference to the exchange of letters between the two men:

Rabbi Wise has gone completely haywire after the passage of the Resolution by the Foreign Relations Committee of the Senate....Wise wrote to several people, including our new Honorary Chairman, Secretary Ickes, asking them to resign because we were using their names only to collect money. Ickes did not resign. I hear he replied to the rabbi and that his reply was a literary gem....[2]

At the height of the feverish activity to pass the Gillette-Rogers legislation, Wise had indeed launched a public attack on the Bergson group. Beginning in March, 1943 with the Hecht pageant and the July 1943, conference in New York, the Bergson group had captured the initiative and headlines. This was followed by the Gillette-Rogers bill. Then Proskauer led his American Jewish Committee out of the American Jewish Conference in October. The *Vaad Hatzala* joined with Bergson in the dramatic Rabbi's march on the White House. Wise's efforts to consolidate Jewish organizations under his control were dissolving.

---

[1]Letter dated 12/27/43, PSCP, Reel 1.

[2]Letter dated 1/11/44, ibid. This letter was written to Arieh Ben Eliezer of the Emergency Committee to Save the Jewish People of Europe, but the name of the signee is unclear.

At the end of December, the American Jewish Conference released a formal statement criticizing the Bergson group:

The American Jewish Conference today identified the Emergency Committe to Save the Jewish People of Europe as one of a "series of fronts" whose leaders had constantly asssumed to speak for the Jewish people in this country without having or endeavoring to secure a mandate from any constituency and whose activities had caused discord, resulting frequently in a disservice to the cause they had assumed to represent....Instead of cooperating with established and recognized national Jewish agencies, they have entered into competition and sought to undermine them. They have conjured up the illusion of activity by press agentry, financed by the appeals for contributions invariably accompanying their advertisements.[1]

This press release by the American Jewish Conference did not achieve the desired results. The *New York Post* editorialized:

We want to rescue as many as possible of the three million Jews still alive in Hitlerian Europe. Moreover, we believe most people in this country would like to do that - or help do it. And so we hate to see such displays of factional spleen as the American Jewish Conference's attack on the Emergency Committee to Save the Jewish People of Europe. The Conference is an important body, but it contributes nothing but dissension when it takes the attitude that it alone can speak with authority for all those who want to get on with the great task at hand. Those of us who think the imminent destruction of three million innocent and helpless human beings was a subject worthy of mention in the Moscow or Teheran Declarations do not propose to keep quiet because the State Department and the American Jewish Conference tell us to hush up.[2]

---

[1]Press release dated 1/26/43, PSCP, Reel 4.

[2]*New York Post*, 1/3/44.

Rabbi Eliezer Silver, of the *Vaad Hatzala,* condemned the statement by the American Jewish Conference and called for support of the Bergson efforts.[1] Senator Gillette wrote to one Jewish leader:

> I regret very much that there has developed confusion and dissension among our citizens of Jewish ancestry....The problem to be solved is big enough for all Jewish people and non-Jewish people to solve without creating dissension among them and without bickering as to whether this organization or that organization shall have precedence or credit for such work as is accomplished....[2]

The monthly publication of the Reconstructionist movement also responded to the attack by the American Jewish Conference, commenting: "the Emergency Committe to Save the Jewish People of Europe...filled a vacuum created by many years of ineffective activity on the part of Zionist bodies and philanthropic organizations." [3]

While the American Jewish Committee had withdrawn from the American Jewish Conference, still uniting them with the American Jewish Congress was the issue of Peter Bergson. An internal State Department memorandum details a visit from Morris Waldman, executive director of the American Jewish Committee, to Wallace Murray, director of the Divison of Near Eastern Affairs:

> [Waldman] inquired whether there was not some way in which the Department could instigate an investigation of Mr. Bergson with a view to curtailing his stay in the United States. He expressed the opinion that upon investigation the Department

---

[1]See Lookstein, op. cit., p. 178.

[2]Letter date 1/13/44, PSCP Reel 1.

[3]*Reconstructionist,* 1/21/44, cited by Lookstein, op. cit., p. 177.

would find that many of Mr. Bergson's activities were little better than racketeering....[1]

But Waldman's conversation with the State Department did not stop with the Bergson group, as the following section of the memorandum indicates:

Mr. Waldman said that in addition to such elements in American Jewish Circles as Mr. Bergson's group, another group whose activities were questioned by the American Jewish Committee was the World Jewish Congress, represented in Washington by Dr. Nahum Goldmann. The World Jewish Congress was the brain-child of the American Jewish Congress, and the American Jewish Committee was unalterably opposed on ideological grounds to the concept of a world-wide Jewish organization of this nature....[2]

The head of the Near East Division dutifully passed this memorandum of his meeting with Mr. Waldman on to Breckinridge Long, Edward Stettinius and Cordell Hull, with additional comment:

I think you may be interested in glancing through the attached rather detailed memorandum of a conversation which we recently had with Mr. Morris D. Waldman of the American Jewish Committee regarding Palestine....The American Jewish Commitee which, as you know, includes among its members the most substantial and influential Jewish personages in this country, is not only bitterly opposed to the present aims of the Zionists to establish a Jewish State in Palestine but, for the first time in its history, has now decided to come out in active and emphatic opposition to any such action.[3]

---

[1]Memorandum dated 1/10/44 can be found in PSCP, Reel 3.

[2]Ibid.

[3]Memorandum dated 1/20/44, ibid.

What is most important to note is that in both the long memorandum about the meeting with Waldman and the report from Wallace to his superiors in the State Department, there is no mention of the extermination of European Jewry. While the American Jewish Conference attacked Bergson, and the American Jewish Committee attacked Bergson and the Zionists, the Bergson group continued to attack the problem of rescuing as many European Jews as possible.

For the first time, there was an official United States vehicle for rescue, a vehicle which would provide a framework for the heroic action of men like Ira Hirschmann, Jacob Griffel and Raoul Wallenberg.

Chapter XI

The War Refugee Board

Ira Hirshmann, department store executive, was off to Turkey. A cable to Ambassador Steinhardt in Ankara included specific instructions to HIrschmann. He was being given "diplomatic status" as Acting Special Representative of the War Refugee Board in Turkey. The most significant section of the cable established the primary change in United States policy which occurred as a result of the formation of the War Refugee Board:

In so far as the Trading with the Enemy Act is concerned, the Secretary of the Treasury has vested in the War Refugee Board and its representatives in the field full authority to communicate with enemy territory to carry out the purposes of the Order. The Secretary of the Treasury has also delegated to the War Refugee Board and its representatives the power to authorize any public or private agencies, who may be subject to the provisions of our Trading with the Enemy Act, to communicate with enemy territory for the purpose of carrying out the Order.[1]

The Bergson group worked closely with the War Refugee Board, providing detailed memoranda of possible rescue activities. In February, 1944, Pehle was active in helping get the necessary papers for Eri Jabotinsky, the son of Vladimir Jabotinsky, to go from the United States to Turkey. He was not a representative of the War Refugee Board but of the Committee to Save the Jewish People of Europe.

---

[1]Morgenthau Papers, Reel 203, Book 700, p. 257.

This relationship between the Bergson group and the War Refugee Board was noted in an internal memorandum of the American Jewish Committee which reported: "We learned the other day that the Emergency Committee to Save the Jews of Europe arranged last week a reception in honor of Mr. Pehle. The dinner and reception took place in Washington at the home of Ernst K. Lindley...editor-in-chief of *Newsweek*."

The writer of the memorandum was impressed with the guest list:

Among the prominent guests, were the following: The entire staff of the War Refugee Board; Mrs. Pehle; the Ambassadors of Holland, Greece, Czechoslovakia, Sweden, Switzerland and Poland. There were also present Senator Thomas, Congressman Celler, Congressman Sommers and many other statesmen and politicians.

The memo closed with the suggestion that the American Jewish Committee "ought to be of greater service...than we have been."[1]

Later in 1944, Pehle the director of the War Refugee Board was asked his opinion of the Emergency Committee to Save the Jewish People of Europe. The request for information came from the Executive Director of the President's War Relief Board:

It is, I believe, fair to state that the Emergency Committee has been a singularly forceful "propaganda" group in calling the attention of a large number of American people to the plight of the Jews in Europe. Through various techniques they have not only inspired a general emotional interest, but they have stimulated many energetic and important people to push vigorously for various types of action in behalf of the Jews of Europe. Since the War Refugee Board was created the

---

[1] Internal memorandum, 2/29/44, YIVO, AJC, Waldman Papers, Box 10, file 207.

Emergency Committee has been most prolific in helpful suggestions as to rescue and relief programs....[1]

At the same time, Stephen Wise was embroiled in another controversy, this time with a new Jewish organization. Rabbi Morris Lazeron and other anti-Zionists organized the American Council of Judaism. Among the organizers were two Reform rabbis, Wolsey and Fineshriber, who were the targets of an attack by Wise in his publication, *Opinion:*

These figures, sinister in the measure of their misrepresentation of American Israel, are "servants of the people" who utterly betray their people. There is a name for them....Is Philadelphia Jewry forever to remain corrupt and content? Philadelphia owes it to the honor of its one time giants to neutralize, if not displace, these dwarfs. They are a blot upon the landscape of a fair and even noble history. Honor demands of Philadelphia Jewry and the Congregations which these men technically lead that it formally disown them.[2]

Attempts to get Wise to apologize for his harsh rhetoric were unsuccessful, and the two Philadelphia rabbis filed a formal complaint with the Arbitration Committee of the Central Conference of American Rabbis. Rabbi Emil Leipziger, the chairman of the committee tried to mediate but could not move Wise. As a result of a formal meeting of the committee, Wise was found in violation of the CCAR Code of Ethics and was told that if no retraction were forthcoming he would be "sharply reprimanded for unethical conduct and that the members of the Conference be appraised of this action."[3] Wise backed down and the issue was closed.

As the work of the War Refugee Board went forward, in March 1944, Secretary of Treasury Morgenthau, Secretary of

---

[1]Letter dated 8/9/44, PSCP, Reel 3.

[2]See Miller, Jonathan, "The Rabbinic Involvement in the Formation of the American Council for Judaism," paper for Near Eastern and Judaic Studies Dept., Brandeis University, May 4, 1976.

[3]Ibid.

War Stimson and Secretary of State Stettinius, who had
succeeded Hull, sent Roosevelt a memorandum:

> We submit herewith for your signature a declaration on the Nazi
> extermination of the Jews. At this stage of the war, if we can
> convince the people in Germany, and particularly the satellite
> countries, of the seriousness with which we view this matter,
> we have a chance of saving many of these people from death.[1]

The State Department had its say on the proposal, reminding
the White House that "this Government has a commitment to the
British Government that if it is decided to issue such a
statement, we would notify them in advance so that they could
consider what to do about it."[2]

Roosevelt decided he did not want a declaration, only a
statement. "He further states that there is too much emphasis
on the Jewish situation and thinks it should be redrafted along
more general terms."[3] The job of downgrading the declaration
to a statement and decreasing its emphasis on Jews was given to
Presidential Secretary Steve Early and Sam Rosenman.[4]

When the statement was issued, Wise's *Opinion* was pleased:

> The nation is grateful to the President for his expression of
> moral and spiritual leadership, and irrespective of politics and
> the pettiness of partisanship, all American Jews bless the name
> of him who, the moment peril approached the surviving Jews of
> Hitler's Europe, spoke out on their behalf not only with the
> strength of his great person but with the moral force of a great
> nation to support it.[5]

---

[1] Memorandum dated 3/6/44, PSCP, Reel 3.

[2] Memorandum dated 3/7/44, ibid.

[3] Memorandum dated 3/8/44, ibid.

[4] Ibid.

[5] *Opinion*, 4/44, cited by Lookstein, pp. 191-192.

Another Jewish publication, *Jewish Spectator*, was not as impressed:

> We are bowed down with grief at the tragedy that has overtaken eight hundred thousand Jews in Hungary. No doubt, the expressions of sympathy of our President, speaking in the name of the United Nations, are a welcome and soothing balm. Nevertheless, our hurt is not assuaged for we know with utter and unshakable certainty that at least half of these doomed eight hundred thousand could have been saved had they been given the opportunity of a haven of refuge in the Jewish homeland.[1]

Was this right? Were the 800,000 Jews in Hungary doomed when, on March 19, 1944, the Nazis occupied Hungary? It was late in the war and a German defeat was only a question of time. The Roosevelt message of win-the-war-first was an appealing "out" for weary, discouraged Jews in the United States, but how many of the 800,000 Jews in Hungary would be alive when victory came. What could be done to save them?

The Bergson group was working hard to set up temporary places of refuge for European Jews still alive to be saved. The question of a Jewish state could wait. How many Jews should be allowed into Palestine on a permanent basis could wait. What could not wait was an emergency, temporary plan for getting as many Jews as possible out of harms way. After the war, it could be decided what the permanent solution should be.

John Pehle, the Morgenthau aide now directing the War Refugee Board, sent Stettinius the following memorandum:

> Persuant to your suggestion, the following are my personal views on the position which this Administration should take in discussing with the British the problem of Palestine as a war-time refuge. I suggest that in their own interests, as well as for humanitarian reasons, the British should immediately take the bull by the horns and announce that any Jew escaping from

---

[1] *Jewish Spectator*, 4/44, ibid.

Hitler may be brought into Palestine on a <u>temporary</u> basis. [Underlining in original document].[1]

The initiative for temporary places of refuge was pursued by the Bergson group in the Congress, the same route that helped lead to the establishment of the War Refugee Board itself. In March, 1944, Pehle reported to Morgenthau about an impending resolution in Congress "which will be put on the basis, solely, of admitting Jews in order to save their lives, and which will put the issue on a different plane. There will be a great deal of pressure behind it, which is probably what should have been done in the first place."[2]

The War Refugee Board provided new hope for those who would not give up on rescue. One was Jacob Griffel. Griffel was an Orthodox Jew from Palestine who had helped the Mossad's *Aliyah B* ("illegal" immigration) efforts. His help for bringing out those Jews selected for immigration by the Socialists was not reciprocated. Griffel writes:

In 1944, while the war was going on in Rumania, news reached us that grave discriminations were taking place against religious Jews, mainly Hungarian refugees in Rumania, in regard to emigration on the boats organized by the Jewish Agency.[3]

Griffel's contention is supported by this secret cable from Ira Hirschmann to the Secretary of State:

The Department's telegram of March 20, 1944, No. 221, cites a case which tends to confirm rumors current in Istanbul for some time as well as statements a number of Jewish refugees recently arrived in Turkey made to me that representatives of Jewish Agency give priority to paid-up members of the Zionist Party with respect to exit visas from the Balkans....I have

---

[1]Memorandum dated 3/20/44, PSCP, Reel 3.

[2]Minutes of meeting 3/11/44, Morgenthau papers, Reel #205, Book 709, p. 3.

[3]Friedenson, Joseph, *Dateline: Istanbul* (New York: Mesorah Publications, 1993), pp. 123-124.

taken pains to investigate the accuracy of those rumors and I am now satisfied that we must soon give serious consideration to eliminating cause for any such complaints.[1]

Griffel's rescue work had come to the attention of the *Vaad Hatzala* in the United States, and his activities were greatly enhanced when he was appointed an actual representative of the *Vaad*, with formal ties to the War Refugee Board. Griffel received this telegram from the *Vaad* in April, 1944:

Our *Vaad Hatzala* Emergency Committee ready transmit financial aid for your rescue work....Give us constructive plan of proposed rescue operations and we will supply necessary funds....Contact Isaac Sternbach and Switzerland committee....Contact American Legation receive and follow Legation's instructions and advise us through Legation.[2]

Griffel, who had been working under the restrictions imposed by the Jewish Agency, now had a new license for action. He met with Ira Hirschmann and briefed him on the desperate situation of Jews in Transnistria.[3]

The Jews in Transnistria were the subject of the Rumanian government offer to ransom Jews reported above. As early as March, 1943, the Jewish Telegraphic Agency reported:

Of the more than 200,000 Rumanian Jews who have been deported to the barren stretches of Transnistria only about 75,000 still remain alive, and they are in imminent danger of death....The children - about 5,000 of them - are in the worst condition of all.[4]

---

[1]Dated 3/23/44, Morgenthau papers, Book 713, Reel 206.

[2]Morgenthau papers, Book 713, Reel 202.

[3]Friedenson, op. cit., pp. 61-64.

[4]JTA, 3/10/43.

Now, in April, 1944, Hirschmann was prepared to use his powers under the new War Refugee Board to help rescue as many as possible of these Jewish refugees. He reports what he learned from his briefing:

> Transnistria is in the southwestern part of the Russian Ukraine, bordering Rumania. It is a buffer region and has been the subject of recurring friction between the Russians and Rumanians. During the period of the German drive on Stalingrad and the Baku oil fields, the Rumanians moved in.

The Rumanians began a forced march of Jews from Rumanian territory into Transnistria. Hirshmann describes their fate:

> Upon arriving in Transnistria, the survivors were put to hard labor and beaten without mercy and without reason. The duty and urgency of saving them weighed heavily on the few of us charged with the task of rescue.[1]

Hirschmann set up a meeting with a Rumanian official, Alexander Cretsianu. He descibes the tension he felt awaiting Cretsianu's arrival at their agreed upon meeting place in the house of Red Cross representative, Gilbert Simond:

> In the sitting room in Simond's home, almost hermetically sealed by blinds, there was a grand piano. While waiting I tried to loosen my tension by playing some pages from a Beethoven sonata. My finders trembled; Beethoven suffered. But the soaring spirit of the music served me well at this moment.[2]

Hirschmann presented the following demands to Cretsianu:

---

[1] See Hirschmann, *Life Line*, op. cit., pp. 47ff.

[2] Ibid., p. 51.

We request first that you disband the disease-ridden camp at Transnistria at once....We ask, second, that you release five thousand children from Rumania, that you facilitate their passage to the port of Constanta on the Black Sea, that you provide exit certificates for them; and that you expedite the debarkation of ships which we will provide for these children to go from Constata to Istanbul and then to Haifa, Palestine. Third, we ask you to arrange to have Antonescu issue, without delay, an order which will put an end to all forms of persecution....[1]

The war was going badly for the Nazis and Hirschmann told Cretsianu that positive action now could help rehabilitate Rumania's tarnished image as a Nazi collaborator:

It should not be necessary to offer anything to a Government to have them free their own citizens. However, if you will stop the massacre of your own people, I offer you the good will of the Government and the people of the United States of America. These moves will receive widespread publicity in the United States and will serve as a significant indication of a change in the policy of your Government away from your Nazi collaborators.[2]

The Rumanians closed the death camp in Transnistria, and Hirschmann made good on his promise of a favorable press for Rumania in the United States. On April 13, 1944, the *Washington Post* reported:

First steps toward mass evacuation of refugees from Rumania and Bulgaria have been completed, the Overseas News Agency was told by Ira A. Hirschmann....Hirschmann revealed that Turkey had agreed to passage of 5,000 children to Palestine. He

---

[1]Hirschmann, pp. 49ff.

[2]Ibid., p. 56.

added that negotiations were nearly concluded for a Turkish ship capable of carrying 1,000 children at a trip.[1]

The Zionist Emergency Committee meeting during this time was to a great extent focused on issues other than rescue. Over one-third of the minutes of the meeting of April 17,1944, is devoted to the Bergson group:

> Mr. Israeli referred to the advertisements which the Emergency Committee to Save the Jewish People of Europe have placed in the Yiddish papers recently with the emphasis on the opening of the doors of Palestine to Jewish immigrants....It was the consensus that something should be done to show up the Bergson group and counteract the effect of their activities among the large group of readers of the Yiddish newspapers....Mr. Cruso expressed the opinion that it was time to work out a systematic campaign against the Emergency Committee....[2]

Whether or not it was part of just such a "systematic campaign," in May, 1944, Nachum Goldmann, leader of the World Jewish Congress and a close ally of Stephen Wise, paid a visit to Gordon P. Merriam, Chief of the Near Eastern Division of the State Department. He complained of the "support the Bergson group received" from the War Refugee Board and that John Pehle, the director, had said their efforts "led to the creation of the Board." Goldmann warned of the possibility of the World Jewish Congress publicly denouncing the War Refugee Board if they did not disavow the Bergson group. Goldmann also reported that Pehle had been told by Wise that Bergson was "as equally as great an enemy of the Jews as Hitler, for the reason that his activities could only lead to increased anti-Semitism."[3]

This visit by Goldmann to the State Department is similar in tone to his visit to the British Embassy only five months earlier. There he engaged in a long conversation with Isaiah

---

[1] *Washington Post*, 4/13/44.

[2] Minutes of 1/17/44 meeting, Silver papers, Series I, folder 86.

[3] See Ben-Ami, op. c it., pp. 329-331.

Berlin who was attached to the British Ministry of Information. Berlin's notes of the meeting were sent by a Mr. Hayter of the British Embassy in Washington to the Foreign Office in London. The report, marked "secret," began: "Dr. Goldmann was unusually full of gossip today, even for him." [1]

The long memo touched on a number of subjects, including a visit to Roosevelt by Eugene Meyer, the publisher and editor of the *Washington Post*. Goldmann reported that the President told Meyer:

> The Jews were really too distrustful of his loyalty - he was their traditional friend and would not let them down whatever happened....He begged Meyer to tell the Jewish leaders to continue to put their faith in him....[2]

The conversation between Goldmann and Berlin inevitably got around to Bergson, with Goldmann reporting:

> The President had been much displeased by the March of the Rabbis instigated by the notorious Bergson, and had used language that morning while breakfasting which would have pleased Hitler himself. Could nothing be done to liquidate Bergson? Goldmann said he might get his committee to disavow Bergson.[3]

It was shortly after this that the American Jewish Conference formally released a statement condemning the Bergson group.

Eugene Meyer's *Washington Post* was responsible for the most bizarre attempt of all to discredit the Bergson group. For three days running, October 3-6, the *Post* carried articles condemning the activities of the Bergson group.

The October 3 story was an inteview with Bergson conducted by *Post* reporters Edward F. van der Veen and Gloria Lubar and

---

[1] Report dated, 11/25/43, British Embassy document E-7355, Public Record Office, London.

[2] Ibid.

[3] Ibid.

was headlined: "Bergson Admits $1,000,000 Fund Raised, Vague on its Use."[1]

The problem with the article was that the interview they were reporting was entirely fictitious. When Bergson held a news conference later in the day, he asked the name of one reporter who was quite caustic. The reporter identified himself as Edward F. van der Veen. As Bergson wrote in a letter to *Post* publisher and editor Meyer:

> To the amazement of all the journalists present, I told him that I was very surprised to meet him for the first time at this press conference. And even the man in question seemed embarrassed when I said, "You were supposed to have interviewed me a few days ago and you even quoted me quite profusely in your story of that interview, though I have never seen nor even talked to you."[2]

Bergson's letter takes up each of the allegations in the fictional interview and responds in detail. The *Washington Post* articles essentially repeated every unsubstantiated attack on Bergson by the "official" Jewish organizations.

Fowler Harper, Solicitor of the Roosevelt Department of the Interior, wrote to Meyer:

> I have been deeply concerned over the recent series of attacks in your newspaper on Peter Bergson and the work which he has been doing....In these circumstances, I feel that the apparent irresponsible attack upon Bergson and the implied discrediting of the work of the Washington group in which I and many other local citizens have been engaged is most unfortunate....[3]

On the defensive, the *Post* put on the front page on October 8, next to a story about the death of Wendell Wilkie, a refutation of its own articles. The refutation was written by Samuel

---

[1] *Washington Post*, 10/3/44.

[2] Letter dated 10/10/44, PSCP, Reel 1.

[3] Ibid.

Merlin, Bergson's top associate. He pointed out the remarkable fact that in only 14 months of operation, the Emergency Committee to Save the Jewish People of Europe had indeed raised $423,252.68 with all of it being accounted for in quarterly public statements.[1] Bergson drew no salary from this committee, accepting only one $45 per week salary from one of the committees with which he was associated.

Bergson's detailed letter to Meyer came two days after the *Post* ran Merlin's response on page one. Not satisfied with this response on the part of Meyer, he points out that several misrepresentations in the *Post* articles had been refuted by individuals quoted by them, including Mrs. Louis Brandeis. Bergson pointed out to Meyer: "already in your follow-up stories...there are clear indications, not only of retreat, but also that you yourself do not believe in the scurrilous allegations in the first story." Bergson pressed for a more formal statement, with a threat to make public his detailed letter to Meyer:

Since you have not found it necessary even to acknowledge the letters, telegrams and statements sent to you by Mr. Samuel Merlin, I feel it my duty to tell you that if this letter does not receive your favorable consideration, I shall be compelled to have it given the widest possible circulation, and also to consider taking other steps to protect the advancement of our cause and our good name.[2]

On October 12, 1944, Rose Keene of the Bergson group visited Alexander F. Jones, the Managing Editor of the *Washington Post*. In a memorandum of the meeting she reported him as "very irritated and intolerant as far as any claim, demand or protest made on behalf of Jews." The memo pointed out that Jones' antipathy was not limited to any one Jewish group: "He doesn't give a damn for Rabbi Stephen Wise either. He never gives him any publicity when he comes to town." The memorandum summed up the meeting: "Yet, in general, he was

---

[1] *Washington Post*, 10/8/44.

[2] Bergson letter to Meyer, 10/10/44 , op. cit.

on the defensive, somehow conceding that the stories were unfair."[1]

Meyer backed down and in an editorial on March 13, 1944, the *Washington Post* reported that "a number of good people" had protested the unfairness of the series of articles. Mentioning the "various agencies which are affiliated...through the person of Mr. Peter Bergson," the editorial writer added:

> One of these bodies, indeed, has been praised in our editorial columns. We refer to the Emergency Committee to Save the Jewish People of Europe. This body, under the active leadership of Mr. Bergson, played a great part in developing public and congressional opinion in support of the Gillette resolution, which resulted in the establishment of the War Refugee Board....

The editorial addressed the allegations of misuse of funds, saying: "There appears, likewise, to be no question about the financing of the Emergency Committee and, in point of fact, the other related committees." The editorial ended by refuting the assertion of its articles that the Bergson group was a front for the Irgun, which by now, under the leadership of Menachem Begin, had declared its revolt against the British in Palestine:

> We do not propose to try to trace any tie-up between the Hebrew Committee and the terrorists in Palestine...the American people are not informed on the politics and internecine feuds among the Jews themselves in Palestine. They are likewise not informed of the manifold Zionist organizations....the Bergson group would contend that the previously established organizations have not been persistent and energetic enough in prosecuting the cause of the refugee Jews. The successful campaigning of the Emergency Committee at least to some extent seems to substantiate this contention.[2]

Johan Smertenko, who had many years earlier been associated with Stephen Wise and praised him highly (see

---

[1]Memorandum dated 10/12/44, PSCP, Reel 1.

[2]Memorandum dated 10/13/44, PSCP, ibid.

Chapter II), was now the chairman of the Emergency Committee to Save the Jewish People of Europe. He worked several hours every day throughout 1944 to prod the Roosevelt administration, the International Red Cross, the Vatican, and other agencies to help rescue Hungarian Jewry. When he visited the Joint Distribution Committee to try to repair some of the damage done by the systematic smear campaign into which the JDC had been drawn, he received a sympathetic hearing. JDC official Joseph Hyman, received this report from one of his colleagues on the Smertenko visit:

Professor Johan J. Smertenko...insists that we have done great harm to a necessary program....He tells a most convincing story, well documented with correspondence from various government officials, to prove that the militancy of the Emergency Committee has made it possible for President Roosevelt to issue the executive order creating the War Refugee Board. Furthermore, the program at Oswego, the work with South American passports, the influence of the Pope on the Hungarian situation and other such measures...according to Smertenko is directly traceable to the propaganda campaign carried out by the emergency Committee....We are in no position to enter into a controversy with the Emergency Committee....[1]

The work of the South American passports mentioned in this memorandum is another example of the cooperation between the *Vaad Hatzala* and the Bergson group. Jacob Griffel, representing the *Vaad* in Europe and working with Recha and Isaac Sternbuch, had acquired a number of South American passports, at first primarily from Paraguay. The Nazis at the time were honoring without question South American passports.

However, the Nazis ceased honoring Paraguayan passports and deported a group of Jews holding these documents in Vittel, France to death camps. At that point, Griffel turned to George Mantello, the Jewish consul from El Salvador, and through his efforts, Salvadoran passports were obtained which saved many more Jews. Friedenson points out that "Raoul Wallenberg, who saved the lives of thousands of Jews in Hungary, made generous

---

[1] Rabinoff to Hyman, Memorandum dated 10/20/44, Ibid.

use of these passports in order to protect Jews in Budapest from deportations by the Hungarian Nazis and Germans."[1]

Another proposal for saving Hungarian Jews came from Rabbi Chaim Michael Dov Weissmandl, who called for bombing of the rail lines to Auschwitz. Mass expulsions from Hungary began on May 15, 1944. Rabbi Weissmandl wrote a letter the following day with details of the process of deportation and the route to Auschwitz. He included drawings and maps showing the topography as they would appear from the air.[2]

Weissmandl sent his letter in code to the Sternbuchs and to Jacob Griffel. In this case of saving lives - *pekuah nefesh* - Griffel travelled on Saturday to Ankara and met with American Ambassador Steinhardt. Griffel records in his diary:

> Steinhardt admired Rabbi Weissmandl's personality from afar, and that evening he was especially impressed by the coded appeal, and the skillful way it had been put together. Steinhardt promised to send the appeal about bombing the roads to Auschwitz on to Washington....[3]

Weissmandl was born in Hungary in 1903. He was a brilliant student of Talmud and, at age 17, wrote three volumes of interpretations passed down by his teacher. During the war years he devoted all of his time to rescue.[4] Another admirer of Weissmandl was Rudolf Vrba who escaped from Auschwitz and wrote a detailed report of the death camp.[5] Vrba recounts his underground meeting with Weissmandl:

---

[1] Friedenson, op. cit., pp. 106-111. Also see Kranzler, David H. *Heroine of Rescue: The Incredible Story of Recha Sternbuch who Saved Thousands from the Holocaust* (New York: Mesorah Press, 1984).

[2] For accounts of this episode, see Gilbert, op. cit., Chapters 23-31, Friedenson, op. cit., pp. 92-98, and Fuchs, Abraham, *The Unheeded Cry* (New York: Mesorah Publications, 1984), 169ff.

[3] Friedenson, op. cit., pp. 92-98.

[4] For a biographical sketch of Weissmandl, see Fuchs, op. cit., pp. 17-40.

[5] For an account of the Vrba-Wetzler report, see Gilbert, op. cit., pp. 202-206.

I had heard strange, romantic stories about Rabbi Michael Dov Weissmandl; how, single-handed and under the noses of the Nazis, he had saved hundreds of Jews from deportation....They took me to his secret school...I passed down a corridor that ran between a line of rooms in which zealous young men were studying the Talmud.

Vrba was struck by the physical appearance of Rabbi Weissmandl:

...I found myself facing a tall, dark man with exceptionally vivid eyes. He was only about forty, but his heavy black beard made him look older. I felt at once that I was in the presence of a very remarkable personality, in spite of his shabby clothes, his collarless, buttonless shirt, his mud-stained trousers and battered shoes. One, I noticed was tied with a string. The other was not tied at all.

Vrba discovered for the first time that Weissmandl had read his report of Auschwitz:

He greeted me in Slovak, which amazed his students because normally he spoke only Hebrew....Then dismissing the students in his room with a gesture, he said: "So you have escaped from Auschwitz. Therefore I must address you as the Ambassador of 1,760,000 people." I understood what he meant. He had quoted the number who died in Auschwitz while I was there, and I knew then that he had already read my report.[1]

In a letter dated May 16, 1944, Weissmandl wrote:

This is the order of events in Auschwitz to which, starting from yesterday, 12,000 Jewish souls - men, women, children, the old, the sick and the healthy - will be taken daily to be choked, to be burned and to be manure for the fields. And you, brother

---

[1]Vrba, Randolph and Alan Bestic, *I Cannot Forgive* (New York: Grove Press, 1964), pp. 258-259.

Jews! And you, ministers of state in all countries? How can you keep quiet at this murder...in the name of the blood of the millions and the tears of millions, we beg you, we plead with you, we claim and demand of you: do something immediately![1]

In the United States, the Bergson group reacted to the reports from Europe. Smertenko wired to Roosevelt:

AUTHORITATIVE INFORMATION REPORTED BY MANCHESTER GUARDIAN AND CORROBORATED BY INSTRUCTIONS BROADCAST OVER HUNGARIAN RADIO STATIONS INDICATE ANNIHILATION OF FOUR HUNDRED THOUSAND JEWS IN HUNGARY AND IMPENDING ASSASSINATION OF ADDITIONAL THREE HUNDRED FIFTY THOUSAND BY JULY TWENTY FOURTH...APPEAL FOR ACTION NOW.[2]

To Arthur Hays Sulzberger, publisher of the *New York Times*, Smertenko protested:

Have Jewish lives grown so cheap and insignificant that impending death of 350,000 is announced on page 12, while crowded holiday traffic is featured on first page? Such callous indifference to fate of Jews must share responsibility for Nazi murders. Surely space devoted to your laudable crusade on behalf of teaching American History is equally justified by attempt to rescue thousands of lives and redeem honor of our civilization.[3]

Shmertenko pressed action through the International Red Cross and persistently prodded its representatives to be more aggressive in their activity. When he ran into reasons why this was not possible from one representative, he wrote to others. Receiving a more forthcoming response from the second source

---

[1] See Fuchs, op. cit., pp. 169-170.

[2] Telegram dated 6/6/44, PSCP, Reel 1.

[3] Letter dated 7/3/44, PSCP, Reel 5.

in the Red Cross, he chided his primary correspondent, a man named Zollinger:

> I was amazed to read the explanation you offer for inaction on the part of the international Committee in response to our cable....I am happy to note that the special communique issued by the International Red Cross indicated agreement with our point of view rather that with the attitude you have expressed. It has taken the drastic action we have requested...without fear that thereby "the general situation of the Jews in Axis-held countries would only be made worse."[1]

The Red Cross attempt to get supplies to Jews in concentration camps met with British obstruction on the basis that these refugees were not covered by the Geneva Convention. But the Red Cross was aware that the British had in fact allowed such supplies to non-Jewish refugees in similar circumstances. An official of the International Red Cross wrote the War Refugee Board for clarification:

> The ICRC would all the more welcome a definite decision as they are puzzled by the fact that the British authorities have replied negatively in the case of concentration camps in Germany, but the Blockade admitted supplies to camps of detained foreigners in Southern France...to whom the Convention does not apply either. It would therefore, in the opinion of the ICRC, be interesting to know the criterion on the basis of which the Blockade allowed the furnishing of supplies to civilian prisoners whose status in no way differs from that of the detainees in the large concentration camps in Germany.[2]

The Roosevelt administration took the usual position that there be no special effort for Jewish refugees; the war must continue as if there were no immediate threat to Hungarian

---

[1] Letter dated 7/19/44, PSCP, Reel 1.

[2] Ibid.

Jewry. Stephen Wise also saw no human course of action: "The issue is in the hands of God."[1]

In the next six weeks, 400,000 Hungarian Jews were killed. Weissmandl asked in another dispatch to the world:

> Why are you silent! And why are you not doing anything? Why are those railroad tracks without a breach, and why have they not been blown up?...Have we not sent you nearly a hundred telegrams and many letters to tell you that every day the expulsion transports travel that route...and Auschwitz still stands in its place and the gas chambers and ovens still operate. What could be easier than to interrupt their operation and blow them up?"[2]

In analyzing the data available to the Allies at the time, Penkower writes:

> Already on May 8, 1944, the commander of the Allied air forces in Italy indicated that the U.S. 15th Air Force based on Foggia had the capacity to attack simultaneously the Blechhammer oil-refining complex 47 miles from Auschwitz and the war industries at Auschwitz....The first mission on June 2 of "Operation Frantic" which allowed American bombers to extend their range by flying between Britain or Italy and Poltava in the Soviet Union, considerably impaired the Hungarian marshall yards at Bebrecen - on a deportation route to Auschwitz. A second shuttle, flying back to Italy from Russia on June 26 to strike the synthetic oil plant at Drohobycz, crossed directly over one of the five deportation lines and trains to Auschwitz.[3]

---

[1] *Opinion*, June, 1944.

[2] Fuchs, op. cit., pp. 184-185.

[3] See Penkower's discussion Penkower, Monty N. *The Jews Were Expendable: Free World Diplomacy and the Holocaust* (Champaign, Illinois, 1983), pp. 214-222.

And Penkower's conclusion? "Had the will to destroy the gas chambers existed, the early data on file could have contributed decisively to their total demolition."[1]

The new circumstances of the threat to Hungarian Jews and the detailed information sent by Weissmandl only evoked the reflex "win-the-war first" response from the administration. The Operations Division of the War Department went beyond these generalities, and issued an incorrect statement that Auschwitz was "beyond the maximum range of medium bombardment, dive bombers and fighter bombers located in United Kingdom, France or Italy."[2]

In July, 1944, allied planes hit within fifty miles of Auschwitz. In August, over 1000 bombs were dropped on factory areas within five miles of the gas chambers, and there were more such strikes throughout the next several months.[3]

Wyman's analysis is in agreement with that of Penkower:

If the killing installations had been destroyed at this stage of the war, it would have been practically impossible for the hard-pressed Germans to rebuild them. At the very least, the death machinery could not have operated for many months...without gas chambers and crematoria, the Nazis would have been forced to reassess the extermination program in light of the need to commit new and virtually non-existant manpower resources to mass killing.[4]

The conclusions of Penkower and Wyman are reinforced by two pilots who took part in the bombing in the summer and fall of 1944. Captain Leonard Cheshire, the commander of a British fighter squadron, spoke in a BBC documentary of the high degree of accuracy that the Air Force had develped at that point in the war:

---

[1] Ibid.

[2] Letter dated 11/18/44, McCloy to Pehle, cited by Wyman, op. cit., p. 297.

[3] Ibid., p. 299.

[4] Ibid., p. 304.

We had to devise a means of eliminating the forthcoming theat of the VC...devise a means of dropping a 10,000 pound bomb from 16,000 feet with an accuracy of 20 yards....we succeeded in doing that.[1]

When asked if it would have been possible to destroy the gas chambers and crematoria at Auschwitz, Colonel Ernest Gentit, Lead Bombadier on the raid on the I.G. Farben plant on August 20, 1944, a raid which actually hit part of Auschwitz also said that, given the maps that were available (but unknown to the pilots), "we could have done a very good job on this."[2]

Meantime, Bergson's lobbying efforts succeeded in pressuring Roosevelt to establish by executive order, June 8, 1944, one temporary shelter in the United States. This shelter, under the authority of Harold Ickes, Secretary of the Interior, received 984 Yugoslav refugees. This was a minimal accomplishment.

Ben Hecht was back in action with a book called *A Guide for the Bedeviled.*[3] In June 1944, the premier of the dramatization of the book opened in Philadelphia to an audience of 2,500 people.[4]

Bergson, having absorbed multiple attacks at the hands of American Jewish leaders, fought back in public for the first time in July 1944. The *Chicago Sentinel* reported:

Peter Bergson...delivered his "first major address" in Town Hall, New York...and the place was crowded with an audience that applauded Bergson's criticism of Dr. Weizmann, Dr. Wise and Jewish leadership in America. Bergson's speech was broadcast over a local radio station, and it created a deep impression....We're telling you this not because we like the Bergson group, but because it must be admitted that the

---

[1] BBC documentary of Martin Gilbert's *Auschwitz and the Allies,* Rex Bloomstein, producer, aired 9/16/82.

[2] Ibid.

[3] Hecht, Ben, *A Guide for the Bedeviled* (New York: Charles Scribner's Sons, 1944).

[4] *Philadelphia Record,* 6/14/44.

Palestinian boys carried it off once more both organizationally and technically.[1]

Bergson suggested that the British establish a temporary haven for Jews in Palestine much as Roosevelt had done with the one shelter in New York. On this subject, Samuel Margoshes, former colleague of Wise at the American Jewish Congress and columnist for *The Day,* wrote:

> ...to save the surviving Jews of Hungary we must act today....If Peter Bergson's suggestion that the Hungarian Jews be brought into Palestine as into a free port, that is as temporary visitors, can make it possible for Britain to expedite the rescue of the Jewish survivors in Hungary, by all means let us all be for it and let it be adopted.[2]

Bergson and his supporters in the Congress continued to pressure the British to be more responsive to the crisis of Hungarian Jewry. Senator Johnson of Utah was particularly pointed in his comments, prompting the Columbia Broadcasting System to censure certain parts of his speech in their report. CBS cut three sentences from the speech. One appealed to the British to allow Palestinian Jews to fight in their own behalf. The other two censored sentences were the following:

> As an American and as a Christian, I venture to suggest to the British government, as the mandatory for Palestine, that it is their inescapable moral duty to answer the Hungarian government through the International Red Cross - that every Hebrew will be admitted into Palestine....This represents the will of practically the entire American nation. Certainly we are all, therefore, for the immediate establishment in Palestine of emergency rescue shelters.[3]

---

[1] *Chicago Sentinel*, 7/27/44.

[2] *The Day*, 8/2/44.

[3] *New York Post*, 8/9/44.

The British would not allow even temporary refugee camps in Palestine, and the Roosevelt administration never pressured them to do so.

The *Vaad Hatzala* kept up their public pressure for action. Rabbi Eliezer Silver, who along with Bergson had led the 1943 rabbis march on the White House, went now, in August, 1944, to the Capitol steps along with leaders of the Greek Orthodox Church. The *New York Times* reported the scene:

> In a ceremony, details of which were recorded by cameramen...the delegation offered to Congress a petition said to be signed by 500,000 persons asking the Government of the United States and of Britain to expedite means of admitting European Jewish refugees, particularly from Hungary, to Palestine at the earliest possible moment.[1]

Orthodox leaders were frustrated in their attempts to enlist the help of Proskauer of the American Jewish Committee to pressure the White House. In September, 1944, Rabbi Avraham Kalminowitz appealed to Proskauer:

> ...we wish to quote telegram received from our committee in Switzerland. Quote: the Germans intend in the last moment to exterminate all internees in concentration camps...we plead with you to do all in your power to rescue the last remnants of our people because it is a question of hours and every moment counts.[2]

Proskauer wrote to Rabbi Kalminowitz in the morning, put in a call to the White House, then wrote another letter to Kalminowitz:

> Since writing to you this morning I have talked with Judge Rosenman on the telephone. He called me to assure me that he was going to do everything humanly possible. He said that he did

---

[1] *New York Times*, 8/30/44.

[2] Letter dated 9/10/44, AJC, Proskauer papers, Emergency Commmittee, 1944 file.

not think there was any practical use in our coming to Washington.[1]

Rosenman had reason to remember Rabbi Kalminowitz. A few months earlier he had refused to see him and two of his colleagues. He agreed only to see one of them. "He [Rosenman] doesn't receive delegates," Pehle explained to Morgenthau when the rabbis showed up at the Treasury Department.[2] Morgenthau agreed to see them immediately and heard an appeal on behalf of the Jews interned in Vittel, France.

Morgenthau picked up the phone and called Cordell Hull to request his help, telling the Secretary of State: "Cordell, Senator Mead and Congressman McCormack asked me to see these three Rabbis, which I did, and the poor fellows broke down and cried here in my office, and we had quite a time."[3]

While these desperate efforts were taking place, American Zionists were focused on post-war planning, not on Hungarian Jewry. The last and most bitter of the personality disputes between Abba Hillel Silver and Stephen Wise broke out at the end of 1944. The context was the American Zionist Emergency Council, yet another organizational vehicle for Silver and Wise. The two Reform rabbis were co-chairmen, but did not easily share the task.

Legislation for a resolution on post-war planning for Palestine was making its way through Congress. Wise and Silver had met with administration officials to press support for the resolution. However, when objections from Roosevelt became known, Wise put on the brakes. Just before he and Silver were scheduled to meet with Secretary-of-State Stettinius, Wise dispatched a telegram to Stettinius without consulting Silver. In the telegram, Wise stated that, while he would like to see the resolution passed, he did not want to take any position contrary to the recommendation of Roosevelt and the State Department. Silver was livid and resigned as co-chairman:

---

[1] Letter dated 9/10/44, ibid.

[2] Minutes of meeting dated 4/6/44, Morgenthau papers, Reel #207, Book 718, p. 86.

[3] Ibid. p. 108.

This, [the Wise telegram] of course, nullified the whole purpose of our visit and more than any other factor was responsible for the shelving of the Palestine Resolution. All too often Dr. Wise has treated the Zionist movement in the United States as a piece of personal property and has bitterly resented any new leadership which threatened his monopoly. His "shtandlanuth" in Washington has been an egregious failure for many years.[1]

Wise, for his part, refused to attend a dinner honoring Silver in early 1945, saying:

I readily acknowledge that Dr. Silver has in the past rendered valuable service to the Zionist cause. I believe, however, that he used extremely bad judgement in his recent persistent and futile endeavor to force the Palestine resolution through the Congress....he or his supporters have prosecuted a vigorous, disruptive campaign among the Zionists of this country for his personal vindication....[2]

One can only wonder if rescue efforts would have been more successful had these two talented men lent their full attention to the effort instead of consuming considerable energy in personal competition.

Hundreds of thousands of Hungarian Jews went to their death with the full awareness of the civilized world. Among them was one of the beloved literary figures of Europe, Yitzhak Katznelson, a friend of Bialik and Brenner. Though the descendent of a long line of Orthodox rabbis, he was a great admirer of the Jewish labor movement and visited Palestine, traveling in the company of his cousins Berl Katznelson and Yitzhak Tabenkin, the two men, who with Ben-Gurion, formed the troika of leadership in the Socialist movement.[3]

Tabenkin was among the freedom fighters of the Warsaw Ghetto when the uprising began. His daughter and the two youngest of his three sons had disappeared into a boxcar to

---

[1]see JTA Bulletin, 1/2/45.

[2]Letter dated 2/23/45, CZA, Wise papers, Reel 117.

[3]See biographical notes in Katznelson, Yitzhak, [English translation by Dr. Myer Cohen] *Vittel Diary* (Israel: Hakibbutz Hameuchad Publishing House, 1972), pp. 11-40.

Treblinka. As the rebellion broke out, his friends spirited Tabenkin through the bowels of the ghetto to the Aryan side of the wall. He and his friends were provided Paraguayan passports which, as mentioned above, to that point the Nazis had honored. But Tabenkin, his oldest son, and many others were transported to Vittel, a resort in Eastern France.

Yitzhak Katznelson's testimony, a poem of over ten chapters, is called "The Song of the Murdered Jewish Nation." In a personal diary written before the poem, he kept contemplating but putting aside the idea of the poem:

I could not draw up this bill of reckoning, the account for millions of murdered lives. I have not the strength for this task and I shall not do it....Whenever I begin to approach the subject, I feel that I shall lose my reason...so I stop.[1]

Katznelson mourned his departed family, his wife Chanah, and his sons Ben Zion and Binyamin:

When I enquire about you, Oh Chanah, my exalted one! My Muse! Oh, my Benzikel and my Binyaminke!...My wonderful children....When I enquire after you my heart grows faint. Then it pounds away as on an anvil and once again the blood is thrust through those depleted channels. Oh, where are you all?[2]

The despairing poet speaks to all of his lost people and summons his courage:

I long to see you all,
I want to behold you,
To behold and contemplate you all.
Oh let me see my people,
My nation that lies murdered.
Grant me just a silent look.
Then shall I sing,

---

[1]Ibid.. p. 29.

[2]Ibid., p. 21.

Yes, give me a harp
- and I shall play a tune.[1]

The Song of the Murdered Jewish Nation was placed in bottles by Katznelson and, while he stood watch, buried near a small pine tree with a cleft in it by Miriam Novitch who survived the war. So too did Katnelson's poem.

And Katznelson himself? On April 18, 1944, Katznelson and his son were transferred to Drancy, and on the 29th of April, they were sent from Drancy to Auschwitz where they were killed. The appeals of Rabbi Kalminowitz to the Roosevelt administration did not help them.

Is this history? Is it fair to invoke the words of a desperate Jewish poet in a work of history, or is it "prosecution" of those who did not save Katznelson. If one does not give Katznelson his place in history, is one an "apologist" for those who failed to save him and millions of other Jewish victims? What is history? Is there a difference between history and "Jewish" history? Who decides what is history?

---

[1] Ibid., p. 30.

PART III

UNDERSTANDING HISTORY

Chapter XII

A Framework for Understanding History

As noted in the Introduction to this work, there has been much conflict among historians writing about the American Jewish response to the Holocaust. How does the reader distinguish between the different versions of history? How can one separate documented fact from polemic, from attempts to shape history by personal argumentation and distortion?

Given a useful framework for evaluation, the reader can make these distinctions. Beginning with a discussion of what historians have written about the writing of history in general, one can construct a paradigm independent of the content issues of any given era. This chapter develops a framework for evaluation. In the chapters to follow, the different presentations of the history of the American Jewish response to the Holocaust are placed into that framework.

To throw up one's hands and say that different interpretations are so irreconcilable that it is not worth trying to make sense of the issue belittles both the craft of writing history and the intelligence of the reader. One historian states it this way:

When interpretations contradict each other, the historian cannot resign himself to these conflicts on the ground that they are inherent in his material, or in the nature of historical research. It is precisely the conflicts of interpretation that are the measure of how unsatisfactory the knowledge of the historical discipline is at this point...it is in any event, reassuring to note that the pendulum of historical interpretation does not always swing with the same vehemence. New facts, better reading of old facts, the elimination of discredited views all bring about a reduction in its oscillations.[1]

It is the goal of Part III to reduce the oscillations produced by the sometimes confusing and contradictory presentations of the American Jewish response to the Holocaust.

In understanding any process, it is helpful to identify points on the spectrum of the process in order to avoid unnecessary black/white, either/or presentations. Language is important, and one does well to be on guard against historians who quickly dismiss ideas that differ from their own in an attempt to try to convince the reader that only they are "right."

There is much discussion among historians on the subject of history as art versus history as science. Many writers distinguish between the natural sciences and the social sciences. Peter Gay speaks to the issue of points on a spectrum in saying that "art and science are not neatly segregated from each other; they share a living, meandering frontier which scholarly and literary traffic crosses with little impediment and few formalities."[2]

Gay goes on to contend that history is science, albeit a "fragile" one. What makes it fragile is that the historian must struggle mightily for objectivity: "The critical distance that other modern scientists take for granted is, for the historian, a laborious victory over sympathy and anxiety."[3] E. H. Carr says that "human beings are not only the most complex and variable of natural entities, but they have to be studied by other human beings, not by independent observers of another species."[4]

The 19th century historian Thomas Carlyle, who emphasized the art of history writing, wrote: "boundless is the domain of man, it is but a small fractional proportion of it that he rubs with Consciousness and by Forethought."[5] And the 20th century historian, George Macauley Trevelyn, whose name honors that

[1]Gay, Peter, *Style in History - Gibbon, Ranke, Macaulay, Burchkardt* (New York: W. W. Norton and Co., 1974), p. 211.

[2]Ibid., p. 188.

[3]Ibid.

[4]Carr, E.H., *What is History* (New York: Vintage Books, 1961), p. 89.

[5]Quoted by Clive, John, *Not By Fact Alone* (Boston: Houghton, Milfin, Co., 1989), p. 115.

of his illustrious predecessor, maintains, as Clive tells us, that history is "more than the accumulation and interpetation of facts." It is necessary that the facts and interpretations be "presented to a wide reading public by the historian in the essential role of literary artist." The role of the historian is to educate - "to cause the minds of men to reflect on the past."[1]

Other historians disagree with Macauley and Trevelyn and make a serious attempt to develop objective laws of history. Their attempts to define history are no more or less serious than those who stress the art of history. One can be aware of the advantages and disadvantages of each approach and arrive at a critical judgement of how to apply each to any given period under study. It is shortsighted to dismiss completely any one philosophy of history and to uncritically embrace another.

The advantage of striving to develop a system as objective and as scientific as possible is that one more nearly approaches the elimination of bias and subjectivity. In examining different theories, It is important to be aware that any theory that can be used profitably can also be misused.

A common analogy is that of the "forest" and the "trees." It is sometimes said of someone that he cannot see the forest for the trees. Other language used is that of "content" and "process." If one is too focused on content, then one does not come to understand the process. There is truth in this illustration with which most everyone can agree, but there are two caveats. One caveat is that both aspects are pertinent - there is a time and place to focus on content, but if one becomes overly focused there, an understanding of the process is lost.

The second caveat is that there are different levels of process - different views of the forest. Withdrawing to the edge of the forest, one can observe the life within the forest - the different types of vegetation, the different species of animals, how the animals relate to one another; one can observe the process of life in the forest. However, from the edge of the forest one cannot see what borders the forest on all of its sides. Rising to 30,000 feet, one can see that the forest borders an ocean one one side, a desert on the other. These topographical restrictions limit the choices of those moving from the forest to other areas of their world.

The price to be paid for this level of observation is that one can no longer see the living forest. Thus more than one level of process is useful in examining historical data.

---

[1]Ibid., p. 280.

Clive has reservations about trying to formulate laws of history. He feels "suspicious" of historians "who think that they can formulate historical laws, thereby eliminating the unique, the contingent, the unforeseen."[1] Carr notes that the discipline of sociology which overlaps with history has trends that err in both directions: (1) of observation from a distance so great that there is "the danger of losing itself in abstract and meaningless generalizations about society in general," and (2) of "confining oneself to so-called 'technical' problems of enumeration and analysis."[2] The second trend is in the direction of super-specialization, for example in overfocusing on demographics at the expense of other factors.

Barbara Tuchman shares Clive's suspicions about those who try to fix historical laws. She writes that she mistrusts "history in gallon jugs whose purveyors are more concerned with establishing the meaning and purpose of history than with what happened."[3] Carr believes that "history cannot be written unless the historian can achieve some kind of contact with the mind of those about whom he is writing."[4]

An understanding of content and process overlaps with other important parts of the paradigm under construction in this chapter. These parts involve human choice or "will" within which is enveloped the issue of motivation. Just as there is overlap between history and sociology, there is overlap between history and psychology. Carr tells us that the historian "needs to penetrate into forms of human behavior in which the will is active....This sets up a relation, which is peculiar to history and the social sciences, between the observer and what is observed."[5]

Dawidowicz, as cited in the Introduction to this work, shares her belief that "history is at bottom an account of what men did and achieved, and the historian's task is to untangle that

---

[1] Ibid., p. 11.

[2] Ibid., p.44.

[3] Tuchman, Barbara, *Practicing History: Selected Essays* (New York: Ballentine Books, 1981), p. 35.

[4] Ibid., p. 27.

[5] Carr, op. cit., p. 89.

meshwork of human character, behavior, and motive whose intertwining creates the very material of history."[1]

Since in sociology, history, and psychology there are human observers and humans who are observed, the factor of will and motivation must be applied to the historian as well as the "players" on the stage of history. Carl Becker points out that "historical facts are not out there, in the world of the past, but in here, in the mind of the historian."[2] To this Carr adds that "the belief in a hard core of facts existing objectively and independently of the interpretation of the historian is a preposterous fallacy."[3]

Peter Gay cites this maxim of Carr in order to challenge it. "It is precisely this preposterous fallacy I wish to defend." Gay believes that the historian can rise to a level of professionalism that will allow him to isolate historical facts from his own interpretation. As professionalism is brought to bear on what the historian studies, so it can also be brought to bear internally:

> Just as it [professionalism] intervenes to regulate the historian's traffic with his culture, it intervenes to regulate his traffic within himself. In establishing stardards of proof and presentation - the full footnote, the honest bibliography, the accurate citation - it compels the historian's sources, reasoning, and conclusions into the glaring light of public scrutiny and serves to discriminate what he owes to others from what he has contributed on his own.[4]

Carr comments on the interaction between the historian and his data, saying it is the historian "who decides to which facts to give the floor, and in what order or context."[5] This issue of which data to bring to bear is also addressed by Dawidowicz who writes that "when historians knowingly or unknowingly

---

[1] Dawidowicz, *The Holocaust and the Historian*, op. cit., p. 146.

[2] Cited by Carr, op. cit., p. 198.

[3] Ibid.

[4] Gay, *Style in History*, op. cit., p. 209.

[5] Carr, op. cit., p. 9.

omit from their historical writing an account of any given course of events, those events disappear from history."[1]

The historian must always keep in the forefront of his or her mind the pursuit of truth. "This historical truth," Dawidowicz writes, "is not, of course, truth in the sense of eternal verity, absolute and unqualified." Emphasizing that this is not an issue one historian can take for granted in analyzing the work of other historians, she adds:

> The historian's task is often to uncover and expose fraud and deceit as it existed in the past and in written history, to bring to light suppressed facts and documents...to strip away the accumulated overlays of myth and legend upon the past.[2]

V.H. Galbraith puts truth at the top of the factors historians must consider. In commenting on the issue of how much of writing history is art and how much is science, he admonishes us: "Write like Macaulay and Gibbon - if you can - but however one writes and whatever one writes about, the basic aim should be to arrive at the truth. Truth and rhetoric are bad bedfellows."[3]

Historians tend to be cautious about drawing lessons from history commenting that each historical period has its own unique qualities, and that one must be careful about drawing conclusions from one period and applying them to another. However, Carr believes that historians are inevitably drawn to extracting such lessons and that doing so involves the need for a legitimate degree of generalization.

> The real point about generalization is that through it we attempt to learn from history, to apply the lesson drawn from one set of events: when we generalize, we are consciously or unconsciously trying to do this...the assumption that men learn

---

[1] Dawidowicz, *The Holocaust and the Historian*, op. cit., p. 1.

[2] Ibid., pp. 144-145.

[3] Cited by, Gay, *Style in History*, pp. 188-189.

nothing from history is contradicted by a multitude of observable facts.[1]

To whatever extent one agrees or disagrees with Carr's assertion that we learn from history, it seems certain that the attempt to extract lessons from history is a striving that is inextricably bound up with the concept of growth.

From the material reviewed above, we arrive at a framework that, in simplified form looks like this:

I. Examine the larger process ("30,000 feet") in order to come to an understanding of the constraints imposed on the players on the stage of history.
   A. Political constraints
   B. Social constraints
   C. Economic constraints
   D. Other constraints

II. Move in ("edge of the forest") to examine the interactive process of those on stage.
   A. With what groups do they affiliate and why?
   B. What are the interactions between the groups?
   C. What are the interactions between individuals within each group.

III. Move in to examine the individuals themselves; what motivates them?
   A. Access to information (what was known)
   B. Power (ego)
   C. Money
   D. Ideology (politics)
   E. Fear
   F. Altruism

IV. Lessons to be drawn from history

This framework is put to work in evaluating the data in Part I and Part II of this work and to draw some conclusions. Since some conclusions are inherent in Part I and Part II, those conclusions and the conclusions of others who have addressed

---

[1] Carr, op. cit., 84-85.

the American Jewish response to the Holocaust are assessed within the above framework. Do Part I and Part II of this work bring new data? Do they facilitate a better reading of old facts? Does applying this framework to the interpretations of other historians move toward a reconciliation of what seem to be contradictory views? If the views cannot be reconciled, does this framework help us identify those views that can properly be discredited?

Chapter XIII

Factors Limiting the Actions of American Jewry in the 1930s and 1940s

With the issue of the limitations within which the American Jewish community labored during the 1930s and 1940s, one arrives at the first point of entry into the debate among historians who have researched and commented on the period. This issue reveals much more about the historians who have written on the subject than about the individuals who lived and made the history.

The restraints that have been mentioned by many historians include the anti-semitism that American Jews faced, disunity among Jews, the anti-alien sentiment that existed in the Congress and in the country at large, and the limits to the effectiveness of ethnic pressure especially in wartime.

Unless one requires absolute answers, and they are difficult to find in history, there is little with which to disagree in the above paragraph. One can give more or less emphasis to the different constraints mentioned. Understanding the constraints within which Jewish leaders of the 1930s and 1940s worked is an important place to begin, but not to end.

Historians have legitimate differences about the degree to which social, political, and economic factors limited the options for American Jews. What is clear is that these restrictions *operated to different degrees on the individuals who lived in the 1930s and 1940s and who worked within those limitations.* This chapter deals with the limiting factors, while the following chapter addresses the choices and motivating factors that defined how much a given individual was constrained by those limiting factors.

Some historians writing from an Orthodox perspective are explicit in saying that not more was done to rescue European

Jews because non-Orthodox Jews are not trained in a "Torah perspective." Thus the implication that the Orthodox Jews did what was required and the non-Orthodox did not. David Kranzler writes that the actions of American Jews were dictated by their differing loyalties:

> ...the assimilationists to government policy and the greater war effort, most of the Zionists to the goal of a postwar Jewish state, most of the Orthodox to the imperatives of Torah law for immediate rescue.[1]

In examining Stephen Wise's actions, Kranzler concludes that Wise's Judaism "was translated into the faith of secular liberalism's primary goal of social and economic equality as epitomized by the welfare state."[2]

Kranzler, along with Rabbi Morris Sherer, was part of the largely failed attempt in 1982 to assemble a commission that would come to some agreed upon report on the American Jewish response to the Holocaust. Sherer writes:

> The decision reached at the Commission's final meeting on September 20, 1983, to take no formal action as a Commission to reach joint conclusions or to approve or disapprove the report, was indeed wise as well as just. There is no way that one can reconcile the divergent views of the Commission about what actually took place in the various circles of American Jewish leadership during the bitter years of the Holocaust.[3]

Sherer then proceeds to provide a narrow ideological look at the restrictions under which American Jews labored:

> When one views events from a Torah perspective, the perception is diametrically different from the experience of

---

[1]Kranzler, *Thy Brother's Blood,* op. cit., p, 1.

[2]Ibid., p. 66.

[3]Finger, Seymour Maxwell, editor, *American Jewry During the Holocaust* (Washington: American Jewish Commission on the Holocaust, 1984), Appendix 3.

seeing the same object through secular eyes. The Orthodox Jew is inculcated from early childhood with a special sense of "arievus" (responsibility) of one Jew for the other and for all mankind.[1]

The individuals who worked with Kranzler and Sherer on the Holocaust Commission included people who gave the particularist input of the various groups that were a part of the history, in some instances the players themselves. Samuel Merlin, Bergson's chief aide, was a participant and took a highly partisan position according to a prominent historian who has written positively of some of the activities of the Bergson group.[2]

Kranzler has provided a major service by researching and preserving for history the heroic acts of some of the people who dedicated their life to rescue,[3] but his narrow interpretation of the data limits the range of his contribution to a broader understanding of the American Jewish response to the Holocaust.

Henry Feingold writes a great deal about the conditions which restricted Jewish actions in the 1930s and 1940s. His seminal work focuses on the response of the Roosevelt Administration to the Holocaust, not the American Jewish response.[4] His contributions to the latter subject have come in the form of commentary in journal articles.[5]

In a preface to the paperback edition of his book on the Roosevelt administration, Feingold writes: "Were I writing this book today I would give a sharper focus to the role of

---

[1] Ibid. The chapters in this loosely edited compendium are not sequentially numbered nor are those in the appendices.

[2] Wyman, David, personal communication, July, 1994.

[3] Kranzler's books include: *Heroine of Rescue: The Incredible Story of Recha Sternbuch Who Saved Thousands from the Holocaust* (New York: Mesorah Press, 1984), and *Solomon Schonfeld: His Page in History* (New York: Judaica Press, 1982).

[4] Feingold, Henry L., *The Politics of Rescue: The Roosevelt Administration and the Holocaust, 1938-1945* (New York: Walden Press, 1970).

[5] Feingold, Henry, "Who Shall Bear the Guilt for the Holocaust: The Human Dilemma," American Jewish History, March 1979, pp. 261-282, and "Was There Communal Failure? Some Thoughts on the American Jewish Response to the Holocaust," American Jewish History, Autumn, 1993, pp. 61-80.

American Jewry."[1] In framing the issue, he provides a narrow definition of the issue of the Jewish response: "I do not believe that the harsh indictment which is emerging is justified. Had American Jewry been more concerned, the charge goes, it would have done more for its brethren in Europe."[2]

The fact that he did not bring a sharp focus to this subject does not prevent Feingold from being unequivocally sure of his own interpretation:

> Ultimately one is forced to conclude that the failure of American Jewry rests as much on the circumscribed impact ethnic pressure is permitted to exercise on policy, especially during war time, as it does on the internal weakness of American Jewry.[3]

I agree entirely with Feingold on two important points: (1) that a harsh indictment of American Jewry is not indicated, and, (2) that the political, social, and economic realities of the 1930s and 1940s severely limited the options available to American Jews. However, within the larger process view that Feingold addresses, one can find examples of relative failures *and* successes in overcoming inherent limitations of action.

Feingold tells us that there is a "circumscribed impact ethnic pressure is permitted to exercise on policy," but, in addition to giving historical examples which support this thesis, which Feingold does,[4] one must also document instances from history which illustrate the success of different pressure groups in impacting policy.[5]

Feingold's language of "indictment" and "charge" frames a legitimate historial inquiry in polemical terms. While his

---

[1] Preface to paperback edition of *The Politics of Rescue*, p. xv.

[2] Ibid.

[3] Ibid.

[4] Feingold, Henry L., "Who Shall Bear the Guilt for the Holocaust: The Human Dilemmma," op. cit.

[5] See Chapters IV and VI of this book for the success of Catholic pressure on Roosevelt, Chapter VIII for the success of pressure from American blacks on Roosevelt policy, and Chapter VIII for the success of pressure by American labor .

point of view is far from that of Kranzler, their analyses have in common a limiting perspective.

If one frames the debate among historians as whether or not American Jewry was "concerned" then one slips easily into labeling some historians as "accusers" and those who dismiss the "accusers" as "apologists." Much of the commentary on the issue of the American Jewish response has taken on this tone as some historians battle to establish their theory as "the" correct theory.

Two important sets of players get lost in this debate - those who lived at the time and "created" the history that historians debate, and the reader; it is the reader who is the ultimate arbiter of the debate among historians.

Those who lived the history were flesh-and-blood people, not "American Jewry." Many used very harsh rhetoric in dealing with one another. There was among the American Jewish Committee, the American Jewish Congress, and the Zionist Organization of America fierce competition to be seen as "the" leading American Jewish organization. And within each organization there was lively competition and even harsher rhetoric among those who vied to be "the" leader of that organization.

Proskauer vied with Wertheim for leadership of the American Jewish Committee and "won." Wise battled with de Haas, Newman, Abba Hillel Silver and many others to gain ascendency in the Zionist movement. The debate between Proskauer and Wertheim was based much more on substantive issues within the American Jewish Committee and much less on personality issues which predominated in the many battles that involved Wise.

The personalities of historical figures help us understand what motivated them, but it is only one of many factors at work in history. To take two examples from contemporary history, much has been written about the personalities of Lyndon Johnson and Richard Nixon. Historians and readers of history can conclude from the historical evidence that these two men had significant personality flaws that affected the conduct of their presidency. Having agreed on that, there is profound disagreement on whether the sum total of their presidency was positive, negative, or more appropriately where on the spectrum between these two poles an evaluation of their historical role lies.

So too, a mature "Jewish" history must take into account personality factors, recognizing that this is only one part of the historical record. The Jewish patriarchs of biblical times were powerful men who made their mark on the historical stage. The Torah does not hide from us their flaws, and there is lively debate even today, for example, about the historical roles of Isaac and Jacob.

Stephen Wise stands out prominently in the Jewish history of the 1930s and 1940s, and, as we saw in Part I, in the 1910s and 1920s as well. Among the battles for Jewish leadership, he was a survivor and served what he proudly called "my people" for close to 50 years. He was bombastic, argumentative, and used the harshest of rhetoric in condemning those he saw as his opponents, whether they were in rival organizations or within his own organizational framework. But it was his strengths, not his weaknesses, for which he was sought out as a speaker for many events; he was not elevated to leadership in many organizations because of the negative aspects of his personality. He inspired many Jews of his era to involvement in Jewish affairs and was a friend to many.[1]

Did Stephen Wise care about his people? - of course he did; he cared deeply. Was he callously indifferent to the fate of European Jewry? - of course not. These are not the historical issues. It is not relevant whether Wise was "a good guy" or "a bad guy."

Stephen Wise, Joseph Proskauer, Jacob de Haas, Abba Hillel Silver, Eliezer Silver, Ben Hecht, Peter Bergson and the many other historical personalities who appear in this book need neither "accusers" nor "apologists." They were who they were, and in trying to understand who they were, one must delve into primary sources. To brand historians who research the primary sources as either "accusers" or "apologists" is to shoot the messenger. The perspective of the historian is part of his work and legitimate territory for debate, but what is most important is the accuracy of the historian's work - to what extent his or her conclusions are or are not supported by the data.

The amount of knowledge one has at a given time in history is obviously a factor that limits ones ability to respond - if one knows nothing about developing events, one cannot respond at all. In moving beyond that absolute, one encounters factors of

---

[1] For the fullest biography of Wise, see: Urofsky, Melvin I. *A Voice That Spoke for Justice* (Albany: State University of New York Press, 1982). Unfortunately Urofsky devotes only 14 pages to the Holocaust. Bergson is mentioned very briefly and the work of the War Refugess Board is given only a sentence. Louis I. Newman, Wise's friend, fellow Reform Rabbi and fellow Zionist, whose choices in responding to the Holocaust were different from those of Wise, does not appear at all.

choice and motivation. If a historical figure knows a little, he or she can chose one of three courses: (1) seek more information, (2) act on the little that is known and not seek further information, (3) suppress what is knows in which case it becomes "unknown" and one cannot act on it. From these transactions one ends up with those who know a great deal, those who continue to know only a little, and those who have been more or less successful in suppressing the little knowledge they began with.

Among the group that now knows a great deal, there are many choices to be made, many different levels of response.

The concept of suppression introduces a psychological concept. Are psychological constructs part of history? It has already been noted that many who write about historiography agree that there is an overlap between the disciplines of history, sociology, and psychology. While those who have researched and/or commented on the American Jewish response to the Holocaust have not stated explicitly where they stand on these theoretical issues, there is inevitable reference to psychological factors.

The historian of necessity deals with psychological and sociological issues. What is most important is to what extent one stays within the data and to what extent one pronounces personal theories in the absence of supporting data. Before taking up the issue of what members of the Jewish commmunity did with the knowledge they had and how they chose to respond, it is pertinent to review what information was available to be known.

One can cite secondary sources, for example, what was written in newspapers and what was on the radio. This type of information is of legitimate historical concern and some historical works are built primarily on secondary sources. One limitation of secondary sources is that one cannot be sure who read the newspaper or who listened to the radio.

In dealing with primary sources, one can eliminate this problem to a great extent. While finding a report in the files of a historical personage does not necessarily mean he or she read the report, in dealing with the reports and letters the individual himself wrote, one legitimately assumes knowledge of what was written.

At this point we are only partway into our framework; by establishing what information was available and when, one does not establish what one "should" or "could" have done with the information.

As Walter Lacquer writes in *The Terrible Secret:* "History is a seamless web and therefore all periodization is arbitrary, and yet lines have to be drawn somewhere."[1] Some historians focus on the year 1942 to address the question of "when did we know?" In order to avoid unwarrented assumptions one must ask: "when did we know <u>what</u>. The question appears to be: "When did we know that the Nazis were systematically murdering thousands of Jews a day." The historical concensus is that this information was widely available late in 1942 and known to many before that date.

Despite the availability of the information, it is entirely possible that many American Jews were not aware of it. When one acquired the knowledge of the daily mass killings or whether one acquired the knowledge at all does not speak to the question of when one knew or could have known that a tragedy of unprecedented proportions was entrapping the Jewish people of Europe.

The reports in the Prologue of this book all were written in the year 1933. This data makes clear that, for several years *before* the death camps went into operation, there was a question of *when did we know* which relates to what Jewish leaders of the time described as an unprecedented Jewish tragedy.

The fact that most of the reports in the Prologue were found in the Wise papers says nothing about Stephen Wise individually other than that he was perhap more conscientious than most Jewish leaders of the time in keeping personal records. These same reports were sent to other American Jewish leaders; Wise himself communicated their content to many others.

The reports from Germany in 1933 speak of "...real middle ages. Many Jews are in prison and it is doubtful if they ever leave it alive," dark cellars, "daily attacks upon people of my acquaintance," people with "broken arms, with broken heads." Later in 1933 comes a report that there was no surcease: "...everything that was true first days of Hitler revolution...now even drasticer."[2]

In letters in which he alerted other Jewish leaders to events in Germany, Wise wrote that he was "going through days and nights of hell...silence is acquiescence," and "It is a war of

---

[1]Lacquer, Walter, *The Terrible Secret*, op. cit., p. 6.

[2]See Prologue, this book.

extermination that Hitler is waging, and it is a deliberate thing planned since...1920, when the Hitler program was first issued....I am looking into the depths of hell. Sometimes I feel as if I could hardly live through it."[1]

Cyrus Adler, then president of the American Jewish Committee received the same or similar reports and gave them credence in writing to Secretary of State Hull asking him not to consider the plight of German Jewry "an internal German question," because it was "an attack upon every Jew throughout the world."[2]

In 1934, Samuel Margoshes, a vice-president of the American Jewish Congress and editor of a Jewish newspaper, traveled to Germany and brought back a first hand report. He told his colleagues that 65,000 Jews had already left Germany, an exodus of more than ten percent of the German Jewish population. The projection was that by the end of 1934, 200,000 would leave.[3]

In 1935, Jonah Wise of the Joint Distribution Committee returned from a trip to Germany and reported to American Jewish leaders that "the situation of Jews in Germany has reached its lowest ebb." He concluded that it was "impossible to draw a picture other than one of the blackest dispair." Perhaps most importantly, he warned that the Nazis were convinced "that the rest of the world does not and will not concern itself about the Jewish question."[4]

A public rally in New York in 1935 brought the plight of German Jews to a wide audience. Each speaker condemned the silence of the Roosevelt administration.[5] In the same year, the Nazis passed the Nuremberg laws prompting the American Jewish Committee to issue a formal report condemning the laws and commmented that "it may be said that all the Jews regard the present situation as hopeless" and that "a new wave of emigration may be looked for."[6]

---

[1]Ibid.

[2]Ibid.

[3]See Chapter III, this book.

[4]See Chapter IV, this book.

[5]Ibid.

[6]Ibid.

Against this and much more data, Finger was still able to write as late as 1984:

> At the outset, it was supposed that Nazism was not essentially different from the many forms of anti-Semitism of the past....The persistent belief of Jews - both leaders and commmon citizens, in Europe and elsewhere - that Nazism was only an especially bad outbreak of anti-semitism was not implausible in the 30s.[1]

For the statement above there are no footnotes, no documentation.

Yehuda Bauer, another historian writing about the American Jewish response to the Holocaust, comments:

> ...from 1935 on, it was clear to the most shortsighted observer that only emigration could afford an answer to the problems of German Jewry. Nevertheless, contrary to claims made after the event, no one knew or could have known what was in store for European Jews. Prophets of doom there were, no doubt, but they prophesied persecution, war, pogroms, economic ruin, and slave labor, not physical destruction.[2]

In a later book, Bauer writes: "And yet one asks the question, whether the Jews of Germany really wanted to leave; and if they did, why did they not leave."[3]

There is some confusion in reporting that all but the most shortsighted person knew in 1935 that Jews had to get out of Germany and citing figures that show an exodus of almost one-half the Jewish population of Germany in the 1930s,[4] yet, on the other hand, commenting that no one "knew what was in store." This is followed, in a separate book, by the implication

---

[1] Finger, op. cit., Chapter III, p. 47.

[2] Bauer, Yehuda, *American Jewry and the Holocaust* (Detroit: Wayne State University Press, 1981), pp. 25-26.

[3] Bauer, Yehuda, *Jewish Reactions to the Holocaust* (Tel Aviv: MOD Books, 1989), p. 32.

[4] Ibid., p. 40.

that German Jews did not want to leave. It is important to note that the comment about Jews not leaving was the more recent of Bauer's cited contributions to the literature. In the following chapter is another encounter with the phenomenon of Bauer presenting in his later writings positions that are at odds with earlier work.

In arriving in this review at the year 1938, one encounters *Kristallnacht*, an epic event in the history of the Jewish people which received front page international coverage; after *Kristallnacht* one who wanted to suppress the knowledge that European Jewry faced a tragic fate of major proportions would have to work overtime to do so.

In 1938, it is four years before the question of what was known about the daily, mass slaughter of thousands of Jews a day can be raised. The historical evidence is overwhelming that from 1933 to 1938 there was a steady outpouring of news of cruel and murderous persecution of the Jews of Europe, not only Germany, but Rumania, Poland and Bulgaria. The news included reports of concentration camps, beatings, and murder; this was news that prompted public protest from American Jews, condemnation by Jews of the silence of the Roosevelt administration, and large-scale emigration of Jews from Germany.

In turning to the psychological factors that limited the ability of American Jews to respond to the fate of European Jewry, one encounters the phenomenon of disbelief. The discussion by historians of this phenomenon comes generally in the context of the news of the systematic, massive killings of the period of 1941-1945. Yehuda Bauer writes:

...We know now that the total murder of a people is possible, but people who were alive in 1941-42 had no such knowledge. In their eyes the news which was beginning to arrive constituted mere war propaganda....The Jewish world could not believe in mass murder and was unwilling to believe in it....This psychological rejection had its roots, not in timidity or in a revulsion from negative or bad news, but because it had such a powerful impact that it might make it impossible to carry on with one's routine life.[1]

---

[1] Ibid., pp. 107-108.

This is bad history and worse psychology. Undoubtedly there were some people who, in 1941 and 1942, dismissed what they heard as war propaganda. However, not only was this not the general response, but primary sources document precisely the opposite.[1]

One can agree with Bauer that "psychological rejection" does not have its roots in timidity, but it does have roots in revulsion from bad news. Saying that the rejection was "because it had such a powerful impact that it might make it impossible to carry on with one's routine life" is but another way to phrase the revulsion from bad news. The bad psychology continues when Bauer writes about testimony from survivors of the death camps:

> These people tell us how the Jews arrived at the gas chambers. It seems that by 1942-43, the inmates should have known about the mass murder, since news about it had already infiltrated the outside world. But those who have survived tell us that the people were utterly surprised and in a state of absolute shock: they simply did not believe their eyes. If this is true of people who were eye witnesses to the Holocaust, what can we expect of those who only heard of it?[2]

The people in the death camps lived amidst conditions to which those on the outside of the camps could not relate, just as none living now can relate to that level of horror. They suffered savage treatment and saw others tortured and murdered day after day while they were forced to watch in silence; they had no means to help their fellow Jews. The need to repress those horrible realities was constant, indeed necessary for survival. The notion that people in the comfort of their homes in the United States had more psychological need for repression and denial than those in the death camps represents a profound misunderstanding of human psychology. Survivors like Rudolf Vrba who escaped from Auschwitz, once

---

[1]See Chapter X, this book and the work of Gilbert, Morse, Freedman, Lookstein, and Medoff, all previously cited. Putting these authors together in this context does not imply that they are all in agreement on their interpretations of the history under consideration; what their works have in common is the presentation of data which documents what information about the Holocaust was available, when it was available, and what were the responses to the data.

[2]Bauer, Yehuda, *Jewish Reactions to the Holocaust*, op. cit., p. 108.

away from the immediacy of the horrors of that concentration camp, did not hesitate to tell the world what was going on.[1]

Bauer is not alone in posing the psychological mechanism of repression and disbelief. Feingold writes:

> Few could fathom that a modern nation with a culture that had produced Goethe, Heine, Bach and Beethoven...had embarked on such a program. It beggared the imagination.[2]

While Jews in the cauldron of concentration camps faced death every moment and had to focus all of their attention on survival, those living far from the horrors of the war dealt with every day decisions of what clothes to wear, where to eat, what business deals to make, and what organizational decisions to make. Those outside Europe who utilized repression and denial were not wrestling with the inability to comprehend the flood of news about the death camps; they were faced with making decisions about how much of their everyday routine to put aside in order to try to mount an effective response to the destruction engulfing European Jews.

Understanding is only clouded by historians who, several years after the fact, ignore what Jews who lived the history said and did and instead substitute their own theories. Jacob Katz expresses an important historical injunction:

> The historian who wishes faithfully to record the external and internal struggle of those involved in the dilemma, and even more if he desires to pass moral judgement upon the decisions taken...has to explain people's behavior on the basis of what they themselves knew at the time, weighing - in the light of accessible information and possible insight - whether the decision was rational, judicious, and moral by whatever yardsticks were conceivably available to the actors themselves. Natually people will be found to have acted on

---

[1]The testimony of Vrba and Bestic can be found first hand in their book, already cited.

[2]Feingold, Henry L., "Who Shall Bear the Guilt for the Holocaust: The Human Dilemmma," op. cit., p. 277.

different levels...they will be found to have revealed different degrees of courage and character.[1]

Those living in the 1930s and 1940s were not blind to the psychological mechanisms they were dealing with; they understood that different organizations and different people arrived at different decisions about how to deal with reality. Richard Lichtheim, as related in Part II of this work, understood the denial of Jews in Palestine, Britain, and the United States and tried to contend with it. He wrote that life in Europe was not pleasant "but it cannot be bettered by those who do not wish to be disturbed by the aspect of ugly things."[2]

Isaac Lewin asked, in 1942, where is the storm of protest against the murder of Jews which has "no parallel in our history," and an editorial in the Jewish press a few months later, reacting to the same news of the massive, systematic extermination of Jews, asks why some leaders "pursue their ordinary ways." These contemporary observers were not commenting on disbelief; they were observing that not all Jewish leaders were willing to put aside pleasurable distractions to deal with the horrible news. So too the writer of another Jewish periodical who found it shocking that some organizations continue business as usual was commenting on conscious choices.[3]

The focus of the major American organizations on postwar planning is not to be condemned as callous and indifferent; it is to be understood in the context of the relative comfort level of addressing postwar issues as opposed to giving primary emphasis to the more immediate, difficult, and painful issue of rescuing European Jews.

Jewish leaders in Palestine, who greatly influenced the agenda of American leaders, also focused on organizational politics and postwar planning. As early as 1938, Moshe Sharett used the word "holocaust" to describe the predicament of European Jews. This took place in a meeting of the central committee of the labor Zionists. Ben-Gurion took the floor to say: "I confess my sin. In these terrible days in the beginning

[1]Katz, Jacob, in Bauer and Rotenstreich, op. cit., pp. 30-31.

[2]See Chapter VII for full quote and reference.

[3]Ibid.

of the disaster that threatens European Jewry, I am still more worried about the elections at the [party] branch in Tel Aviv."[1] Ben-Gurion was making an honest, *conscious* statement of his priorities; he was neither denying nor repressing the bad news.

The coordinator of the Rescue Committee of the Jews in Palestine also addressed conscious choices within a full recognition and acceptance of the news of the Holocaust. This was after the news of the daily, massive killings was widely disseminated in 1942:

Should we help everyone in need, without regard to the quality of the people? Should we not give this activity a Zionist-national character....The current refugees lack [material possessions]...and we can only expect more of what we have already seen from a large portion of German Jewry: complete alienation and sometimes hostility to the Land of Israel....[2]

There are many indications from Griffel, Hirschmann, and others who were involved in rescue activites in Europe that this "selective" rescue was indeed the policy pursued by the Rescue Committee of the Labor Zionists.[3]

The ugliest part of this tendency toward elitism was that it persisted even after the war and led to condemnation of the survivors. The newspaper *Ha'aretz* commented: "The few that remain to us in Europe are not necessarily Judaism's best."[4] David Ben-Gurion was more explicit:

Among the survivors of the German concentration camps were those who, had they not been what they were - harsh, evil, and

---

[1] Minutes of Mapai Central Committee meeting, 12/7/38, cited by Segev, *The Seventh Million* (New York: Hill and Wang, 1993), p. 105.

[2] Ibid., pp. 100-101.

[3] See Chapter XI, this book.

[4] Segev, op. cit., p. 119.

egotistical people - would not have survived, and all they endured rooted out every good part of their souls.[1]

This sentiment was also expressed by David Shaltiel, another of the *yishuv's* leaders:

I believe that those who remained alive lived because they were egotists and looked out for themslves first....The fact that a person was in a camp is not reason enough to send him to Palestine.[2]

The different parts of our framework for evaluating the data from the 1930s and 1940s overlap. This chapter is concerned primarily with the limitations within which American Jewry struggled in the 1930s and 1940s. The next chapter focuses more closely on issues of choice and motivation.

---

[1] Ibid.

[2] Ibid., p. 118.

Chapter XIV

Factors of Choice and Motivation

The knowledge of the Holocaust that was available at any given time was the same for most Jewish leaders. What they did with the knowledge involves choice and motivation, factors which are inextricable intertwined. Eva Fogelman, in an important study of non-Jewish rescuers notes:

> The ability to see clearly, to strip away the gauze of Nazi euphemism and recognize that innocents were being murdered, is at the heart of what distinguishes rescuers from bystanders. It was the necessary first step that made the ensuing rescue activity possible and, in some cases, inevitable.[1]

Most of the non-Jewish rescuers in Europe were in a situation intermediate between Jews in the death camps and Jews in the United States. They did not witness beatings and killings daily, but those who chose to hide Jews, or to help them in other ways, faced the possibility of summary execution were they found out. The Jews in the United States faced no such dire consequences if they chose to actively pursue the rescue of European Jewry.

In the process of history one deals with choices. "The" American Jewish response to the Holocaust is a theoretical construct. In any historical period, when one leader or group of leaders disappoint those looking for leadership in a particular area, other leaders will be found, other avenues for expression of the needs of the time will arise. Samuel Margoshes, who was

---

[1]Fogelman, Eva, *Conscience and Courage: Rescuers of Jews During the Holocaust* (New York: Doubleday, 1994), P. 55.

editor of *The Day* and who served with Stephen Wise as an officer of the American Jewish Congress, expressed an understanding of this process in the midst of the trauma of 1943:

> When the recognized leadership is dormant and sleepy there appear forces which accomplish wonders, without the authority and the earmarks of collective responsibility which should be behind every public act of ours in this responsibility-laden hour.[1]

The American Jewish response to the Holocaust encompassed the activities of many different people and organizations. No one organization represented American Jewry.

In 1944, a detailed article appeared in the magazine *Common Sense* entitled "Who Speaks for the Jews?" The article spoke to the diversity among the five million Jews in the United States. Of the five million, "only about one million...belong to some sort of Jewish organization." The author gives this picture of Jewish religious life:

> Of this million, at least half are members of the 3,728 synagogues in the country. Most of the synagogues are small Orthodox congregations; the rest are Conservative and Reformed. The time, money and energy of Jewish organized life is devoted mainly to worship and philanthropy.[2]

As for Zionist organizations, the article reported that there were about 250,000 members, with the 100,000 women of Hadassah being the largest single group. All active Jewish groups are reviewed including the work of the Bergson group.

Whatever the diverse leadership of the Jewish organizations did or did not do need not be a subject of moral judgement, though one understands that readers of history make their own judgements about such matters. An accurate accounting of what

---

[1] Cited by Medoff, op. cit., p. 131.

[2] A copy of this article can be found in PSCP, Reel 4.

American Jewish leaders did and did not do is part of the responsibility of the historian to a pursuit of truth.

One of the limitations often mentioned in connection with the 1930s and 1940s is the lack of unity in the American Jewish community. This issue arises more properly in this chapter than the last chapter, because it has more to do with choice and motivation than with inherent limitations.

Just as one must clarify the question of "when did we know" by asking "when did we know *what*," one must clarify the "unity" issue. On *what* issues did American Jewish leaders show disunity, and on *what* issues did they come together?

There was a clear lack of unity between the American Jewish Committee and the American Jewish Congress on the question of Zionism. Within American Zionism, as documented in Part I of this book, there were different points of view in the 1930s between the "A" faction which supported Chaim Weizmann and the "B" faction which supported Vladimir Ze'ev Jabotinsky. In the late 1930s and 1940's, the two towering personalities in Zionism were Stephen Wise and Abba Hillel Silver. These two Reform rabbis were united in their opposition to "illegal" immigration, yet their personality conflicts led to significant disunity in American Zionism.

It has been documented in this book that there was significant unity among the major national organizations on many questions relating to rescue. Joseph Proskauer, Stephen Wise, Abba Hillel Silver, and Eliezer Silver of the *Vaad Hatzala* were in agreement that rescue was an important value. More to the point of choice, they were in agreement with Peter Bergson and his backers that the United States and the Allies could do much more than they were doing to rescue European Jewry *without* harming the war effort. Proskauer and Wise together sent to the State Department in May, 1943, the following:

...we desire to convey the sense of despair of the American Jewish community over *the failure of our government to take any effective steps to save the Jews in Nazi occupied Europe* from the certain death that awaits them...it must be stated that in all circles of Jews there is the deepest sense of disturbance and even of apprehension over what appears to be the determination of the United Nations to *continue a bankrupt policy*....[italics added].

Addressing the issue of whether or not Jews could be saved without interfering with the war effort, Proskauer and Wise were explicit:

> It is the conviction of the American Jewish community that *without retarding by one moment the military victory* of the United Nations the governments of the United States and Great Britain *can take such action* as would succeed in saving at least a substantial remnant of European Jewry [italics added].[1]

One might guess that this memorandum was written by Peter Bergson or Yohan Smertenko of the Emergency Committee to Save the Jewish People of Europe. These two men and their supporters agreed with every word that Proskauer and Wise wrote. The difference is that while there was unity on these issues *in private,* the Bergson group proclaimed the same beliefs publicly and acted aggressivly on those beliefs, while Proskauer and Wise publicly supported Roosevelt's win-the-war-first policy, condemned Bergson and acted aggressively to discredit him.

In the framework constructed in Chapter XII, it was noted that common factors that motivate behavior include altruism, power, politics, money, and fear. Altruism is a characteristic all American Jewish leaders had in common; the difference lies in the degree to which other factors overrode humanitarian instincts.

Money can be ruled out for all of of the leadership; in the decisions that were made there was no financial gain for individual leaders nor for their organizations. Questions of politics and power entered into the picture as factors in the behavior of men like Proskauer, Abba Hillel Silver, and Stephen Wise. These factors inhibited their altruistic instincts, while for men like Eliezer Silver, Irving Bunim, Ben Hecht, Ira Hirschmann and Peter Bergson the instinct to save Jewish lives was the overriding factor.

Bergson, Hecht, Hirschmann, and many others like them, present a problem for *both* sets of historians - those historians who write that the motivating factor in rescue was whether or not one was a "Torah Jew" and those historians who

---

[1]Memorandum dated 5/13/43, AJC, Proskauer papers, Emergency Committee, memoranda; material file.

write that there was little to be done by any American Jewish leaders.

Bergson, Hecht, Hirschmann and many others who actively pursued a rescue agenda to the exclusion of all other factors were far from the practice of the Jewish religion. In this sense they were among the "assimilated" Jews against whom Stephen Wise thundered. From the time that Yitshaq Ben-Ami, the first of the Bergson group to reach the United States, began working with American Jews, he found common purpose with Irving Bunim and other Orthodox Jews. The common purpose was not religion; it was rescue.

Within the Roosevelt administration, Henry Morgenthau, Jr., and Sam Rosenman were two Jews who had direct access to the President. Neither was an Orthodox Jew, neither was a Zionist. The careers of both men were tied directly to Franklin Roosevelt; his success was their success.

Samuel Rosenman's mother was a religious woman who kept a kosher home. Roseman himself "scrupulously obeyed the dietary laws" and put on tefillin until a year after his Bar Mitzvah, "but after that I gradually left it all behind."[1] In this sense, he was similar to Bergson who grew up in an Orthodox setting but as an adult did not continue religious practices. Morgenthau did not grow up in an Orthodox home, but had as a role model his father who was President Wilson's ambassador to Turkey during World War I. At the time of the Armenian massacres, Henry Morgenthau, Sr. fought a reluctant State Department to prod the Wilson administration toward efforts to stop the Armenian genocide. A generation later, the internal dynamics of the State Department were much the same, but the son was in Washington and was more successful with the President he served than the father was able to be from his post in Turkey 30 years earlier.

Morgenthau and Rosenman were affected differently by the news of the death camps. Rescue became a central issue for Morgenthau, while Rosenman was one of the obstacles to be overcome in pressing for a rescue agency.

The above examples demonstrate the folly of trying to ascribe complex human issues to one or two causes. If one grants that all of the Jewish leaders cared about rescue - had altruistic instincts - then it becomes a question of how these instincts interacted with other motivating factors to determine a course

---

[1] AJC, oral history section, interview with Sam Rosenman conducted in two sessions, July 9, 1970, & Sept, 1971.

of action for each individual. Morgenthau's altruism appears to have overcome his concerns about his power and position in the Roosevelt administration and natural fears that his standing would be adversely affected by approaching his President with a strong condemnation of his own State Department.

Social and psychological research into the altruism of non-Jewish rescuers identifies independence, the willingness to be different and competency as important factors in pursuing resuce. One study identifies competency as "a necessary precursor to helping." This is reinforced by other research which concludes that when rescuers "strongly believed they could influence events [this] made them feel that what they did, or failed to do, mattered a great deal."[1]

One finds a strong sense of independence, confidence, and willingness to be different among those who aggressively pursued rescue. These qualities are enveloped in the understanding of the yiddish word *chutzpah*. Bergson, Hirschmann, Hecht, Bunim and Griffel were all men who were able to put aside fears of personal consequences in order to pursue rescue.

Hirschmann is one of the purest examples of altruism. Without any affiliation with Jewish organizations to suggest to him a path to follow, he spontaneously supported, in the 1930s, a boycott of German goods by the retail industry. Called on the carpet by his boss, he was able to convince him to join the boycott movement. When Hirschmann's efforts brought him to the attention of Zionist leaders who tried to involve him in Jewish organizational work, Hirschmann declined to do so.

Hirschmann's independence and competence were admired by Fiorello LaGuardia. When LaGuardia was elected mayor of New York and offered Hirschmann his choice of four administrative positions, Hirschmann again decided to retain his independence, and declined a paid position in city government. When he accepted a volunteer position on the Board of Higher Education and came into conflict with La Guardia, Hirschmann followed his conscience even though the result was a year's hiatus in his friendship with the powerful mayor.

In the war years, Hirschmann was not satisfied merely with joining a Jewish organization to work for rescue, but left his comfortable position in the retail industry to go to Turkey to directly involve himself in rescue efforts.

---

[1]Fogelman, op. cit., pp. 58-59.

Hirschmann shared these characteristics of an altruistic personality with Raoul Wallenberg, another rescuer who worked within the aegis of the War Refugee Board. Wallenberg had a comfortable existence in a family of noted financiers, but opted for the dangerous work of rescue. His co-worker and biographer describes his assets:

He was a clever negotiator and organizer, unconventional, extraordinarily inventive and cool-headed....At heart, he was a great idealist and a warm human being.[1]

The certainty of lost income and lost comfort did not deter these men from their course.

In eliminating power and money from the factors motivating the Bergson group we have the extensive documentation of the failure of the attemps to discredit Bergson in the 1940s. Bergson came to the United States as a representative of the *Irgun*. His leaders were Jabotinsky and David Raziel. Within a year, both died. The Bergson group operated independently in the United States from that time forward.

During the war years, the various committees that supported the attempts to rescue Jews "on the high seas" (see Chapter VI), to lobby for a Jewish army and to lobby for resuce were given tax-free status and were audited on a quarterly basis. No money went to Palestine for weapons for the *Irgun* or for any other activity in Palestine. Non-married workers received $45 a week salary and married workers received $55. After World War II, Bergson and his followers were involved, as were many Jewish leaders, in the effort to get weapons into Palestine.

The editor of the most powerful newspaper in the nation's capital, the *Washington Post,* was forced to print a rebuttal of charges of misdeeds made against Bergson which the paper alleged in a series of articles. The rebuttal, written by Bergson aide, Samuel Merlin, was published on the paper's front page. A few days later, the *Post* published an editorial that stated there

---

[1] Anger, Per, *With Raoul Wallenberg in Budapest* (New York: Holocaust Library, 1981), pp. 49ff.

was "no question about the financing of the Emergency Committee and, in point of fact, the other related committees."[1]

The most difficult place to find altruism is in the efforts of some Jewish leaders to discredit the efforts of the Bergson group. When there is agreement on a goal - rescue, but disagreement on strategy and tactics, cooperation at some level is still possible.

There is the example of Jabotinsky and Weizmann early in the 20th century. Both favored the formation of a Jewish legion to fight in World War I, but Weizmann could not follow Jabotinsky in his aggressive lobbying campaign. Instead of undermining Jabotinsky's efforts, Weizmann told him: "I cannot work like you, in an atmosphere where everybody is angry with me and can hardly stand me....Better let me act in my own way. A time will come when I shall find a means to help you."[2] And he did find a way to help Jabotinsky.

So too was Wise unable to work in an atmosphere that brought the displeasure of Roosevelt, but instead of quiet cooperation, he allowed questions of ego, power, and Jewish politics to overrule his altruistic instincts and lead him to undermine the efforts of those whose altruistic goal of rescue was the same as his own.

Unfortunately, the attempts to discredit the Bergson group did not end with the war. Lucy Dawidowicz, one of the Jewish historians that this writer admires and to whose work he is indebted, wrote as late as 1962 that Bergson "...set up the Emergency Conference to Save the Jewish People of Europe, another in a series of *Irgun* fronts to raise money for arms to fight the British."[3] This statement is made with no supporting documentation and in the face of a great deal of documentation to the contrary. Possibly Dawidowicz was influenced by loyalty to the American Jewish Committee; it was as a researcher for that organization that she began writing on Jewish affairs.

The War Refugee Board creates a special problem for historians who want to discredit the Bergson group, as well as for historians like Feingold and Bauer who present the view that rescue was not possible due to the limitations of the historical era. The War Refugee Board is widely credited with

---

[1]See Chapter XI, this book.

[2]Schechtman, Vol II, op. cit., p. 224.

[3]*Commentary*, March 1962 Vol 3, #33 p. 262.

saving 100,000 to 200,000 lives. Chapter XI of this book contains the extensive documentation of the connection of the work of the Bergson group with the formation of the War Refugee Board.

If one wishes to discredit the Bergson group or present a unitary theory that rescue was not possible, one must minimize the accomplishments of the War Refugee Board and/or the connection of the Bergson group and the *Vaad Hatzala* to that Board.

In the sentence after the incorrect statement above about the Emergency Committee to Save the Jewish People of Europe being a front to raise money for arms for the *Irgun*, Dawidowicz writes of the Emergency Committee: "Its one accomplishment, as far as I know, was that its proposal to establish a United States Commission to rescue European Jews brought about the creation of the War Refugee Board."[1] Writing on the same subject at a later date, Dawidowicz gives credit to Morgenthau and his aides for the founding of the War Refugee Board and contradicts her earlier statement about the "one accomplishment" of the Bergson committee by writing the following concerning the Bergson-initiated Senate resolution and the creation of the War Refugee Board:

Exploiting the coincidence in timing [between the Senate resolution and the Board] the Irgunists now falsely claimed credit for the creation of the War Refugee Board.[2]

This 1983 *Commentary* article was published only one year after Dawidowicz wrote the following praise of Bergson:

Bergson and his friends embarked on a campagin that enlisted the support of prominent Americans....With stunning success they dramatized the issue of Jewish life and death....The Bergsonites were probably the most potent influence, seconded

---

[1]Ibid.

[2]Dawidowicz, Lucy S., *What is the Use of Jewish History* , edited by Neal Kozodoy (New York: Shocken Books, 1992), p. 195. This book is a collection of Dawidowicz's works; this quote is from an article originally published in *Commentary* in June, 1983.

by Henry Morgenthau's staff in the treasury department, in Roosevelt's creation of the War Refugee Board....[1]

Bauer joins in giving credit to the Bergson committee with one hand and taking it away with the other. In a book published in 1981, he writes that the creation of the War Refugee Board was

not pure humanitarianism by any means. The president yielded to a combination of public pressure, organized largely by the Emergency Committee of the Irgun and, quite independently, by a small group of non-Jewish Treasury officials exercising constant pressure on Secretary Morgenthau.[2]

Writing in another book, published in 1989, Bauer gives sole credit for the War Refugee Board to:

a small group of officials in the department of the treasury, none of them Jewish, including John Pehle, Josiah E. Dubois, Jr. and Raymond Paul....From the American point of view, this was a complete reversal, due to the initiative of three non-Jews who were in positions of power and could wield infuence - unlike the Jewish organizations which were begging from door to door with no success....[3]

Bergson, along with the many other Jews and non-Jews who worked with him, has disappeared from Bauer's history, apparently in the service of trying to show that there were no historical choices within the Jewish community itself.

Henry Feingold's seminal work was published in 1969. This book reflects extensive research into primary sources, and significant space is given to the activities of Bergson and the

---

[1] Dawidowicz, Lucy, "A Century of Jewish History, 1881-1981: The View from America," in the 1982 *American Jewish Year Book,* pp. 72-73.

[2] Bauer, Yehuda, *American Jewry and the Holocaust: The American Jewish Joint Distribution Committee, 1939-1945* (Detroit: Wayne State U. Press, 1981), p. 402.

[3] Bauer, Yehuda, *Jewish Reactions to the Holocaust,* op. cit., pp. 117-118.

Emergency Committee to Save the Jewish People of Europe, especially in association with the formation of the War Refugee Board.[1] Yet in the preface to the paperback edition, written in 1980, he writes of "the failure of the Jewish rescue advocates to gain credibility,"[2] and in 1993, in a 19-page journal article, entitiled: "Was There Communal Failure? Some Thoughts on the American Jewish Response to the Holocaust," the War Refugee Board is not mentioned.[3]

It appears that with both Bauer and Feingold we have historians of note who, in their primary research into the period of the 1930s and 1940s, find much evidence of the activities of the Bergson group, their accomplishments and their connection to the War Refugee Board, but who later find some of the data they originally reported inconvenient for the theories they are defending.

Lost too in the recent historical commentary of Bauer and Feingold are the efforts of Orthodox Jews working through the *Vaad Hatzala*. These efforts are not lost in the history of Kranzler, Rakeffet-Rothkoff, Friedenson, Penkower and other historians. Penkower writes:

In a savage world that claimed six million of their people, some Jews understood that morality transcended man-made laws....Kalminowitz, Kotler, Tress, Bunim, Lewin and their associates [on the *Vaad Hatzala*] merited War Refugee Board director Pehle's postwar encomium: "for imagination and constructive ideas, for courageous programs, for ingenuity and singleness of purpose, the *Vaad Hatzala* need bow to none."[4]

Are there lessons to be drawn from the history of the diverse responses of the American Jewish leadership to the Holocaust? We turn to this issue in the next and final chapter.

---

[1]Feingold, *The Politics of Rescue*, op. cit., pp. 208-247.

[2]Ibid, Preface to the Paperback edition, p. xv.

[3]Feingold, Henry L."Was There Communal Failure? SomeThoughts on the American Jewish Response to the Holocaust," op. cit.

[4]Penkower, Monty N. *The Jews Were Expendable: Free World Diplomacy and the Holocaust*, op. cit., pp. 287-288.

Chapter XV

Lessons of History

When historians express reservations about drawing lessons from one period of history and applying them to another period, they tend to relate to broad historical processes - the geopolitical situation at the time of the 1930s and 1940s with worldwide depression, the growth of communism, and a world war are unique to that period of time and will not be reproduced in another era. Thus it is difficult to draw lessons from this period and apply them to the present or the future.

There is much with which to agree in the above proposition. From other levels of the historical process, however, it is heuristic to draw conclusions and speak of lessons of history. These lessons can be applied by the reader of history who is conscious of his or her role in history as an organizational leader, as an individual conscious of his or her role in history from outside an organizational framework, and by those individuals who are not conscious of themselves as actors on a historical stage (and perhaps are not at all interested in defining themselves as such), but who enjoy reading history and want a framework for drawing lessons from one period of their reading and applying them to another.

The first lesson to be drawn from reading the works of different historians, and thus a lesson for those writing history, is that overemphasizing any one level of historical process at the expense of the others necessarily limits one's perspective. This is not a new lesson, but one that has to be learned and constantly relearned. Peter Gay, who makes an important contribution to history from his perspective as a historian and as a psychoanalyst, emphasizes this point:

To say that all history is psychohistory is not to say that subjective causes are somehow privileged and always determinative. Again and again, theorists of history have posted one-way signs to regulate the traffic of cause and effect: Carlyle his heroes, Marx his relations of production. Yet again and again, other theorists, or the pressure of historical evidence, have compelled their removal. The graveyard of historiography is strewn with the untended monuments of monocausal systems....I have no intention of adding another.[1]

Perhaps the most difficult lessons to deal with for both the writer and the reader of history are moral lessons. Can one extract such lessons? Should one even try? Where is the line between drawing moral lessons and being judgmental; what right does one have to be judgmental?

Historians who write about historiography address this issue, and none make a case for ignoring it. It is an issue that is not seen very well "from 30,000 feet," but even those historians who confine themselves to the larger historical process address the issue of morality. Feingold aspires in his book on the Roosevelt administration to go "beyond" moralizing, but adds that "to go beyond the moral aspect is not to ignore it. One soon discovers that the role of witness is burdened with a moral freight that cannot be ignored."[2]

When it comes to the history of nations and the relationships between nations, the tendency for issues of power, money, and self-interest to rise above ethical and moral issues has long been recognized. As documented in Part I of this book, some of the Jewish leaders active in World War II were leaders also at the time of World War I. The indifference of the State Department to the Armenians and Jews during World War I was well known to them as was the fact that this phenomenon was no different during World War II.

The lesson that governments respond not to pleas, but to pressure, had already been learned by leaders active during World War II, but it was a lesson that was applied only by some of them.

When one researches the interaction between and within the organizations and between individuals within each

---

[1] Gay, *On Causes in History*, op. cit., p. 19.

[2] Feingold, *The Politics of Rescue*, op. cit., p. ix.

organization, it is not possible to ignore the moral aspects. The Jewish organizations and individual Jewish leaders of the 1930s and 1940s engaged in a great deal of self-justification, finger pointing, and sharp personal attacks. In order to avoid moral issues, the historian must suppress important primary sources.

To dismiss the work of Morse, Medoff, and Friedman[1] as moralizing is, as mentioned above, to shoot the messenger. It is legitimate historical debate to critique their presentation of the data, what data they included or left out and the conclusions at which they arrived, but to dismiss their research out of hand is to reinforce the impression that one is pushing the ascendency of one's own ideas at the expense of examining the perspective of others. Thus one falls into the trap of reproducing in the present the mistakes of the Jewish leaders of the 1930s and 1940s.

Feingold, with no evaluation of their data, dismisses the work of the three researchers cited above.[2] Lucy Dawidowicz not only uses discredited charges to attack the Bergson group, but also finds fault with David Wyman's *The Abandonment of the Jews*, in part because, in her view, Wyman "puffs up" the Bergson group and in part because he implies that the Roosevelt administration was indifferent to the fate of the Jews.[3]

Wyman is one of the few non-Jewish historians to research the history of the Roosevelt administration's attitude toward the Holocaust. His account, highly praised for its scholarship, has found a broad readership.[4] Dawidowicz finds Feingold's book on the Roosevelt administration more to her liking,[5] yet Feingold, in discussing the War Refugee Board, comes to the same conclusion as Wyman, writing that the policy of the War Refugee Board "did mark a sharp departure from the previous

---

[1]Morse, *While Six Million Died*, op cit., Medoff, *The Deafening Silence*, op. cit., and Friedman, *No Haven for the Oppressed*, op. cit.

[2]See Feingold, *The Politics of Rescue*, op cit., p. ix, Feingold, "Who Shall Bear Guilt for the Holocaust: The Human Delimma, op. cit., p. 262, and Feingold, "Was There Communal Failure? Some Thoughts on the American Jewish Response to the Holocaust," po. cit., p. 60.

[3]Dawidowicz, *What is the Use of Jewish History*, op. cit., pp. 157-178.

[4]Dawidowicz acknowledges, on pages 161-162 that Wyman's work has "been embraced by book reviewers, even by some who profess to be historians, and by a large reading public, including many Jews."

[5]Ibid., p. 158.

policy of indifference and inadvertant collusion with the Nazis."[1]

Without dealing with moral issues, one can easily minimize the Holocaust. Biographer Kenneth Davis, in his volumes on Roosevelt, deals directly with moral themes and writes a great deal about the fate of the Jews in the 1930s and 1940s. By contrast, James MacGregor Burns, the author of a multivolume biography of Roosevelt, is 395 pages into his volume about the years 1940-1945 before there is any mention of the Nazi treatment of the Jews. He devotes three pages to the subject and never returns to it.[2]

Burns, Davis, Wyman and Feingold have all researched and written history on the subject of the Roosevelt administration. No one of these works is the "right" history; they all make a valuable contribution. One obvious lesson for the reader of history is that one cannot confine oneself to a single writer if one wants to understand complex, differing perspectives of history.

Another lesson from the history of the American Jewish response to the Holocaust is that group norms may conflict with an individual's evaluation of what is right and wrong. One adheres strictly to group loyalties only at the expense of one's own altruistic instincts. Research for this work reveals that many individuals in the 1930s and 1940s were alert to this potential conflict.

While some leaders of the "official" Jewish organizations condemned the Bergson group and refused to have anything to do with them, others within the American Jewish Committee, the American Jewish Congress and the Jewish Labor Committee met on a number of occasions with members of the Bergson group to try to find common ground for rescue work. As documented in Chapter XI, Jacob Pat, of the Jewish Labor Committee, did not hesitate to sharply criticize the inaction of the umbrella committee which included his own organization. Going beyond criticism, the American Labor Committee often went outside the framework of the umbrella group to work with the *Vaad Hatzala* on plans for rescue.[3]

---

[1]Feingold, *The Politics of Rescue,* paperback edition, op. cit., p. 247.

[2]Burns, *Roosevelt, 1940-1945,* op. cit., pp. 395-397.

[3]See Kranzler in Finger, Seymour Maxwell, editor, *American Jewry During the Holocaust* , op. cit., Appendix 4-2, p. 19.

It is for these reasons that not only does one miss much history by overly generalizing about "the American Jewish community," but one also misses much history by over generalization even about one organization within the Jewish community.

At an individual level, one examines the behavior of historical personages to find role models. Hook, who addresses the concept of the hero in history,[1] understands both that there are limitations to the concept of heroes in history *and* that we inevitably seek role models. Seeking to balance the overly heroic model of a Carlyle with an overly restrictive view of social determinism, he writes:

Many of the might-have-beens of history were beyond human control. It is hard to see what human beings could have done to realize these might-have-beens...other might-have-beens were within human grasp....They were lost because of the failure to be more intelligent, more courageous, more resolute - sometimes a little more of each.

The triumphs of intelligence and will never violate natural and social necessities. Intelligence and will supply, by their own effort, some of the conditions upon which the transition from the "might be" to the "is" hangs....Among the most poignant tragedies of history are those in which men have cried "impossible" too soon, and for want of vision have summoned up energies sufficient to win the day - too late.[2]

Speaking to the issue of moral responsibility and the qualities of the hero in history, Hook adds:

Moral responsibility in history consists in being aware of the relevant ifs and might-be's in the present, and choosing between alternatives in the light of predictable consequences. We may lose even after we have chosen intelligently and fought

---

[1]Hook, Sidney, *The Hero in History: A Study in Limitation and Possibility* (New York: The John Day Company, 1943).

[2]Ibid., p. 146.

bravely....But intelligence and sustained courage will win much more often than drift and fitful bursts of effort. If there is any ethical imperative valid for all historical periods it is awareness and action.[1]

In Hook's work we encounter the value of generalization, properly constructed. The commments quoted above were made in a general context and have no reference to the American Jewish response to the Holocaust, yet their applicability to our subject is obvious.

Hook's observations are not fact, rather his own interpretation of history, an interpretation which this writer shares. Within our framework for evaluation, my own interpretation is that there were realities that severely limited the ability of the American Jewish people to rescue their fellow Jews. No different reaction by any one leader or group of leaders would have prevented the overwhelming tragedy we know as the Holocaust.

Within this reality, there were different courses of action, choices to be made. The choices that some people made saved lives. From a broad perspective, one can minimize, as some historians do, the accomplishments of the War Refugee Board, but for others, including this writer, it is difficult to minimize the saving of 100,000 to 200,000 lives and difficult to avoid Ira Hlrschmann's conclusion that "history will tell that our government achieved marked success through the War Refugee Board in rescuing the remnants of persecuted minorities and in checking their slaughter," and his conclusion that more lives would have been saved "had we acted vigorously and decisively at an earlier date."[2]

Why the Jewish community has so diligently sought to document the rescue activities of non-Jews and has not hesitated to label them "heroes," while assiduosly avoiding such efforts where rescue by Jews is concerned is a fascinating question. By ignoring the heroic actions of some Jews, we bypass the uncomfortable necessity of characterizing contrasting behavior. This is no reason to deny Jewish history its heroes.

---

[1]Ibid.

[2]Hirschmann, Ira, *Life Line to the Promised Land*, op. cit., pp. xv-xvi.

Those who persevered and seized the limited opportunities to rescue their fellow Jews in a historical period obstructionist and hostile to their actions deserve the mantle of heroism.

Those whose altruistic impulses were overridden by other instincts and did not aggressively and single-mindedly pursue all avenues of rescue failed to rise to the historical opportunity to make the contribution they could have made. That failure does not, to this writer, make them antiheroes.

Those who persistently and aggressively used energies that could have been summmoned for rescue to instead undermine the efforts of those so engaged warrant the mantle of antiheroes.

When asked by a friend: Who is the intended audience for your research - for whom are you *really* researching and writing this history, my response was that, at the deepest level, the effort was for myself. While I would like to think that, had I been an adult in the 1940s, I would have joined those actively pursuing rescue, my fear is that I would not have, that I would have been among those who found it easier to do less.

BIBLIOGRAPHY

Anger,Per, *With Raoul Wallenberg in Budapest* (New York: Holocaust Library, 1981),

Barnard, Harry, *The Forging of an American Jew: The Life and Times of Judge Julian W. Mack* (New York: Herzl Press, 1974).

Bauer, Yehuda, & Nathan Rotenstreich, editors, *The Holocaust as Historical Experience* (New York: Holmes & Meier, 1981).

Bauer, Yehuda, *American Jewry and the Holocaust: The American Jewish Joint Distribution Committee, 1939-1945* (Detroit: Wayne State U. Press, 1981).

Bauer, Yehuda, *American Jewry and the Holocaust* (Detroit: Wayne State University Press, 1981).

Bauer, Yehuda, *Jewish Reactions to the Holocaust* (Tel Aviv: MOD Books, 1989).

Ben-Ami, *Years of Wrath, Days of Glory: Memoirs From the Irgun* (New York: Robert Speller and Sons, 1982).

Burns, James MacGregor, *Roosevelt, 1940-1945: The Soldier of Freedom* (New York: Harcourt Brace Javanovich, 1970).

Carr, E.H., *What is History* (New York: Vintage Books, 1961).

Chernow, Ron, *The Warburgs: The 20th-Century Odyssey of a Remarkable Jewish Family* (Random House: New York, 1993).

Cohen, Israel, *The Zionist Movement* (New York: Marstin Press, 1946).

Cohen, Naomi, *Not Free to Desist: The American Jewish Committee, 1906-1966* (Philadephia: Jewish Publication Society of America, 1967).

Cohen, Naomi, *The Year After the Riots* (Detroit: Wayne State U. Press, 1988).

Davis, Kenneth S., *FDR, The New York Years, 1928-1933* (New York: Random House, 1979).

Davis, Kenneth S., *FDR, Into the Storm, 1936-1940* (New York: Random House, 1993).

Dawidowicz, Lucy, *The Holocaust and the Historians* (Cambridge: Harvard U. Press, 1981).

Dawidowicz, Lucy S., *What is the Use of Jewish History*, edited by Neal Kozodoy (New York: Shocken Books, 1992).

Finger, Seymour Maxwell, editor, *American Jewry During the Holocaust* (Washington: American Jewish Commission on the Holocaust, 1984).

Fogelman, *Eva, Conscience and Courage: Rescuers of Jews During the Holocaust* (New York: Doubleday, 1994).

Feingold, Henry L., *The Politics of Rescue: The Roosevelt Administration and the Holocaust, 1938-1945* (New York: Walden Press, 1970).

Friedenson, Joseph, *Dateline: Istanbul* (New York: Mesorah Publications, 1993).

Friedman, Saul S., *No Haven For the Oppressed* (Detroit: Wayne State U. Press, 1973).

Fuchs, Abraham, *The Unheeded Cry* (New York: Mesorah Publications, 1984).

Gay, Peter, *Art and Act: On Causes in History - Manet, Gropius, Mondrian* (New York: Harper and Row, 1976).

Gay, Peter, *Style in History - Gibbon, Ranke, Macaulay, Burchkardt* (New York: W. W. Norton and Co., 1974).

Gilbert, Martin, *Auschwitz and the Allies* (New York: Holt, Rinehart and Winston, 1981).

Gurion, Yitshaq, *Heroes on the Gallows* (New York: Brit Trumpeldor, 1950).

Hamilton, Thomas J, *Appeasment's Child: The Franco Regime in Spain* (New York: Alfred A. Knopf, 1943).

Hecht, Ben, *A Child of the Century* (New York: Simon and Schuster, 1954).

Hecht, Ben, *A Guide for the Bedeviled* (New York: Charles Scribner's Sons, 1944).

Hirschmann, Ira, *Caution to the Winds* (New York: David McKay Co., 1962.

Hirschmann, Ira, *Lifeline to a Promised Land* (New York: Vanguard Press, 1946).

Hook, Sidney, *The Hero in History: A Study in Limitation and Possibility* (New York: The John Day Company, 1943).

Jabotinsky, Vladimir, *The Story of the Jewish Legion* (New York: Bernard Ackerman, Inc., 1946).

Katz, Shmuel, *Days of Fire* (Jerusalem: Steimatzky's Agency Ltd., 1968).

Katz, Shmuel, *Jabo* [Hebrew], Vol. I & II (Tel-Aviv: Dvir Publishing House, 1993).

Kranzler, David H., *Thy Brother's Blood: The Orthodox Jewish Response to the Holocaust* (New York: Mesorah Press, 1964).

Kranzler, David H. *Heroine of Rescue: The Incredible Story of Recha Sternuch who Saved Thousands from the Holocaust* (New York: Mesorah Press, 1984).

Kranzler, David H. *Solomon Schonfeld: His Page in History* (New York: Judaica Press, 1982).

Lacquer, Walter, *The Terrible Secret* (Boston: Little, Brown, and Co., 1980).

Lipsky, Louis, *Memoirs in Profile: A Memoir of Early Days* (Philadelphia: Jewish Publication Society, 1975).

Lookstein, Haskel, *Were We Our Brothers' Keepers?: The Public Response of American Jews to the Holocaust* (New York: Random House,1985).

Medoff, Rafael, *The Deafening Silence* (New York: Shapolsky Publishers, 1987).

Melson, Robert F., *Revoloution and Genocide: On the Origins of the Armenian Genocide and the Holocaust* (Chicago: University of Chicago Press, 1992).

Morgenthau, Henry, III, *Mostly Morgenthaus: A Family History* (New York: Ticknor and Fields, 1991).

Morse, Arthur, *While Six Million Died* (New York: Random House, 1968).

Newman, Louis I., *Biting on Granite* (New York: Bloch Publishing Company, 1946).

Offer, Dalia, *Escaping the Holocaust: Illegal Immigration to the Land of Israel, 1939-1944* (Oxford: Oxford U. Press, 1990).

Perl, William R., *Operation Action: Rescue from the Holocaust* (New York: Ungar Pub. Co., 1983).

Rakeffet-Rothkoff, Aaron, *The Silver Era: Rabbi Eliezer Silver and His Generation* (New York: Feldheim, 1981).

Reed, Anthony and David Fisher, *Kristallnacht* (New York: Peter Bedrick Books, 1989).

Reinharz, Jehuda, *Chaim Weizmann: The Making of a Statesman* (New York: Oxford University Press, 1993).

Schechtmann, Yosef, *Jabotinsky, a Biography*, Vol I & Vol II (Tel Aviv: 1957).

Schlesinger, A., *The Crisis of the Old Order : 1919-1933* (Boston: Houghton, Mifflin Co., 1956).

Selden, Harry L., *A Digest of The Rape of Palestine by William B. Ziff* (New York: American Friends of a Jewish Palestine, 1940).

Shapira, Anita, *Berl: the Biography of a Socialist Zionist* (Cambridge: Cambridge U. Press, 1984).

Shirer, William, *Berlin Diary: The Journal of a Foreign Correspondent* (New York: Alfred A. Knopf, 1941).

Simpson, Christopher, *The Spendid Blond Beast* (New York: Grove Press, 1993).

Teveth, Shabtai, Ben-Gurion: *The Burning Ground, 1886-1948* (Boston: Houghton Mifflin Co., 1987).

Thomas, Gordon and Max Morgan Witts, *The Voyage of the Damned* (Greenwich: Fawcett Publications, 1974).

Thomas, Hugh, *The Spanish Civil War* (New York: Simon & Schuster, 1986).

Tuchman, Barbara, *Practicing History: Selected Essays* (New York: Ballentine Books, 1981).

Urofsky, Melvin I. *A Voice That Spoke for Justice* (Albany: State University of New York Press, 1982).

Vrba, Randolph and Alan Bestic, *I Cannot Forgive* (New York: Grove Press, 1964).

Walworth, Arthur, *Wilson and His Peacemakers* (New York: W.W. Norton & Co., 1986).

Watkins, T.H., *Righteous Pilgrim: The Life and Times of Harold L. Ickes* (New York: Henry Holt and Company, 1990).

330   Heroes, Antiheroes & the Holocaust

Weizmann, Chaim, *Trial and Error* (New York: Shocken Books, 1949).

Willis, James F., *Prologue to Nuremberg: The Politics and Diplomacy of Punishing War Criminals of the First World War* (Westport: Greenwood Press, 1982).

Wise, Stephen S. and Jacob De Haas, *The Great Betrayal* (New York: Brentano's, 1930).

Wyman, David S., *The Abandonment of the Jews: America and the Holocaust, 1941-1945* (New York: Pantheon Books, 1984).

Ziff, William B.,*The Rape of Palestine* (New York: Argus Books, 1946).

INDEX